Badness

Badness

GARY JUBELIN

with Dan Box

HarperCollins*Publishers*

All dialogue and other direct speech in this book are taken from interviews conducted by the authors, publicly available records tendered during the relevant court proceedings or, in some instances, from the memory of those involved. In particular, the material described as having been captured on both authorised and unauthorised listening devices used to record Paul is taken from records tendered in the local court proceedings involving Gary Jubelin during February 2020.

Dan Box is a Walkley Award–winning journalist who has worked for *The Australian*, as well as London's *Sunday Times* and the BBC.

HarperCollins*Publishers*
Australia • Brazil • Canada • France • Germany • Holland • India
Italy • Japan • Mexico • New Zealand • Poland • Spain • Sweden
Switzerland • United Kingdom • United States of America

HarperCollins acknowledges the Traditional Custodians
of the land upon which we live and work, and pays respect
to Elders past and present.

First published in Australia in 2022
by HarperCollins*Publishers* Australia Pty Limited
Gadigal Country
Level 13, 201 Elizabeth Street, Sydney NSW 2000
ABN 36 009 913 517
harpercollins.com.au

Copyright © GKJ Phoenix Pty Limited and Dan Box 2022

The right of Gary Jubelin and Dan Box to be identified as the authors of this work has been asserted by them in accordance with the *Copyright Amendment (Moral Rights) Act 2000*.

This work is copyright. Apart from any use as permitted under the *Copyright Act 1968*, no part may be reproduced, copied, scanned, stored in a retrieval system, recorded, or transmitted, in any form or by any means, without the prior written permission of the publisher.

A catalogue record for this book is available from the National Library of Australia

ISBN 978 1 4607 6053 6 (paperback)
ISBN 978 1 4607 1390 7 (ebook)
ISBN 978 1 4607 4273 0 (audiobook)

Cover design by Christine Armstrong, HarperCollins Design Studio
Cover images by shutterstock.com
Typeset in Bembo Std by Kirby Jones
Printed and bound in Australia by McPherson's Printing Group

For William Tyrrell
26.2.2011 –

It's not what they are doing to you, rather it's why you have been chosen.

... You can't win against the system by adhering to the rules chosen by the system.

So this moment in time is what you make of it.

Enjoy your day

Text message sent by Adam Watt before I gave evidence in the Supreme Court

Contents

Prologue

1

Round One

5

Round Two

121

Round Three

219

Postscript

335

Acknowledgments

338

PROLOGUE

The Brute of Katingal

I was a cop; he was a crook. We're not supposed to understand one another.

It's January 2020 and, only a year ago, Bernie Matthews was still shut in his cell, watching the sun set on his latest, decade-long, prison sentence. This time around, he'd been jailed for selling drugs and guns. Previously, he'd been inside, more than once, for armed robbery and escaping from prison. Around the same time – January 2019 – I was working out my last few days as a Homicide detective, unaware that I was the target of a criminal investigation by my employers, the New South Wales Police Force. The same force that had arrested Bernie.

Back then, if you'd asked me who he was, I'd have told you he was a hardcore crook. I was just a kid when Bernie first made headlines, escaping from Sydney's Long Bay prison, and the newspapers back then said he was dangerous and not to approach him. When I was in my teens, Bernie was again on the front pages: part of a group of inmates one paper called 'the brutes of Katingal'. Katingal being the country's super-maximum security prison complex.

These brutes were so violent, according to the newspaper, that a fortress was needed to contain them. They could not be allowed to mix with other prisoners. And, as a cop, I would have agreed with that assessment; during his time in prison, Bernie tried to rip a guard's throat out using his teeth, beat another inmate close to death for giving evidence against him, and tried to burn down one of the workshops with himself inside it.

In early 2019, I would have told you there was no place for men like Bernie in the world outside of prison. Today, experience has changed me.

I handed in my police badge and warrant card in July 2019, after being charged myself with criminal offences. The same month, Bernie was released from prison. Six months later, the two of us are meeting here as equals, sitting across the table from each other in an upmarket Sydney coffee shop, him drinking his hot chocolate, me with my green tea steaming in its cup. I'm here on the recommendation of a mutual friend, who told me there's more depth to Bernie than the newspaper stories ever let on.

Also, I'm here because I'm curious about what it is like to sit down facing a crook like this. Watching him wipe the chocolate from his white moustache, I wonder if, maybe, I'd been wrong about him. As a cop, I've faced down many men like Bernie across the interview room table. Always, I was trying to catch them lying, or to snatch a confession from them. But this time, it is different. For a moment, the two of us just sit here, looking at the other. *It's like looking in a mirror,* I think. Nobody moves. Nobody speaks.

Bernie says he knows who I am, also. He knows some of the cases that I worked on, or at least he knew the people I was going after. Bernie was mates at school with Terry Falconer, he tells me. For years, I led the investigation after Terry's body was discovered, dismembered, his limbs and torso wrapped in plastic bags, floating in the Hastings River.

Bernie's also seen me in the papers, he says, in the stories about my upcoming trial, which is due to start next month and where I will be the one accused of doing something criminal. The charges are four counts of illegally recording my conversations with a witness. To Bernie's mind, he says, I'm still a cop, whatever the court outcome.

'This has never been done before,' he growls. 'Where two of us from the opposite sides are sitting down and actually talking.' He says the scene reminds him of the gangster movie *Heat*, where an armed robber played by Robert DeNiro is sitting in a diner, over coffee, facing Al Pacino, who's playing a career detective.

In the movie, you can tell the two men like each other. Each of them confesses something. Pacino talks about his failing marriage. DeNiro says a guy once told him to never let yourself get attached to something you're not prepared to walk out on.

I don't have anything else, says Pacino.

Neither do I.

I don't much want to either.

Neither do I.

Pacino says that now they've sat there, face to face, if he had to put DeNiro away, he won't like it. But, as a cop, if he had to, if it meant saving another innocent life, then he would kill DeNiro.

DeNiro nods. He says there is a flip-side: What if he has to shoot Pacino?

Bernie looks straight at me and I know what he's thinking; what if he and I had come face to face with one another, back when we were working? As a young cop, I was part of the Armed Hold-Up Squad, set up to target crooks like Bernie. The squad got a reputation for shooting first and asking questions later. Bernie would have been a desperate man, ready to do anything to secure his freedom.

It would have been simple.

Now, everything is complicated. Bernie has done his time in prison. He's going straight. A month from now, in February 2020, my trial will take place inside a confined, windowless Sydney courtroom. Two months after that, in April, the magistrate will deliver his judgment. He'll find my evidence is 'unbelievable'. My actions were 'above and beyond legality'. I will be disgraced. Found guilty on all four charges I am facing.

Meaning I will become, like Bernie was, a criminal.

Round One

On the Side of the Angels

I worry that this might go badly. I don't want to provoke old hurts for both of us so, before calling Kathy Nowland, I decide that, if the conversation starts going where I fear it might do, I will say something innocent like, 'I have to go, just checking in', and cut it short, leaving her alone.

But Kathy wants to talk to me.

'I've been thinking about you,' she says when I call in April 2020, a few days after being found guilty in court and a few months after my meeting with Bernie Matthews. Kathy says that she's been watching the news about my trial on TV. She asks how I'm coping.

Badly, I think. Before, I had a clear idea of who I was. I was a detective. I caught killers. In the cops, we used to say we were on the side of the angels. Now I've been judged; I am the crooked former detective, convicted of recording conversations with a witness. But I'm convinced I did the right thing. Those conversations took place when I was leading the investigation into the disappearance of a young boy, three-year-old William Tyrrell, who went missing in September 2014. In them, I was talking to a witness, asking about things that troubled us in his evidence, trying to work out if we should rule the man in or out of our investigation. That was my job. I was a detective.

I first met Kathy ten years before William went missing, when I was leading the investigation after her daughter's body was discovered in February 2004, lying in bushland near some playing fields in western Sydney.

Neither case has been solved yet.

'Thank you for remembering about me,' says Kathy.

'Of course,' I say. Her voice is a comfort, reminding me of when the world was simple, divided into good and bad, with me on the side of the innocents. I've needed reminding of that. In court, the magistrate said I went too hard in my investigation into William's disappearance; that I was pursuing the investigation at all costs when I recorded those conversations on my mobile; that I belittled a witness. That I humiliated him. I tried to crack him. That I 'controlled the chess pieces'.

I tried telling the magistrate that those recordings were for my own protection, so the man couldn't later accuse me of saying something that I didn't. And when the man himself was called to give evidence in court, he did accuse me of saying things I hadn't – including a threat to arrest him that I never made. I also tried to tell the magistrate that we already had a warrant to use listening devices and that I never used the phone recordings of those conversations in evidence. The magistrate dismissed this.

So had I done wrong? As a young detective, I'll admit, I might have been too eager. I wanted to be the gun cop with the crack arrest record, so if someone broke into a house, I would pursue them as if they had committed a murder. But by the time I was a Homicide detective, I had learned. I still went hard, sometimes to the point of obsession, but always within the rules. Otherwise, what's the point? The people you are locking up have lawyers. Do the wrong thing and those lawyers are going to use your rule breaking to get their clients released from prison.

In court, what the magistrate could not seem to understand was that people do get hurt during murder investigations. Sometimes they become targets of suspicion until you've found the evidence to clear them. That can cause them stress and upset. Their friends and families might start to look at them differently. And, as a cop, it is right that you do that to them because, ultimately, you are trying to catch a child killer. But I doubt the magistrate will ever think that, unless he has stood where I have, on the brown, withered grass of the Town Centre Reserve in a suburb like Mount Druitt, looking down at the swelling, blackened body of Kathy's 13-year-old daughter. That's the reason you go hard when you're trying to solve murders. It's because there are people out there who leave children's bodies lying half-naked and discarded.

When you've seen that, the world seems simple.

That's why I wanted to call Kathy now, because, after speaking to Bernie, everything seemed complicated. For me, this conversation is a first step. I'm out of the police force and have a new job, working as a journalist for Sydney's *Sunday Telegraph* newspaper. I took it, partly, because I had bills to pay and partly because I still see myself as one of the good guys, whatever they said in court about me.

I try to explain that, now I am a reporter, maybe I can write something about Kathy's daughter, Michelle Pogmore.

I can try to bring some attention to what happened. That, even though I am no longer a detective, there's still something I can do to help her.

'That's the difference,' Kathy says. 'You still care.'

***

Kathy closes the screen door behind me, shutting out the noise and dust coming from the construction site next door. Her house is a brick, two-bedroom building in one of those worn-out western Sydney suburbs that get sunburned every summer and shiver every winter. Inside, everything is neat, tidied and silent. Kathy herself looks tired, more drawn than when we last met, her long black hair tumbles down over one shoulder.

'I see the photos of Michelle around,' I start. They're everywhere. Framed photographs in her school uniform. Wide-eyed. Her hair tied back. A snub nose and pale pink lips like flower petals. Recognisably her mother's daughter. In one, Michelle's face is superimposed on a sunset above a bunch of red roses.

'I've even got her bedroom set up still,' says Kathy.

That comes as a shock. *It's so long now, since Michelle died,* I think to myself. *Sixteen years, maybe. No, seventeen.*

'I can't shut it down,' Kathy says. 'I can't shut it down,' she says again.

She shows me her daughter's bedroom. The room is small: bare boards; a wooden chest of drawers; the single bed, made up and ready, with its sheets tucked in place and smoothed down. But Michelle never slept here. Kathy has moved, she says, from their old house at Bidwill, where they were living at the time her daughter went missing. Kathy couldn't stay there, not after everything that happened, so she came here, bringing Michelle's soft toys and ornaments, then setting them all up as if nothing was different.

'I need to keep her alive still,' says Kathy. She feels her daughter's spirit in the house sometimes, she says. Things move, as if Michelle has touched them. So Kathy wants to show her daughter just how much she loves her. Beside the bed, there is a dresser, on which sits a teddy bear wearing a pretty dress. There is a stack of presents, still in their bright, multi-coloured wrapping paper. A toy angel with shiny wings hangs from the ceiling in one corner, sitting on a wooden swing suspended above the empty bed.

Looking around, I count five or six pictures of Tweety, the wide-eyed yellow canary from the Warner Bros cartoons, as well as two ornate butterfly decorations and a dream catcher.

'So this is all Michelle's?' I ask.

'Yeah,' Kathy sighs. 'It's hard Gary,' she says, not for the first time since I walked into her house this morning. I'm not sure if she means it's hard being in here, or that Michelle will never be here, or talking about what happened to her.

Maybe it's all of those at once.

* * *

It was hot that weekend I remember. My team in the Homicide Squad were on call, meaning we had to be ready to respond to every new suspected killing across the entire state of New South Wales. My phone rang when I was driving back from the police academy at Goulburn, more than two hours southwest of Sydney, where I'd been lecturing to detectives. I had my kids in the car with me. When the call came, I had to take them home then turn around and drive back out to the crime scene at Mount Druitt, meaning I was tired and hot and late by the time I made it. I didn't want to be there.

But then, no one wants to be there.

Michelle's body was lying about 35 metres from the car park. She looked like she'd been dumped, her arms outstretched, her head resting on one side. She was naked from the waist down, other than her white socks. At the time, we didn't know who she was but the local cops said that a 13-year-old girl called Michelle Pogmore had been reported missing two days earlier, on the Friday. Michelle was always going missing, they said. She ran away from home. She smoked, she drank.

According to her friends, Michelle was sexually active. Some of them had previously seen her pushing a stroller round the streets and thought it was her baby. She was still a child herself, of course, and some of the cops who said they'd known her were protective. Michelle's mother didn't let her drink or smoke at home, they said. Most likely it was a doll in that stroller. During one of our briefings at Mount Druitt Police Station, I said something about Michelle sleeping around, meaning we'd have to look at those men as potential suspects. A uniformed cop at the back of the room interrupted: 'She's not like that. She's a good girl.'

We worked late on that Sunday, after the discovery of her body, handling forensics, the search of the crime scene, and overseeing the initial door-to-door inquiries. We learned that Michelle was born in Brisbane, the youngest of Kathy's four children. Her parents had met at a pub and her dad had asked Kathy to marry him twice, but both times she knocked him back.

They moved to Sydney's western suburbs and, when Michelle was five, into a four-bedroom weatherboard house in Bidwill, provided by the Department of Housing. As Michelle grew up, her parents fought. They split up a few times, then got back together for whatever reason. Her dad drank. The relationship was toxic. Sometimes the police were called in.

It made me sad, learning her story. My own son, Jake, was 12 coming up on 13, and my daughter, Gemma, was 10, a few years younger than Michelle. I thought about how much safety and security they needed.

At the local public school, one of her teachers said Michelle was a well-behaved student but had some learning difficulties. She didn't interact well with other children and found it difficult to make friends. Although she got through the first few years of school without any real problems, something changed when Michelle was around 10, we learned. She'd wet the bed, or blow up into rages. Yell and scream. Slam doors. Around this time, the police came to talk to Michelle about hitting another girl but let her off with a warning. Her mum thought she had her father's temper.

When Michelle was 11, Kathy called the police to say she'd been assaulted by her daughter during an argument. Kathy also told the school that she wasn't coping with Michelle at home. A teacher offered to take the schoolgirl in during the weekends and, for a while, that helped. Her behaviour got better. But sometimes, when Michelle was back at home, this teacher would speak to her on the phone and could hear her father in the background, shouting.

Michelle started to run away. Sometimes daily. When she did, her mum would call the police and often they would find her, sometimes drunk, one time sleeping in a parked car with two men. The police once called Kathy to say Michelle was at Sydney's Central Station, trying to get on a train to Queensland. Another time, Michelle got bashed and ended up in hospital. Learning this and knowing how her life had ended, it was easy to think that Michelle was always heading in the one direction.

Diagnosed with attention deficit hyperactivity disorder, aged 12, Michelle took an overdose of the prescription meds that she'd been given. The next month, out riding her bike, she was hit by a van. Aged 13, in January 2004, she told police that she'd been raped. She said the man was somewhere between 40 and 50 years old, with a moustache, a beer belly, big hairy chest, wearing blue overalls and driving a late model Ford Falcon. The police thought it might be someone in the family but the investigation stopped when Michelle said she was unwilling to continue. The man was never found.

Afterwards, Michelle became more angry. Kathy didn't know how to make her happy. On Thursday, 19 February 2004, she bought a pair of shoes Michelle had wanted. For Kathy, it had been the way her daughter asked her: 'Can you *please* buy me a brand new pair of shoes?' They were pink and blue runners from Payless Shoes and cost her $24.99. Michelle was so happy. She said thank you.

That evening, Kathy saw her daughter walking down the street, alone. Michelle yelled, 'I'm going out.'

'I don't want you to go out,' Kathy told her.

'I'm going.'

Kathy didn't know how to stop her. That night, the police called to say they'd seen Michelle hanging around the taxi rank at Mount Druitt train station. Kathy couldn't get there, so she said the cops should put her daughter in a jail cell for her own protection. If they had done, according to Kathy, her daughter might still be here.

Michelle did not come home the next day. Her mum reported her again as being missing. That was the Friday. On the Saturday, the police came to Kathy's house and told her it was her job to keep an eye on her daughter.

The next day Michelle's body was found.

Forgotten

Standing in that dusty park, looking at the body lying abandoned on the dirt ground, I knew this was something awful. In the cops, we called it badness, for the evil that we could not understand. And yet I had to face it.

We didn't question it back then; evil existed. That helped justify those missed weekends, or holidays, or birthdays, all those late nights when I didn't come home because I was working, or when I was physically at home but not really present because mentally I'd brought my work home with me. To my mind, it also helped to justify my actions at work, like when I pushed a junior detective to work harder, or blew up at a senior officer, telling them to get fucked because they wouldn't agree to my request for more time, or staff, or money.

We were facing evil and it was our job to catch those who did it. Nothing else mattered.

On the Monday following the autopsy, I went to meet Kathy Nowland for the first time, to tell her we believed the body discovered lying in the reserve was her daughter. It was a girl's body, I told her. She'd been wearing a blue T-shirt with a picture of Tweety on it. Kathy said it was her daughter's. She loved Tweety. I said the body we'd recovered had pierced ears but no earrings. Kathy nodded. I talked about releasing some CCTV footage we'd recovered from the shopping mall that showed her daughter on the night that she was last seen, in the hope some witnesses would come forward. I asked Kathy about releasing Michelle's name and a photograph, in case anybody recognised her.

I stayed in the house there longer than I needed. I promised that I'd do everything I could to find who had been responsible. When I told Kathy what clothes we'd found with Michelle's body, she couldn't understand why her daughter's shoes were missing. Who would take her shoes? Who would do that to a person? I knew it was up to us as cops to find the answers. Later, back at the police station, a junior detective came up to me, saying, 'Boss, I'm going to tell you this but you're not allowed to react.'

'What?'

He said one of the other cops involved in the investigation was sitting in the local police station playing cards on his computer. This was amid the chaos of those first few days, when witnesses' memories are freshest; when physical evidence has still not been destroyed by rain, or wind, or time, or simply lost; when any suspect might already be covering their tracks behind them; when everyone on this side of the fight between good and evil should be standing up and saying, 'This goes no further'.

'Don't unleash on him,' said the junior detective. 'He's a good bloke, really. Everybody likes him.'

I did what he asked me. Didn't unleash. And that lazy fuck just sat there, getting paid and playing games in the middle of a Homicide investigation.

That was a kind of badness, also, I think, looking back.

***

It saddened me that Michelle's death didn't get enough attention. Other child killings got front-page headlines and rolling, day-after-day coverage on the evening news. Hers didn't. I wondered what about this case was different.

I'd seen the same lack of response with another case I worked, the murder of three Aboriginal children in Bowraville, a small town on the New South Wales Mid North Coast. Those children's families had told me then that, if it had been three white kids who were murdered, there would have been a sensation. The police would have had to find the killer. As it was, those murders, like Michelle's death, remained unsolved.

A year before Michelle died, in 2003, a US scientific study looked at this difference in reaction. It looked at the reporting of 640 homicides that took place over almost a decade in one American city – Columbus, Ohio – and found that some deaths did receive much more attention, measured either in the number of mentions in the daily newspaper or in how many of those reports were on the front page. Those that did tended to be killings where the victim was white and female, and the offender was black and male. The scientist, Richard J. Lundman, called this 'selection bias'. I'd call it prejudice.

To explain it, the study suggested certain homicides might get attention because they fitted the stereotyped beliefs of journalists working on the paper. As a result, these killings were seen as being more 'newsworthy', and the journalists who made these decisions 'rarely have the time or the inclination to take a reflective look ... at their own work'. Other killings got forgotten; those that did not fit the journalists' prejudices about race and gender. It made me sad to think that something similar might be going on in Sydney.

Michelle had dark skin. Kathy told me people were always asking if her daughter was Aboriginal, although in fact, the family had Spanish heritage. Michelle also grew up in a rough suburb. She'd run away from home before. Maybe all that would have made it harder for the mostly white, mostly relatively well-off journalists I saw covering the crime beat to identify with her as a person. I wondered if some reporter, or one of their bosses, had somehow decided this girl's death was less 'newsworthy', meaning it could more easily be overlooked.

'It depresses me to watch TV,' says Kathy as we leave her daughter's bedroom and walk through to her lounge room. She sees the TV news stories about other children's deaths, while her daughter's is rarely, if ever, mentioned. There are also a whole heap of cases, she says, where the police have recently announced a million-dollar reward for information, while the reward in Michelle's case is one-tenth of that amount, the same as it has been over the 17 years since her body was discovered.

'It just feels like it's a forgotten case,' says Kathy, but she cannot forget it. It's crowded in her lounge room, even with only the two of us in there. There's a bowl of faded, brittle, flower petals on the bookcase. Kathy sees me looking at them. They're from Michelle's funeral, she says.

As it turned out, I led the investigation into this death for a few days only. Like every Homicide detective, I had other cases and my bosses soon decided I should focus my attention on those. The case was passed to someone else, a detective senior constable in the local cops, who as far as I could tell did work hard on it. After almost two years, there was an inquest, where the coroner worked with police to formally establish how Michelle died. By then, I'd left the Homicide Squad and been promoted to a desk job at a police station in the north of Sydney, an hour's drive in traffic from Mount Druitt. The coroner's findings took up a single paragraph on an A4 sheet of paper:

> I find that Michelle Pogmore died sometime between the 20th and 22nd day of February, 2004, in the State of New South Wales. As to the place of death, the manner and cause of death, from the evidence adduced, I am unable to say.

I've never been able to forget it. I look at Kathy, sitting hunched and wide-eyed, as she did that first time I met her, when she looked to me for answers. *Did we ever do enough?* I wonder. *And if we didn't, is that a kind of badness, also?*

Eventually, the case was sent to Unsolved Homicide, meaning it was one of hundreds assigned to a small team of detectives whose job it was to review them. Most of those cases stayed unsolved, the files stacked in heavy cardboard boxes that people rarely opened. Once or twice a year, sometimes at night and sometimes at the weekends, Kathy would call me, asking what's happening with the investigation? When I got back to work the next day or on the Monday, I'd find out who was in charge of the case now and ask them, 'Could you at least phone her up, or maybe go out and see her?'

Every Christmas, Kathy took a hamper to the Mount Druitt Police Station and gave it to the cops who worked there, both to thank them and in the hope that it would remind them of her daughter. Over the years, she says, the faces behind the counter changed. The ones who'd worked on Michelle's death moved on. Their replacements didn't recognise Kathy. One year, when she turned up with her hamper, they asked what she was doing.

Today, 'nothing is being done', she says. She means nothing is being done to find her daughter's killer. 'Why isn't anything being done?' she asks me.

Because it isn't in the papers, I think. No journalist or politician is asking, 'What happened to Michelle Pogmore?' There is no pressure on the police force to pick this case out of the hundreds of others they have to work on. So it is being forgotten.

This is, perhaps, where I can help her.

Badness

Kathy Nowland shows me a photo on her iPad. In it, she is standing beside her daughter's grave, holding tight to 30 multi-coloured balloons that the wind is blowing sideways. The balloons look ready to take off into the bright blue sky behind her but are trapped by their trailing, pink ribbons, which have wrapped themselves around Kathy.

'I never got to see her body,' she says. 'I never got to say goodbye, or let her go.' The photos are from Michelle's last birthday. 'She's 30 now.' So, 30 balloons.

I ask if she can send me a copy of the photo and Kathy says she'd text it but doesn't have any credit on her mobile. I take a picture on my phone instead and think about the cost of all those Christmas hampers. Kathy shows me another photo, of Michelle staring into the camera. It takes me back to that first, frantic evening of the investigation, when I saw the CCTV footage of Michelle walking through Dawson Mall on the night she went missing, which we released to the media in the hope it would trigger someone's memory of having seen her. In the footage, Michelle is walking straight towards the camera. You could see her face, getting closer.

'Every time I walk through the mall, I walk in Michelle's footsteps,' Kathy tells me.

Then Michelle disappeared out of the frame.

On her iPad, Kathy pulls up a Facebook page she set up, called Justice for Michelle. On it, she posts photos of her daughter, along with birthday messages; sometimes she begs, sometimes she demands that anyone who knows what happened to Michelle come forward.

In Kathy's messages, and in the replies left on the page by other people, Michelle is described as a beautiful girl, a sweet angel, an innocent. Her killer is evil, a dog, scum, a bastard and a monster. This is good and evil as I knew it in the cops.

'If I had a gun I'd shoot him,' Kathy says. 'Put him in front of me and I'd beat the crap out of him if I can't shoot him. I hope he rots in fucking hell for what he did to my daughter.'

I don't blame her. Kathy is an innocent, just like her daughter, but I still understand her wanting to do violence. I felt the same thing after being forced out of the police.

* * *

The investigation into William Tyrrell's disappearance was the most high-profile in the country. It was one of those the newspapers and TV stations ate up; a three-year-old white boy who disappeared from his grandmother's house on one edge of the country town of Kendall. In the family photos released to the media, William could have been anybody's son or nephew. He was a little, non-stop kid who loved the bike he'd been given for his birthday, had a cheeky smile, a wicked sense of humour and suffered from mild asthma, meaning he sometimes needed to use a Ventolin inhaler. In truth, William was a foster child. He'd been taken away from his biological parents when he was seven months old — too young for him to remember. His older, biological sister had also been removed from their care. Growing up in his new home in north Sydney wasn't always easy; sometimes he would hit, or bite, according to his foster parents, or seem to be unsettled, especially after the mandated visits with his birth family organised by the State Government. He was cautious. Not the sort of child to wander off and get in trouble. William knew not to cross a road alone.

By chance, Kendall is about an hour and a half's drive south from Bowraville, on the New South Wales Mid North Coast, where those three Aboriginal children were murdered. But, unlike those kids, the media did not forget William. One particular photo of him — taken shortly before he went missing — showed him playing in his Spider-Man costume. That picture was on all of the newspaper front pages and, night after night, on every channel on the TV news.

In that photograph, William looks like he is happy but there was something about his sad life story and about *this* disappearance, unlike so many others, that struck at people's heartstrings. When he went missing from his foster nanna's place, where the family were staying for the weekend, hundreds of volunteers turned up to help with the search.

In contrast, few people saw his foster parents in public. The fact William was a foster child meant there were legal restrictions preventing the couple being identified, so they could not go on camera, even to ask for help to find him. Instead, the police filmed a single interview with the couple in which they were not named and seen only in silhouette. The problem was that too few people knew the reason for this, which bred suspicion. In the days following William's disappearance, everyone was talking about the case, even in the corridors at police headquarters and in the lift up to the offices of the Homicide Squad. Other cops were asking why his parents weren't speaking out in public? What was it that was being hidden?

Despite all this attention, when I took the case over in February 2015 – five months after William's disappearance – it was in a mess. The previous lead investigator was retiring. There were too few staff left working on it; on paper there were supposed to be 12 detectives and an analyst, in reality there were never 12 of us together. The number was always fewer and all of us were also working other cases. When I started, there were also over 1250 separate reports, statements or other records on the investigation database which had not yet been reviewed. With few staff to work through them, we seemed to be going backwards as more information kept on coming in.

I was told both sets of William's parents – biological and foster – had been cleared as suspects by the previous lead investigator, who had decided instead to focus on a local white goods repairman. The cops had even launched a raid of this man's home and business, despite my objections that his alibi had not yet been checked out and that there was no strategy in place for any covert surveillance of his reaction, or any plan to deal with the press when they found out.

The media feasted on those raids, with TV cameras filming as uniformed police trawled through the repairman's house and garden, even emptying the septic tank on camera. But the search came up with nothing. And now he knew the cops were looking at him.

In my first investigation log entry after taking over, I wrote that our best approach now was to throw everything we had at trying to find evidence either of the white goods repairman's involvement, or to finally exclude him. The longer this investigation went on, I wrote, the broader it would become and the more difficult to manage. If the repairman 'is not the person responsible for the disappearance I would suggest the investigation will go for years'.

I worked that case for four years. We drew up lists of everyone with any possible connection to Kendall or to William's family, which ran to hundreds of names. With each, the strategy was to rule them in or out and then move on. Among them, after the white goods repairman, were local sex offenders, then others who got our attention because of their behaviour, their proximity to the place where William was last seen or because we couldn't prove where they were at the time. One man who lived near where William went missing had what seemed to be a kind of shrine at the end of his bed, made from a photograph of William. Another neighbour, Paul, lived opposite the house where William disappeared and seemed erratic, like you could never guess what he might say or do next. That morning, while others searched together for the young boy, this man said he walked up into the forest behind his house to search alone – meaning we could not be certain he was really doing what he told us. To rule him in or out, we needed to know more.

We got court warrants to put surveillance devices in Paul's home and car. Listening to the recordings, we learned that Paul often talked to himself. At times he seemed to be talking to his dead wife, who he called Mum. Although the devices sometimes failed, or the recordings were unclear and crackling, we heard Paul saying, 'Great, they're gunna find something Mum, don't dob on me OK?' We didn't know what he meant by that, but I wanted to find out.

We called him in for questioning, where I went hard, asking Paul to explain where he was that morning. Afterwards our listening devices recorded Paul saying that I'd locked him into the interview room – which wasn't true – and saying I was as low as the bastard that took William. 'OK Mum, oh, oh, oh, oh Mum, oh Mum, oh Mum, what do I do?' the recording continued. 'Cos everything he said to tell me is all lies, you know ... I'm sorry.'

In another place, the tape was indistinct, with parts where some of the detectives who listened to it thought they could hear different words. 'No, yeah, well I'm gunna run into your property too,' I thought Paul was saying. 'This is my place, you're in my place, you do what I want,' he rambled. 'Don't want to take too much crap, hey, I'm not interested in your bullshit, mate ... you're a little boy, you're nobody. You're just a little boy, you're nobody ... You don't tell me, I'll tell you, I did tell you.'

Paul was on his own when that recording was made, we were certain. So who was the little boy that he imagined he was talking to? I didn't know.

Because there was no way of knowing what Paul might say or do, or who he might next accuse of some mistreatment,

I used my mobile on four separate times to record our conversations. I did not ask his consent to do so. In my mind, it was a backup; if he accused me, I could say there was proof that what he claimed didn't happen. I didn't hide what I was doing from the other cops on the strike force. During one of the recordings, two other detectives were in the same room with me. One of them even pressed record on my mobile. Another time, when Paul and I were going to be alone together, a third detective from the team showed me how to make the recording myself.

In November 2018, someone in the strike force made an anonymous complaint against me. The cops launched an investigation and brought me in for questioning three months later. Once there, sitting on the other side of the interview room table from the one I was used to, two detectives from Professional Standards told me I was accused of recording private conversations without lawful authority and also of creating false affidavits – meaning sworn statements used in court as evidence. Those charges of tampering with evidence could easily have been checked and found to be false but instead they were leaked to the press, who swallowed them, destroying my reputation. They were later dropped for lack of evidence, but this seemed to barely get reported.

I was taken off the investigation into William's disappearance, weeks before we were due to start an inquest into what happened to him. While still in charge, I'd said to the coroner that Paul should be put in the witness box at the inquest and asked to publicly explain what he said in those listening device recordings. After I was gone, that didn't happen.

Nor was I called to give evidence at the inquest, which felt strange. After all, I had been the lead investigator for the past four years. The coroner would later say that I had instead given evidence in writing, which was true – shortly before being taken off the case, I'd written up a formal, 22-page statement, setting out everything we'd learned during that time: who was where on the morning William went missing; details of the initial police response and the four-week-long forensic search we had conducted in 2018; what each of the dozens of local witnesses told us; the CCTV footage that we seized; the work we'd done questioning every known sex offender in a 30-kilometre radius; the thousands of alleged sightings of William we'd chased down; and the hundreds of people we'd identified as 'persons of interest' – like Paul – and what we knew about them.

For every one of these persons of interest, we'd tried to find evidence that might rule them in or out of the investigation. I'd sent this statement to the lawyers working on the inquest but, to my knowledge, it was not included in the briefs of evidence later sent out by the coroner's team to those involved, like William's foster parents.

Instead, the couple were told by senior police that I'd given a handover to the detective who replaced me as head of the investigation, allowing me to pass on what I knew, including the different tactics we were using and how each piece of the investigation fitted into the next one. That handover never happened. When William's foster parents later asked for me to give evidence to the inquest in person, the coroner said it would be a 'significant distraction'.

In May 2019, I resigned from the police force, a month before being told they intended to charge me over those four recorded conversations. I hated that decision. I loved being a detective. Each morning at work I would sit down at my desk and look at a photograph of William I'd put there because it gave me purpose. One of the hardest things to leave behind was the knowledge that, when I left it, the strike force into William's disappearance still had thousands of hours of surveillance recordings that no one had yet listened to. To this day, I do not know what happened to those tapes.

The magistrate who found me guilty said there was no evidence against Paul: 'No DNA ... no fingerprints ... no leads. There's nothing.' He said my own evidence was 'make believe'. *That's his opinion*, I thought. What he didn't seem to understand is that, in the Homicide Squad, we don't get the easy cases. If you've already got your suspect's DNA and fingerprints, that case stays with the local police.

And then, what about all the Supreme Court judges who signed the warrants authorising us to use listening devices to record Paul's conversations? None of them thought we had made up what was written in our applications. What about the email I received from the Director of Inquests at the New South Wales Department of Justice suggesting I apply for another order, this time to search Paul's home? Without a search, that email said, 'should any person be charged in future, such person could reasonably say that a necessary step to eliminate Paul from suspicion has not been taken'. I provided that email to the police when I was under investigation. The magistrate didn't mention it.

Listening to him convict me, I felt violence boiling up inside me. Walking out of the courtroom, through the pack of TV cameras and newspaper photographers, someone on the footpath yelled out: 'You're going to be fucked up when you go inside!'

He meant inside prison.

At first, I couldn't see the man, I could only hear him.

'The boys are waiting for you!'

I turned and saw him, standing no more than two metres from me, finger pointing. *That grubby fuck.* His face was twisted into something vicious. *He looks like a petty crook*, I told myself. I'd dealt with plenty like him in the cops. Men who could not control their tempers. Men who threatened to do evil.

'We're going to fucking do you!' the man shouted. But I wasn't in the police any longer. I was just a crook, like he was.

I took a step towards him.

He fell silent. We stared at each other. I pictured my fists landing in his face. The sound of breaking cartilage. The red blood bursting out.

I would enjoy that feeling.

Fuck this. If I'm a criminal already …

I might have done it, if it weren't for the TV cameras waiting on the top step of the courthouse. I would have liked it.

I walked away.

I wondered where that badness in me came from.

* * *

I stay with Kathy longer than I expected, just like I did that first time, when I went to tell her Michelle's body had been discovered.

Before leaving, Kathy says that she'd like me to be there if anyone is ever caught and put on trial over her daughter's murder.

'Of course,' I tell her. She goes into her kitchen, returning with a bottle of wine that she offers to me. She's not drinking at the moment: 'Would you like it?'

I take it, trying to measure all her kindness against the little that I can do for her. I'll try to tell Michelle's story, I tell Kathy. In the hope that maybe someone still knows something.

Maybe, all these years later, something will be different. Maybe, this time, people will pay attention. Maybe someone will come forward.

* * *

Leaving Kathy's, the quiet of her lounge room and of Michelle's bedroom are replaced by the sounds of building work from next door and the cars tearing past outside it. Walking away, I feel confused and troubled. My thoughts going back over the memories of standing in that park in Mount Druitt, looking at Michelle's body, and of being in the courtroom where I was found guilty.

For an old cop, that's not an easy thing to come to terms with. Before the trial, I thought the law would protect me. The experience of being convicted has shattered something deep inside me. Outside the cops, as a criminal, it is harder to hold on to the thought that I was ever on the side of the angels.

Maybe that is what brought me back here to meet with Kathy. Because in that one, old, unresolved case, everything was simple. And I still want to be a detective. I want to be back where I was, standing in the Town Centre Reserve looking out through the unforgiving sunshine across the dust, the withered grass to the houses that surround it, casting shadows, and thinking, *Someone out there knows something. I just have to find them.*

I shake my head. I can't look at things the way I used to. This is what the world looks like from where I am standing today: crooks like me believe they did the right thing, while cops play solitaire at their computers; the murder of a 13-year-old girl can be forgotten and the reward for information about one child's death is $100,000 yet the death of another child attracts ten times that amount. Getting into my car, I pull away into a road full of ugly traffic. I drive, staring forward, lost in my thoughts.

I still want to make a difference. I'm grateful for this second chance, to become a reporter, but if I'm going to make this career work, it must also have a purpose. *The one thing I'm still qualified to do is look at badness,* I think. Few people out there, if any, have ever seen what I have; from trying to solve the worst kind of crimes to what it's like to be sitting in the suspect's chair during a criminal investigation.

Maybe I am guilty of having looked at the world too simply when I was a detective, I think to myself. If so, then I can put that right. My new role can be to really try to understand it. What is it that makes people commit crimes? Where does that evil come from? Are criminals born or made? Or is badness something we all carry in us?

If so, who among us is capable of the kind of crimes committed against Michelle Pogmore and William Tyrrell? And is there any way back once evil has been committed?

This is something that I can do.

Behind me, in the rear-view mirror, Kathy Nowland's brick home recedes into the distance. Inside it, I'd asked her if she ever got any support to help deal with the pain of losing her daughter.

'I've got my music,' she told me.

'What type of music?'

'Guns N' Roses,' she'd said. Angry music. Anything to drive away the silence.

I think of that photograph of Kathy at her daughter's graveside, wrapped up in multi-coloured balloons for Michelle's birthday. Wrapped up in hope and anger. Hope that one day we will catch the monster who did that to her daughter. And only Kathy knows for certain what she'll do then.

Grab a Pencil and Come Running

I start with the detectives. At the *Sunday Telegraph* I set up a podcast series in the weeks after my court trial. In it, I'm interviewing cops, the ones I reckon were the real detectives, who I looked up to myself. It's one-on-one, sitting across a table with me asking the questions, just like I used to do when I was interviewing crooks.

Dennis O'Toole arrives neatly dressed in a dark suit and tie, every inch the retired Homicide detective. He has wide, open eyes, revealing the white around the iris, and which seem to see deep inside you. He's seen more than anyone should have to. Dennis led the investigation of the Granny Killer.

As if this really were me interviewing a suspect, I begin the recording saying, 'The time is 10 am, I'm Gary Jubelin. Sitting opposite me is Dennis O'Toole. Dennis, for the purposes of voice identification, can you tell me your full name and service history?'

He grins at me. 'Well, my full name is Dennis John O'Toole and I did just short of thirty-five years in the New South Wales police.'

'And do you agree you are here of your own free will?'

'Well, I'm not so sure about that.' He grins again.

'I'll be running this interview, Dennis,' I tell him. 'You let me run the show please. Now, one very, very important thing, you do give me permission to record this don't you? In light of recent events.'

He laughs.

I keep the joke running: 'Could you say it loud and clear? "Yes".'

'Yes.' Dennis agrees to be recorded.

We're laughing but I'm serious about this. For me, having somebody of Dennis's standing happy to be interviewed by me in public is a way of saying 'Fuck you' to the police. That not everyone's convinced I did the wrong thing.

'It's been a while,' I say.

'Yes, you've aged well.'

OK, I think, *I'm going to enjoy this.*

***

The media came up with the name 'Granny Killer'. At the time, between 1989 and 1990, no one knew his real name. All they knew was that a serial killer was preying on elderly women across Sydney's north shore. They were brutal murders, says Dennis, bad enough to shock even hardened detectives, and they kept on coming, six in total that we know of. The police were chasing shadows, telling themselves: We've got to stop this. How do we stop it? What are we missing? What aren't we doing properly?

Dennis knew the longer that it took him and his task force to find answers, the more people would be murdered. One time, he says, they'd worked all day, all night and most of the next morning when his boss said, 'Come on you blokes, go home, you've got to get some sleep.' Dennis had just about accepted his boss was right, they had to stop, and had ripped the top off a beer in an attempt to wind down when a phone call came in: 'We have another body.'

'I just couldn't believe it,' he says. That was one of the low points.

Dragging himself to the scene of another murder, the elderly victim lying bloody and broken, Dennis simply couldn't figure out who could do this. It was the work of a monster but the cops had so little to go on. At the scene of one killing, he says, a potential witness said she'd bumped in to someone on their way out who, looking back, they figured had to be the killer.

'She gave a description of the shoes, of the trousers, of the belt and the shirt. This well-dressed, middle-aged man,' Dennis tells me. So, not obviously a monster. Later, when they did arrest the killer, the cops would find those clothes hanging in his wardrobe.

The breakthrough came, Dennis continues, when he walked into the office around seven o'clock one morning, and one of the other detectives was in there before him working through a stack of documents.

'He said, "I've got your murderer",' Dennis tells me. 'I said, "What?" He said, "I've got your murderer. I don't know who he is, but I've got your murderer."'

Dennis sat down and the detective showed him how the same description of an elderly, grey-haired man kept turning up in different witness statements, not only from the murders, but also from other attacks and sexual assaults on elderly women over the past few years.

He seemed so ordinary that no one had noticed him. When they put a name to that description – John Wayne Glover – the man turned out to be a father, in his 50s, married and later separated, who worked as a seemingly sedate sales rep for the Four'N Twenty pie company. This job meant that John visited retirement villages on business. They welcomed him in.

Listening as Dennis describes how they'd been looking for a monster and found a pie salesman, I think, *This is the first lesson: evil people can seem ordinary*. Dennis tells me how they put John under surveillance, following him to the home of a 60-year-old divorcee, Joan Sinclair. The cops watched as Joan opened the door, gave John a peck on the cheek and welcomed him in.

Dennis breathes out. He closes his eyes for a moment. 'We sat with the observation squad for a number of hours until it started to get dark,' he says. From outside, there was no way of knowing what was going on behind that closed door. Dennis had to make a decision; should they knock and risk letting their red-hot suspect learn he was being watched, or wait and risk what might already be happening to Ms Sinclair?

'It was getting more desperate as the hours went by and there was a dog inside the house and the dog was barking,' he says. Eventually, they knocked. No answer.

Dennis says they went in through the back door. Inside the place was in darkness.

Joan was lying, dead, in the hallway with a hammer on the floor beside her. Knowing that nobody had left the building, the cops had to step over her body and go through it room by room, fully expecting the killer to be sitting, waiting, ready with a loaded shotgun.

'We checked each room, calling to each other,' Dennis tells me. 'We went to the bathroom and he was in the bath, it was a full bath, actually over-flowing.' An empty bottle of scotch whisky was standing beside the tub. John's nose was just visible above the waterline. 'I grabbed him. I took hold of his hair and gently raised his head from the bath.'

My eyes widen when he uses the word 'gently'.

Dennis sees this and smiles, then adds, 'He would not agree with that description.'

* * *

In September 2020, I am in court again, trying to appeal my conviction.

I lose.

The judge repeats the magistrate's decision: I went outside the law. I'm guilty.

After the court hearing, I get a lift to Sydney's Star Casino in Pyrmont and look out at the flat, black expanse of Darling Harbour. I think how Sydney is a complicated city, built on blood and corruption since the first European ships arrived here to establish a penal colony. Behind me are the bright lights of the casino, but I'm not there to drink or gamble. Instead, I've been invited to give a speech to some of the staff and executives at News Corp, the company that owns the *Sunday Telegraph*.

This is still a new world to me and I often feel like an imposter. I still get nervous writing newspaper articles, or preparing for a podcast interview, thinking that thousands of people are going to read or listen to them. I wish that I had paid more attention in school.

I try not to let it show, though. Turning back to the casino, I bump into an old mate from the cops, someone with whom I went through the police academy as a recruit and one of the few who still talks to me now I'm on the outer. Not wanting to show him my true feelings, I laugh off the appeal court decision. I do the same later with the compere for the News Corp evening, Matty Johns, the former footy player and TV host, who approaches me off stage to ask how I am going. For a moment, walking out into the stage lights, I look at myself through the eyes of the audience. They see a crook, I am certain. There is no way of disguising that fact now, not after the appeal verdict. Anger flares again inside me, just like it did after the first trial, where I was convicted. I stand there, preparing to speak and silently imagining myself inflicting bloody violence on those people who'd been involved in the decision to suspend me, or to charge me, or had given evidence against me in court.

I picture myself exchanging punches with those others on the strike force investigating William Tyrrell's disappearance, who also knew about the phone recordings. This morning, outside the appeal courtroom, I'd asked one of the detectives who investigated me if any of them had been charged yet, or disciplined for having knowledge of a crime.

'Um,' he mumbled, 'no, they haven't.' I wish all of them were on stage in this casino with me in this moment. Along with my old bosses, including my old Homicide Squad commander, the man who put me in charge of trying to solve William's disappearance and who later made the decision to charge me. He's since said it was his hardest decision in the police force and that he had no choice but to make it. I'd like him up on the stage with me now, to explain that. I'd also like to see his successor as Homicide commander, who was running the squad at the time I was forced out. Finally, I'd like to be facing the police commissioner, who oversaw the whole thing.

I'd show them how I am hurting.

That's not what I say in my speech, though. Instead, I joke and entertain the audience and make them believe I am far from broken. To their applause, I walk off stage and out of the casino, losing myself among the crowds around the water. As the day's emotions seep out, people leaving the bars and restaurants come up and stop me to say they know me from the TV news, or from seeing my photo in the paper. They ask for a selfie together. I smile and joke, keeping my mask in place, just like I had on stage, so they won't see how lost and violent I feel behind it.

Still walking by the water, I get a phone call from Mum, asking about the court hearing. How am I doing? I tell her not to worry. I'm going for a drink with friends, I tell her. I am fine.

The pub is in the city centre, near Chinatown, where neon lights up the darkening sky with artificial colours. When I get there, I keep walking, killing time, not wanting to arrive too early and having to wait, alone, for people to join me. It works. When I return, I see familiar faces.

'You want a beer?' they ask.

It's time, again, to put my mask on.

'Of course I'll have a beer,' I tell them, laughing. 'I definitely need one.' We take over the pub's top floor and drink too much. I've told people this will be a celebration. An evening in place of the traditional retirement booze-up I would have had if I'd left the police the way that anybody else does.

Instead it feels like we are mourning something.

***

For years after John Glover was arrested, Dennis O'Toole kept visiting him in prison. While John had been found guilty of six murders, Dennis was convinced there were others. Dennis tells me that when he first told John he wanted to talk about unsolved murders, the killer replied, 'Which ones?' It made Dennis hope he would admit to something and that might, at least, provide some comfort to the victims' families.

But, right from the start, John started playing silly games, always changing the subject when Dennis tried to tie him down to any detail.

'He'd say, "There is a dark part of my mind there, you know that. At any time it might unlock. If I find the key to unlock it, grab a pencil and paper and come running." There is no doubt that he enjoyed those little games,' says Dennis.

It's chilling to hear him describe this. I ask if he walked away from those exchanges feeling drained, remembering how, after similar conversations that I had with killers, I'd always wanted to wash afterwards, as if the darkness had seeped inside me while we were talking.

Dennis says it drained him, but that didn't stop him from going back, even after he'd retired from the police force.

'A couple of times I went there by myself,' he says. John would talk about murder as casually as if he was going to buy a pie in the shop but he would never cough to any that he hadn't already been charged with.

Even when Dennis pleaded with him, John said nothing, sitting comfortably behind the official explanation that he had killed six people only. 'I'd leave the jail up there at Lithgow, go out into the car park and I'd just sit in the car for fifteen, twenty minutes, trying some deep breathing or whatever, thinking, "You bastard",' says Dennis.

John also never revealed what drove him to murder. But Dennis has a theory that it went back to when John was young and found some photographs of his mother during the war, where John could see her bare flesh, and had found out she'd had a number of affairs.

That had a deep effect on him, says Dennis. John hated older women from that moment.

But he never got a proper answer from the killer. Instead, the Granny Killer took his own life. The monster who looked like a pie salesman was found hanging in his prison cell in May 2005.

He left behind a partial explanation.

Just like Dennis, I want more.

Evil Isn't Helpful

Frank Abbott looks like a proper monster. Coarse skin, neck jowls, belly hanging over the belt of his trousers. A convicted paedophile, he's twice stood trial for the murder of a 17-year-old girl found buried near a timber cutters' road to the southwest of Sydney. The first jury failed to reach a verdict and the second found him not guilty. In 2014, Frank was living in a caravan not far from where William Tyrrell went missing and we started to look at him when I was still running the investigation, back in January 2019. At the time, I was more focused on the neighbour, Paul. But the police now running the inquiry seem to have given up on that pursuit and are chasing Frank in its place.

In October 2020, at the inquest into William's disappearance, different witnesses are called to the stand, describing Frank as a 'dirty old man' who used to boast he beat a murder charge in Sydney. One says he was always friendly with children. Another thinks he had sex with her pet dog. All of these suspicions are repeated on the evening TV news and in the morning papers. The inquest also hears outright hearsay, which is then repeated by the reporters outside it, with one channel reporting: 'William Tyrrell was killed by a local paedophile and his body stuffed into a suitcase and buried.'

That 'startling claim', the news report continues, 'came from two women who heard it from two boys who blamed a man named Frank Abbott'.

That isn't evidence, I tell myself. *It's rumour.*

I don't remember seeing anything during my time on the investigation that proved Frank was in the area when William went missing. Nor have we heard any evidence at the inquest that proves this. I can't understand why they seem to be trying to build a case against him in public, or why the reporters seem so willing to repeat it. When Frank's face appears on the TV news now, I change the channel, trying to find something else to capture my attention. When people ask me, 'What about Frank Abbott?' I shrug and tell them I know nothing. *I need to put this past behind me.* But when I see the breaking news that police are searching bushland near the old sawmill where Frank once had his caravan, I can't help myself. Like everyone across the country, it seems, I'm interested.

The TV cameras show a line of dark blue police uniforms advancing through the shadows as the sun sinks through the forest. There are also sniffer dogs involved, according to the news reports. The cops have brought brush cutters and spades, meaning they expect to be digging.

The journalists repeat more of the claims made at the inquest: that somebody said Frank once said he smelled something he thought was a 'dead human' in the bushland; that Frank had said the police were searching in the wrong place when William went missing; that one of Frank's fishing buddies said he gave his best mate a lift in his car, along with a young boy, who might have been William. Only, the fishing buddy has died now, so cannot answer questions.

What gets me is how these claims get reported without examination. As if, right from the start, there's been an expectation in the public mind that only someone evil could have taken William. And all the reporters covering this case now seem to be accepting what the cops and lawyers tell them. They're probably thinking, *These are the good guys – they must be right,* and *Frank looks evil.*

***

'Evil isn't helpful,' Dr Sarah Yule says, when I call her. Sarah was the police forensic psychologist I worked with on the investigation into William's disappearance. Maybe it's because I'm reading about the case in the papers over breakfast, but when I find myself asking questions about evil like this, she is the first person I want to talk to.

I pause, unsure what to make of her answer. I thought it was a simple question.

Sarah fills the silence: 'I mean, it's not helpful to talk about evil.'

I say nothing.

'Evil is a weird construct, and it's non-scientific,' she continues, sensing my confusion. 'For one thing, it's subjective,' she says. Everyone has their own definition of what evil is. Some might say there's a difference between an evil thing and an evil person. 'You might say the murder of a person is an act of badness. But that doesn't mean the person who did that murder was always a bad person.'

Or say that somebody gets drunk and caught up in a fight. They throw a punch. The other person falls and cracks their head. They die. The person who threw the punch now is a killer, but might otherwise have been kind, a loving parent, a good person.

OK, that's fine, I say. I'm happy to accept that. But some people kill deliberately. Surely that is different?

Well, yes, but then are there degrees of evil? Sarah asks me whether the person who lashes out in anger is less evil than someone else who plans a killing.

'Yes, they are,' I say. That's simple.

And is that person, in turn, less evil that someone else who choses to kill once and then again?

'Yes,' I say again. Which suggests that being truly evil involves both doing harm to others and choosing to do so.

'But why would someone choose to hurt another person?' I ask Sarah.

'That's more complicated,' she says, laughing. As a forensic psych, her world is the mind and how it dictates criminal behaviour. Among the first to explore this territory was a man called Cesare Lombroso, an Italian army medic, then psychiatrist and prison doctor, who is seen as the founder of criminology and came up with the idea that there are people that he called 'born criminals'. These criminals, Cesare said, had different brains from other people. They were dangerous individuals with physical and psychological abnormalities that were throwbacks to more primitive stages of human evolution.

You could tell them from other, 'healthy' people by these physical defects, which were also obvious from the outside: smaller, deformed skulls; crooked noses; sloping foreheads. Put crudely, born criminals were monsters.

Ideas change. Cesare's anatomy of violence was all but abandoned during the twentieth century. Today, Sarah's world looks very different.

'There are no monsters,' she says, 'at least not as Lombroso found them. There are, instead, only people. Some people might be born with some kind of predisposition, like a fault line in their make-up, but that alone does not give you a proper explanation. Something needs to shake that person, something bad enough to force that crack wide open.'

I trust Sarah. Though she's now left the New South Wales Police Force, over the years she was pretty much embedded in the William Tyrrell investigation. Her insights into how people think helped us devise our different strategies, including how we would approach potential suspects in person. She pioneered this role, advising directly on police operations and, in doing it, she has seen some of the worst humanity can offer. Other cases she's worked on include the 2009 murder of five members of the Lin family in northwest Sydney and the years-long search for the fugitive killer Malcolm Naden, who was eventually captured in 2012.

Before joining the police force, Sarah spent years studying the badness that we do to one another. She wrote her Ph.D. thesis on profiling patterns in serial sex crimes and later studied different international approaches to offending, including under some of the people who first developed forensic profiling at the FBI. These pioneers included Roy Hazelwood, part of the FBI's Behavioral Science Unit (BSU), who, in 1980, developed one of the fundamental concepts in understanding murderers, the distinction between *organised* and *disorganised* killers.

To explain it, an organised killer is one who plans his killing. He's Freddy Krueger, the figure from your nightmares. A disorganised killer isn't like this. He doesn't plan. He acts out of impulse, or because he thinks the circumstances demand it. Maybe his first crime was to rob or sexually assault his victim. Then he realises that victim can identify him, so he panics. He kills to stop them talking.

Shortly after Roy joined the BSU, they began a famous research project, visiting prisons across the US to sit down with and interview 36 convicted murderers, who, between them, were known to have killed 118 people, mostly women. These were the worst of the worst – men like Edmund Kemper, Richard Speck and David Berkowitz. It was the first time anyone had done this kind of research and, back then, in the late 1970s and early 1980s, police forces around the world had little understanding of these killers, or others like them. It was a member of the BSU who first came up with the phrase 'serial killer'.

As well as speaking to these serial offenders, the FBI looked at their histories, their IQ and school performance, the wealth or poverty they grew up in, and their sexual experiences. What they found was that many were not simply monsters. Instead they often had ordinary things in common. Most came from families with a history of alcohol or drugs, the FBI discovered. They talked about physical abuse or neglect during childhood, or of having fractured relationships with their parents.

Patterns started to emerge among the killers' answers. Using their responses, the FBI drew up a table listing the frequency of different behaviours during childhood, adolescence and adulthood. These included: daydreaming; compulsive masturbation; isolation; chronic lying; enuresis (bed wetting); fire setting; cruelty to animals; and convulsions. Three of these – bed-wetting beyond the normal age, fire-starting and cruelty to small animals – were thought to be behaviours that could predict violent behaviour in adults. They became known as the homicidal triad.

Like with most things, others disagreed with the FBI's conclusions. Sarah stresses that the scientific research has also developed hugely since those early days. But what they did was pioneering. They showed that badness might be hard to understand for those who had not themselves committed acts of evil. But it could be made sense of. In fact, it could be studied.

At first, some of these killers' acts still seemed senseless: Edmund Kemper took one of his victim's heads and buried it in his mother's garden, facing up towards her bedroom; David Berkowitz had claimed to be obeying the orders of a 3000-year-old demon in the form of a black dog belonging to his neighbour. That story became a sensation, repeated in newspapers, on TV and even in the movies. But when the FBI sat down with David, he admitted the dog had been a hoax. A wind-up. His real motivation was anger at how he had been treated by his mother and other women, the FBI concluded. Edmund also described a bitterly unhappy relationship with his mother, a domineering alcoholic who would mock and abuse him. Asked why he buried his victim's head in her garden, he replied that his mother always wanted people to look up to her.

It was a kind of twisted explanation.

Sarah waits, again, as if she expects me to ask a question, but I'm silent. That, then, is my second lesson: that monsters can be understood, if not forgiven.

* * *

Having learned her lessons overseas, from different police forces, Sarah brought her own ideas to the New South Wales Police Force. At the beginning, she says, people called her Clarice, after Clarice Starling, the fictional FBI student from *The Silence of the Lambs*, who gets sent by the BSU to interview Hannibal Lecter. Slowly, Sarah was accepted. When they saw how she could help them understand the people they were chasing, different detectives asked to work with her. In 2017, three years after William went missing and when we were deeply involved in the investigation to find him, she was named Employee of the Year. After about 17 years with the cops, when Sarah left to take up a chief psychologist's position with the State prison service, she wasn't Clarice any longer. She was cherished.

Which is why I thought she could help me. Only, nothing is ever simple when you are talking to Sarah.

'An offender might not even completely understand why they've committed an offence,' she continues over the telephone. Instead, they might be driven by impulse, without thinking. 'And even if they think about it, a criminal might not really know what's driving them to do it.'

She describes another case she worked on, a brutal murder. The violence involved made the cops think whoever did it must have been motivated by some powerful emotion. A suspect was arrested and Sarah watched him being interviewed by a detective, who kept asking, 'Where does that anger come from? Have you been angry like that before?'

As time passed and the detective kept on using the word 'anger' the suspect seemed to get confused. He struggled to find answers. Sarah was worried that he would eventually stop talking.

During a break in the interview, she told the detective to stop asking about anger. Instead, she said, ask their suspect why he did it.

'I just felt that I had to,' said the killer. A feeling had come over him, although he didn't seem to understand it. Watching, Sarah thought this made sense. The killer was right – he just felt he had to, but he did not know why he had that feeling. As a psychologist, Sarah thought you could explain it; he was driven by a desire to kill and had a fascination with violence, but it wasn't anger. It was exploratory. Experimental.

Asked again to explain what happened, the killer said, 'I just did it.' Even he didn't really understand it, thought Sarah, but on some deep level, the killer wanted to have power over someone.

'Can you then say that what he did was evil?' she asks.

Yes, I think. *It was*. But if he didn't know why he was doing what he did to his victim, does that make him less evil or more evil than another violent killer?

Sarah laughs. She laughs a lot during our conversations, I realise. Without that, I don't know how she could keep doing the work she does. 'That's it,' she says. 'That's why I don't like talking about evil.' It's a strangely shifting subject. Everyone, when asked whether one person is more evil than another, can come up with a different answer. There's no science to it, she says. That's why you won't find the word evil in any psychological or psychiatric textbook.

* * *

I remember Sarah saying something about the different reasons people kill to me before, when I was heading out of the strike force's headquarters, towards Benaroon Drive, the dead-end street that disappears into deep forest, where William went missing.

Looking up at the tall, two-storey, brick home where William was last seen, I'd tried to think myself into the mind of whoever was to blame for his disappearance. This might be a pre-planned crime, I'd thought — an organised killing. Or it might be a the work of a disorganised killer, acting out of impulse. It might also be that William died by accident, say in a fall. If so, the real evil might be the act of covering up after his death, instead of the act of killing.

If so, the most likely suspects were those inside the house when William was reported missing. But when I took over the case, the previous lead detective told me his foster parents had already been discounted as potential suspects. I did not accept that. Instead, I looked at them again, trying to find something to either rule them in or out. There was nothing to make me think that the couple were guilty, so we were back to looking for someone from outside the family.

As a detective, you try to put yourself there when the crime happened; to picture what was going through the crook's mind. What did he see? What did he do next?

Studying the outline of the house, against the trees, the white line of the verandah running around the top floor, high above where the ground slopes away beneath it, I kept coming back to the idea of an abduction. The road leading up to the house was quiet, with the few other houses spaced out over semi-rural blocks the size of horse paddocks. There was no reason for anyone to drive up there unless they were visiting one of these isolated properties. That meant few witnesses if someone took a child. But, also, that anybody waiting on the road, planning to abduct the toddler, would more likely be noticed.

Could someone just happen to have been there?

I remembered years before, when I was driving home at night and our neighbours had young children, twins, about 11 months old. Somehow, one of them was in the road. I nearly ran over the child. I jumped out, grabbed the kid and was holding them in my arms when my neighbours came out, saying 'Thank God!', having just realised the child was missing.

What if you were driving up the road here, I thought, *and, just as you came past where that sign is there on the tree, a three-year-old kid runs down the hillside from the house towards you?*

What would you do?

You'd slow down.

Then what?

You'd wait.

Then what? What if the kid doesn't say anything and no one is coming out to find him?

You can't just leave the kid. You pick him up. You put him in the car with you.

Then what?

He's lost. You found him on the roadside. Maybe you start the engine, planning to take him to one of the houses, or to a police station. Maybe you turn the car round. And still, there's no one out here looking for him. The boy wearing the red and blue Spider-Man costume is sitting in the front seat.

Only then do you think this is an opportunity. It might not be something you've ever thought of doing. You've had these thoughts before, but never acted on them. After all, you're not a monster. But, with a car, you could be five kilometres away from here in minutes and then, if anybody asks, you could say: I found him. No one was there. I couldn't leave him.

You look around. So far, you've done nothing wrong. Even if somebody is watching, no one is going think that you are up to something evil. Maybe you don't really understand just what it is you're doing now. You're in the car. The kid is looking at you.

Hey Spider-Man, you say to him. You have always been good with children. You press down on the accelerator.

Then you panic.

***

It was only a theory. But for a moment, looking up at the tall house with the white verandah, I could imagine that it might have happened. And it wouldn't need a monster, or Frank Abbott, to do it.

'It might be because I'm out of the cops and looking at things differently,' I say to Sarah over the phone. 'But it's almost like when someone does a bad thing, I always used to say they were a bad person.'

'Yes.' She waits for me to continue.

'But you're saying that is not the case. You're almost saying that anyone might be capable of doing a bad thing.'

'Yes, that's probably right. Given the right circumstances, perhaps they are. It depends what the thing is,' she says. 'Although there are some heinous acts, most of us couldn't do those.'

I think about how I've had people come up, including cops I used to work with, and tell me I am shameful, or that I am a bad person, after the courts decided I was a criminal.

'Are you comfortable with saying there are some people who are just beyond redemption?' I ask Sarah.

'Ummm, probably. Yeah. I mean, I guess,' she answers. 'Maybe it's my profession, but we're not trained to look at it that way. I look at things in terms of risk.' If anybody can commit a crime, what is the risk that *this* person will do so?

'It's hard to know who is capable of doing badness before they commit their first crime,' Sarah says. But once they have offended, once you have had a chance to study their history, their motivations, maybe to work with them in prison, then it is easier to work out their risk of re-offending. 'So I think in terms of this person being high-risk of committing another crime, rather than this person being evil,' she continues.

'Can't you just look at things in black and white?' I ask her.

She laughs again.

With Frank, you can see how someone might make that calculation. He's already been in prison for sexually abusing children. It's easy to think he may have done the same again with William. But there's no real evidence he did so. At best you can say Frank is high-risk. You'd want to know more about him. You can't say he is evil. You cannot say he did it.

Hanging up, I turn on the television. The same images are repeated across every channel: Frank, pictured with white hair bursting out from beneath a baseball cap, skin creased, his belly sagging; William, in the Spider-Man costume he was wearing on the morning he went missing; a line of uniforms advancing across an empty field.

This Ideal Young Girl

In late October 2020, I call Ian Kennedy and ask to meet him for a coffee at a place in Mascot, not far from my home in the city centre. When he arrives, Ian's still the same bear-like man I remember from the police academy; when I was one of a roomful of young, aspiring detectives he'd been sent down to teach how to investigate a homicide.

To me, sitting in the audience, Ian seemed to be the archetype of a policeman. He was gruff. A hardarse. Someone who could hold his own. Outside work, he played rugby union for Randwick, a tough game of confrontation, and it was from playing rugby that he earned his nickname, 'Speed'. He was one of the few detectives whose face people outside the force would recognise, mainly from TV reports about the latest act of badness. When you saw him on the evening news, your first thought was, 'Oh, Speed's on it. Now they're playing first grade.'

As he fills the doorway of the café, I can tell he's older now, of course, and long out of the police force, but I still see the same old, hard-charging cop in his lined face and in the set of his shoulders. Smiling a greeting, I stand up. His fist fills mine. We shake hands.

This Ideal Young Girl

I tell Ian how I'm working on the podcast and ask if he'll agree to take part in an interview. I know it won't be easy, I say. It will also be hard listening for the audience, but the story of how he arrested Michael Murphy is legend in the police force. Ian burst into the house where Michael was sitting in the lounge room and pointed a shotgun at him. He told Michael to lie down. Then Ian stood there, with his size 11½ boot on Michael's head until the house was clear, before handcuffing his suspect.

That kind of violence always leads to questions. When asked in court how the defendant got the red mark visible on his cheek, the big man answered: 'Probably when I had my foot on his head as he lay on the floor.' And no one criticised him for it. By then, Michael was one of five men accused – and despised – over the murder of a young nurse, Anita Cobby. That was in February 1986, my first full year in the police force. It remains the one killing that every Homicide detective in Sydney has heard of, no matter how young or old they are.

I remember the reaction across Sydney when Anita's body was discovered. The streets had never been so quiet. Women were scared they'd become the next victim and no longer felt safe to walk outside alone. Men would drive their wives, or girlfriends, daughters, sisters to work and drive them home again. It changed us as a city, as if we lost our innocence that summer. Even today, when cops speak of Anita's murder, they call it the worst crime they have heard of. They look at you in incomprehension that anyone could do that, and they shake their heads.

Ian led the investigation. I tell him that I want to ask about how he responded to that kind of badness. What it takes to face it and what you do when you have found the people who carried it out. Anita's death should not be raked over without reason, I tell Ian. I'm not here to celebrate it. But nor should it be forgotten.

Ian looks at me and nods.

***

We meet up again to do the interview at a hotel, the Keg & Brew, a few streets away from where I work at the *Sunday Telegraph*, and where the mid-morning sunlight streaming through the old, sash windows casts dark shadows around the walls and heavy, wooden furniture. The pub is empty. Ian and I are face to face across a table.

'OK,' I say as the recording starts. 'Now excuse me again for the formalities, but are you here of your own free will?'

'Yes,' he answers, smiling with recognition at the opening words we used to give the crooks when we were in the job.

'No threat, promise or inducement has been held out to you to participate in this interview?'

'I wouldn't worry about a threat from you, mate,' he says, and grins.

'Is that a challenge?'

He shrugs, still smiling, and leans forward into the sunlight. A cloud passes when I start to ask about Anita's murder. His eyes fall to the table.

'OK,' he starts, and stops. 'Well.' Looking for the right beginning. 'Anita was a nurse, which is tragic in a sense because nurses are there to help everyone.'

I nod. The newspapers ran photos of her after the murder happened. Bright-eyed, as if looking forward to the rest of her life. I wait for him to continue the story.

This Ideal Young Girl

It was a hot February, he says, in Blacktown, western Sydney. So hot that a dairy farmer called John Reen was sleeping badly. A few nights earlier, on maybe the Saturday, 1 February or maybe Sunday, 2 February, John was woken by the sound of screaming coming from one of the paddocks where he kept his cattle. But it wasn't unusual to hear loud noises coming from the Boiler Paddock. Young people went there to party. The place was isolated, with a deserted road running between the fields and out of sight of any nearby houses. John turned over and tried to get back to sleep.

On the Tuesday morning, 4 February, John noticed his cattle were acting strangely, all gathered around one corner of the paddock. He went to look and found a woman's body lying on her stomach, naked. John raced back to the house and called police.

Ian got the call just before 1 pm, when he was sitting at his desk in the Homicide Squad offices. It was rare, back then, for Homicide to get involved in a case so quickly, but Ian says this was different. 'The officer-in-charge of the detectives at Blacktown, when they said we've got a naked girl's body in a paddock, he thought it was pretty extreme.'

He drove out to the Boiler Paddock and knew at once that this was more violence than one person could have committed. The bruises. The blood. The deep cuts to her neck. This was the work of a group, Ian thought. A pack. The worst part was when the doctor arrived and began his examination. 'She was lying face down and we rolled her over and the head just about fell off because that's just how severe the cut was.'

Ian closes his eyes, as if trying to shut out the memory. 'When you see something like that,' he says. 'That's tough.'

It doesn't matter then how big and rough you are yourself, it never leaves you.

With the doctor, Ian looked at the dead woman in more detail. Her shoulders seemed to have been dislocated. Her eyes were swollen, as if she'd been punched. There were more cuts to one of her hands, where two fingers were almost severed. Ian thought that these looked like defence wounds – caused when someone raises their hands to protect themselves from an attacker; evidence that the woman fought back. Elsewhere, her body carried more evidence of being beaten. There were sexual injuries. To the detectives' eyes, it looked like a sadistic attack.

The cops' first task was to find her name, and then her family, but without her clothes, without her purse, there was no easy way of knowing who she was. Checking the local Missing Persons reports, they found a man called Garry Lynch had reported his daughter Anita missing the evening before, on the Monday. Anita hadn't turned up for work at Sydney Hospital, he'd told police. They were worried. Their daughter would never let anyone down like that.

Ian says he drove to the family's home, taking a wedding ring the dead woman had been wearing with him. I feel a chill just thinking about that moment, when you knock on someone's door, knowing that the person behind it will have to open up for you to break their world to pieces. When he arrived, Ian told Garry that he was sorry but the police had recovered a body that they thought might be Anita. Garry physically sagged, says Ian, as if ready to collapse. Ian showed them the ring. Time stood still for her family. Ian says he stayed with them for as long as he could, while they told him about their daughter.

This Ideal Young Girl

Anita had grown up in Blacktown. A model student. She raised money for charity and won the Miss Western Suburbs beauty pageant. She'd been married for a year or so and her husband, John Cobby, arrived at the family home soon after Ian got there. He and Anita had met while the two of them were training to be nurses.

Ian learned that the newlyweds had separated weeks before, although they were getting back together. As he listened, Ian says, he was already thinking about the work ahead to find her killers. All those details of her life would help to drive him. 'We had this ideal young girl, a beautiful nurse, young daughter, young married woman, you know, we really wanted to catch them.'

Back at Blacktown Police Station, more than 20 other cops had gathered and begun working. The feeling was one of shock, and fury, and a need to find the people who could do that to Anita. They started piecing together her movements, speaking to everyone who knew her. They worked so many hours, over so many days, without any let up, that Ian once drove home early one morning after leaving the office and pulled into his driveway before falling asleep, dead to the world, slumped against the car seat.

As a young uniformed constable working in a different part of Sydney, we were also focused on Anita's murder. Every day, as the summer sun beat down, I'd read the papers, looking for the headlines about the killing. Each afternoon, the heat would worsen. Out in the streets, working on unrelated jobs, we'd discuss what we would do if it was us who found the killers. It felt as if the whole city was seething, getting ready to lash out.

Everything in My Power

Three days after the discovery of Anita Cobby's body, a radio presenter called John Laws read out the findings of her autopsy on air. As he spoke, rage erupted among both the police and the public; John was the uncrowned king of Sydney's talkback stations, with hundreds of thousands of people listening as he described those sickening, bloody details. This was no ordinary killing. Anita had bled to death after her neck was cut open.

Autopsy reports are usually kept private, for good reason, and never before had I heard grim details of a murder being detailed in public like this. To this day, I cannot imagine why someone would have leaked it. Were they driven by their own anger at what happened? Did they want to provoke a reaction? If so, it worked. People started calling for the return of the death penalty. The police commissioner was demanding a report on the investigation every 24 hours. The New South Wales Premier was also getting daily briefings.

As the lead detective trying to find Anita's killers, Ian Kennedy was working until 10 pm or later each night, pushing through his own exhaustion, using his own sense of rage as motivation.

I've been through that myself, I say to Ian, where the bosses want a daily report and you've just worked for 18 hours, you need to sleep, you've lost your motor skills so you can't even type, and you're still sitting there trying to put a report together. It takes absolute conviction. Without that, you can't keep going.

At the same time, you must accept your limitations. Anita's father, Garry Lynch, was constantly on the TV and radio channels, says Ian, asking for help, despite the weight of his own grief and horror. It would have been natural for Ian to want to comfort him. To promise that they'd find the killer. But he couldn't make that promise. When I was running Homicide investigations, I say to Ian, I'd tell the victims' families that I'd do everything in my power to find the killer, but never that I would definitely find them.

'Because if you make a promise to them that you can't keep that's going to cause more trauma,' I say.

'That's exactly what I said,' Ian agrees.

Their first real breakthrough came when they found two teenage witnesses who'd been on Newton Road in Blacktown on the night Anita went missing. One of them had heard screams and run outside, to see a dark-haired woman being dragged into a car by two men. It looked like a dirty white or maybe a grey Holden.

If that had been Anita, Ian thought, then they were looking for at least three people; the two who forced her into the car and one other who was driving. And if there were at least three people – a pack, just like Ian had feared when he first saw Anita's body – then that could help them. It meant there was more chance that someone out there must know something. Or that one of the three might turn on the others.

It meant the media attention could help also. Maybe there was already someone out there wrestling with the idea of coming forward. That person might be overcome, for now, by fear or the idea of betraying a friend or family member. But all these headlines, all this public anger, might help that person's conscience make a comeback.

So Ian fed the media tidbits, enough to keep the headlines coming. Garry did his part, also, never knocking back an interview request. They kept Anita's murder on the front pages. As hurtful as all the attention must have been to deal with, Ian thought Garry understood what they were doing. When you're out there going head-to-head with something evil, it might be a decision to do the right thing, made in the heart of a total stranger, that can make the difference.

* * *

In this case, someone did step forward. That person told police to look at an 18-year-old named John Travers, calling him an evil man, the kind who could have carried out an act like murdering Anita. Ian says the cops learned John had a criminal record going back to his childhood. He was wanted in Western Australia over a rape at knifepoint. Those who knew John also told a story about him; how, once, he had sex with a sheep in his backyard, slit its throat then cooked and ate the animal.

Ian did not know whether to believe it.

The cops learned that John was one of a group of men who'd been at a party on the night Anita went missing, but had left it and, later, come back. Each had given different accounts of what they'd been doing. A day after Anita's funeral, on 11 February 1986, the police were told that John and two more men, 18-year-old Michael Murdoch and 23-year-old Leslie (Les) Murphy, had recently stolen a car matching the one in Blacktown that witnesses described seeing a woman get dragged into.

All three men, John, Michael and Les, were young, two of them barely adults, Ian says, but all were already established crooks with a rat cunning. Like rats, they were hard to catch. They rarely stayed at one place for long, the cops learned, instead moving between houses belonging to family or friends, spending their days drinking and getting stoned, often paying for the booze or pot with money they had stolen.

After 10 long days spent looking for them, on Friday, 21 February, the cops gathered in the operations room of Blacktown Police Station and were split into two groups. Each was given an address. Ian warned the officers in the room against getting carried away with their emotions. Outside, people were still calling for Anita's killers to receive no mercy. Ian didn't want anyone inside the room deciding to take vengeance.

One of the two teams went to a house belonging to John's uncle and dragged the 18-year-old out of a bed that he was sharing with Michael. The other team, led by Ian, arrested Les. All three were charged over stealing the car. During the interviews that followed, the cops also asked about the murder, but all three denied it.

John, particularly, was cold, says Ian. Like he had no emotions. John asked to see his uncle's partner, who he called his aunty. Ian saw an opportunity.

The police called John's aunty, who Ian says he cannot name and instead refers to only as Miss X.

'I said, "He wants some cigarettes. We've got cigarettes, we'll give them to you but if you come in would you be prepared to wear a listening device?"' says Ian.

The woman told him, 'Yes. If he's responsible for what this girl got then he deserves whatever's coming to him.'

They sent Miss X to visit John in his jail cell, Ian tells me. 'She said to him, "Here's your cigarettes, what have they got you in for?"'

John told her they were asking questions about Anita's murder.

'Did you do it?' Miss X asked him.

John told her, yeah. He even bragged about it. He told her there were five of them involved, himself and Michael Murdoch, Les and also Les's older brothers, Gary and Michael Murphy, who was himself on the run from prison over an armed hold-up.

All of them had raped Anita, John told Miss X, unsuspecting that his aunty was now working with the detectives. He seemed to be uncaring. At one point, says Ian, Miss X even had to ask John to stop laughing.

John said the other men told him, 'Do your thing', after they raped Anita. The cops could only guess at what he meant by this. They'd heard about the sheep he'd killed by cutting its neck open.

Miss X walked back shaking, Ian tells me. 'She came out and she collapsed in my arms and said, "It's him, it's him."' But this was not a victory. Not really.

That's the thing with Homicide investigations; everybody loses, because you start out with a murder. Finding out who'd killed Anita couldn't take away the anger at what was done to her, nor the grief that had swallowed up her family.

Also, the police work wasn't finished. The cops now knew there were five men involved but none of them had been charged over the murder. Two of them, Les and Michael Murdoch, had to be released on bail as they had, so far, been charged only over the car theft. The cops kept John locked up because he was wanted for the rape in Western Australia, but even with his confession to Miss X, Ian knew they did not have enough evidence against him.

I can imagine Ian's thought process in this moment, knowing that a good defence lawyer could always claim that John's confession to Miss X was actually a lie, or a boast, or was tricked out of him. The cops still had more work to do on this investigation to make good on Ian's promise to do everything in his power to find the killers.

I Go in First

The cops confronted John Travers in his cell shortly before 4.40 am on Sunday, 23 February, three weeks after Anita Cobby's murder. By then, based on Miss X's recordings, they had re-arrested Les Murphy and Michael Murdoch, this time over the killing. Both had told police that it was John who carried out the murder. Waking the 18-year-old, the detectives told him they now had new information.

John did not deny it. Instead, he looked at them with the coldest eyes they'd ever seen and asked, 'Who gave us up?'

Inside an interview room, two detectives led him through his formal confession. John admitted that they'd forced Anita into their stolen car. That they had raped her. After taking her purse, they bought petrol at a local servo, holding Anita down inside the car so nobody outside it could see her. Then they drove out to the Boiler Paddock.

For Ian Kennedy, one of the worst moments was following John's confession. He drove out to Anita's parents' house. Her father, Garry Lynch, opened the door.

Ian told him, 'Look Garry, just to let you know we've got three of them.'

'Oh my God, how many were there?'

Hard as this was to deliver, it was better that Anita's parents heard the news from him in person. Better anything than have them read about it in the next day's paper without warning.

News of the arrests drove people into a frenzy. A mob gathered outside Blacktown Police Station as John, Les and Michael Murdoch were taken to court for a brief, formal appearance. The crowd wanted vengeance. People carried placards reading 'Hang the bastards' and tradies fashioned nooses out of ropes and hung them over the sides of buildings opposite the police station. The crowd was rocking the police car carrying the three men, trying to get at them. Hearing Ian describe this, I'm sure that, on any other day, most of the people in that crowd would have found it hard to believe that they themselves could carry out a murder. But the horror of what was done to Anita meant they were now clamouring for death.

***

I wonder if we are all capable of violence. On the last day of the inquest into William Tyrrell's disappearance, I sat in court, watching his foster parents present the black-gowned coroner with a book of family photos they had taken of the three-year-old. The coroner's face was drawn in a grim line as William's foster mother – who still could not be named or pictured in public – said the photos were like memories, evidence of her son's innocence, as well as the love the family had for one another.

My replacement as the lead investigator, Detective Chief Inspector David Laidlaw, sat impassively throughout the inquest hearings, his eyes hard to read, staring forward. At times, he would reach up to run one hand over his greying moustache. When William's foster parents had themselves given evidence – his foster father for about an hour, his foster mother over almost two days – they had said the family's relationship with the police went from 'empathetic' to 'cold' after I was taken off the investigation. I had always encouraged them to call me on my mobile phone if they wanted to talk but William's foster mother said she was told not to call David, but to go through other members of the strike force instead. There were also fewer police working the case now than when I led it, she told the inquest. She feared the force was losing interest.

'No other family member should ever feel the need to fight tooth and nail in order to maintain commitment to find out what happened,' William's foster mother told the inquest. It was now 19 months since the inquest started and, sitting there, it seemed to be flailing around, trying to find a suspect. The searches near Frank Abbott's caravan had found nothing, or at least nothing we were told about in public. Other possible explanations for William's disappearance had been raised, repeated in the press, then seemingly abandoned. Like the witness who said he'd seen a LandCruiser speeding past outside his home in Kendall on the day that William went missing. Inside the car, he claimed, was a young boy in the back seat wearing a Spider-Man costume. Or the evidence about another man who worked in a local Caltex servo a few minutes' drive from Kendall. He'd done time for sexual assault, the inquest heard, and there was some confusion over his timesheets. Had he been at work when William went missing? For a moment it seemed that he might also be a potential suspect. Once again, it went nowhere.

Sitting in the coroner's court, it felt like the cops still working on the case looked at me with suspicion. After being taken off the investigation, I'd been told not to be there. William's foster parents had asked the police if I could attend it with them, saying they trusted me, despite what had happened. They told me they'd left telephone messages for the police commissioner, without receiving an answer. In the end they had written to him, saying it was with 'profound sadness' that they felt compelled to put in writing their many requests to speak or have him personally respond to their concerns.

In that letter, William's foster parents called him 'our son', and said he had been the victim of a heinous crime. 'We and William's birth family are all victims.' Over the four years of heartbreak since his disappearance, they wrote, I had been their rock, helping give them confidence that the police would leave no stone unturned and would work tirelessly to find the missing boy, 'with care and compassion for our son and those of us who have been left behind'.

The letter said the family had been supported by the New South Wales Police Minister, Troy Grant, Premier Mike Baird and others in both the State and federal parliaments. It described how the foster parents helped set up a national Where's William? campaign that put his name and face on posters, billboards and social media across the country, asking people to come forward with information.

William's foster parents said they would 'continue to lobby influence ... to ensure the wider community recognises our need to find our boy', the letter said – a line I wonder now if senior police might have seen as threatening. It continued, saying the foster parents had taken comfort knowing the police had always had William's best interests at heart and that their 'primary purpose' was solving the mystery of his abduction. Having me attend the inquest would not not change or impact its direction, they wrote, which had already been redefined after I was taken off the strike force.

The last paragraph of the letter was the most likely to provoke a reaction. It talked about those responsible for removing me from the investigation, saying 'we hope they can put aside any personal or political agendas or media concerns to ensure that Gary will be there for us, sitting beside us to support us throughout this harrowing process.' It concluded with a direct request to the police commissioner, asking that he overturn the force's decision not to allow me to attend the inquest in person. The last line was, 'Please accept our sincere appreciation for giving our request your deepest consideration.'

The letter went unanswered.

In the end, the only reason I could be at the inquest was that I had left the police, so they couldn't stop me. That meant the alliances within that courtroom were different from what I was used to. I was no longer sitting with the cops. I wondered whether they saw William's foster parents differently also.

Frustrated at the silence from the police force, William's foster parents had given one public interview, on a podcast series about their boy's disappearance produced by Network 10. In it, they were angry. His foster mother said the commissioner's lack of a response to their letter 'speaks volumes about the leadership of that organisation. Speaks volumes about what they see as important.' She said that they had been ignored or dealt with unprofessionally and without empathy by senior police. She said they had been told that William's disappearance would eventually be sent to Unsolved Homicide, just like the disappearance of Michelle Pogmore, where the files would gather dust inside rows of cardboard boxes, being pulled out every six months or so for a review.

'We cannot let this happen,' said William's foster mother in that podcast. 'Because this is what's going to happen; it will go to inquest and the coroner will say, "The police have done a great job, thank you very much," and deliver an open finding. The police will go, "Great, we did a really good job, let's push that over onto Unsolved."

'And it's going to sit there and people are going to forget about it and every so often they're going to pull it back out again ... and someone will have a look at it: "Hmm, yes, nothing new's come through. We'll put it back in that box." So who forgets? Police will forget. People will forget William ... We can't let people forget William. We can't. He's a three-year-old boy that was abducted. How can we, public, police, say that's OK and let it go?'

She had said the same thing in court during my own trial, after being called as a witness. There, William's foster mother told the court how the then head of the Homicide Squad had said the case was going to be sent to Unsolved Homicide. The same senior officer had also told her there had been a formal handover between myself and David, when he took over the investigation.

'He told me Gary Jubelin was doing a handover with David,' she said in court. But she then spoke to David, who told her there had been no handover. That he was not allowed to talk to me.

'I am angry,' William's foster mother had told the court. 'Angry with those running the police force.'

By saying this in public, I'd feared that she would make herself a target. I wondered what the response would be.

***

Ian says that more than 50 armed police were gathered for the raids in which they arrested the last two men suspected of Anita Cobby's murder. Once more, he felt the need to remind the cops to control their emotions, that their job was to deliver justice for Anita's family, not vengeance. Then they went in.

'One bloke had a sledgehammer,' Ian says, 'and he's the entry man, so he smashes the door in. I'm number one, I go in first, I look to the right as I'm going through, number two behind me looks to the left, so he covers me.

'I had a shotgun,' Ian continues, 'we walked into a small hall and then there was a lounge room.' Gary and Michael Murphy were sitting inside, and Michael had a kid sitting on his knee.

Gary jumped up and ran outside, straight into some of the surrounding police, who tackled him, smashing his face against the back fence. Inside, Ian pointed his shotgun at the eldest of the Murphy brothers.

'The reason I did that was Michael was a prison escapee and he'd been serving time for an armed robbery,' he tells me.

'I didn't know if he had a gun or anything. So I said, "Michael, put the kid down and lie face down on the floor," which he did. I stood on his head, I waited until people weren't running around and everything was quiet. And I handcuffed him and took him away.'

In court, the five accused men smirked and whispered to each other. Both Anita's father, Garry, and her husband, John Cobby, have admitted that thoughts of murdering these men came to each of them, unbidden. After the trial, when the jury walked into the court to give their verdict, the vast, echoing room fell silent.

Then it came. Guilty. All five of them. Guilty of Anita's murder.

Members of the public wept.

***

Was Ian right to stand there with his boot on the head of Michael Murphy? It was violent and, today, we often think of violence as being wrong, as if it itself is an act of badness; the product of our darker, illicit urges. The courts routinely brand people as criminals for using violence and give out higher prison sentences to those who do violent crimes, like a robbery at gunpoint. But when I was training to become a cop, sitting in the lecture hall at the police academy, we didn't learn a lot, if anything, about *why* criminals used violence. My memory is that the lecturers seemed instead to want to shock us by telling us of the violent crimes they'd dealt with, so we would understand just how dangerous the world was that we were heading into.

They taught us self-defence and hand-to-hand combat, so we could deal with violence when we had to. Wanting to know more about its source, I've since started learning about a US forensic psychiatrist, Dr Dorothy Otnow Lewis, who studied child development and violent crime, and has appeared as an expert witness in the trials of several serial killers, including Ted Bundy, Joseph Franklin and Arthur Shawcross. Dorothy has described how, during her own training in the mid-twentieth century, she was taught children grew up to commit crimes because they had bad parents or because of poverty and social inequalities in the world around them. Violence was the product of these unnatural forces. It was something they learned.

Dorothy was not convinced, though. She spent time in a nursery school, studying normal child development and one morning, watched a little boy who was bored with making bubbles ask three times if he could go and play elsewhere, without success. He upended his basin of bubbles. This was an act of violence, Dorothy says, committed out of desperation. And if a normal, nursery child could resort to violence, then, surely, it was also normal. Meaning any one of us could do it.

My son, Jake, is a soldier. He has been deployed overseas, to places where the use of violence is not just legal but necessary. I used to box, a legal sport that relies on violence. Ian played rugby union, another game of physical confrontation. Police work also often involves confronting violence. Sometimes you have to put the boot in. Think of Ian putting his boot on his suspect's head. That was an act of violence but not done to hurt Michael Murphy. It was done to prevent him escaping while Ian made sure of his own safety during the chaos of that raid when no one knew how many other, potentially armed criminals there might be in the house around them. Ian used violence in that moment to *enforce* the law.

Think also about Ian warning the other cops involved in that raid on the house, before entering the building, not to take the law into their own hands. *That is another lesson*, I think. *We all have violence in us.*

Times change and, by the time I'd become a Homicide detective, I would have been suspended if I'd put my foot on a suspect's head in order to arrest him. But I've done other things that some might find unpleasant.

I can use the violence in me. Sometimes you might go in and sit down opposite a crook and look like you're just itching to do them badness, but every twitch is deliberate, it is an act to make them feel uncomfortable. Sometimes you might go in seeming cold and uncaring. You might even provoke somebody to tears with your questions. At other times, you might seem to be on their side. You might try to understand them: sympathise with your suspect, even if he's a paedophile or killer; you might say, 'If I was in your position, I might have done that also'; you might laugh when your suspect cracks a joke.

If it took that to get a confession, then I'd do it, even if it left me feeling sickened after. So, no, I don't have a problem with Ian putting his boot on Michael Murphy's head to arrest him. It was honest. Ian was using the violence inside him to catch someone who'd done evil. The difference between Ian and his suspect wasn't that only one of them used violence, it was that Ian could control it.

I ask him if there was any point during the investigation into Anita's death when it got too much for him. When he woke up one morning and thought, *I can't do this – I don't want to go out there and deal with this badness.*

He looks at me.

'No', says Ian. 'You get up and go to work each morning because you have given your word to the victim's parents that you will do the best you can.'

***

Investigating William Tyrrell's disappearance, we did arrest someone; the white goods repairman. He'd visited the house where William went missing a few days earlier to fix a washing machine and, months before I took over the investigation, the police received a tip-off that he'd been previously accused of sexually assaulting children.

Those claims had been pursued decades before and no action taken but we looked at them again, spoke to his alleged victims and found medical evidence that seemed to support what they were saying. Confronted with a potential crime, we charged the white goods repairman over these allegations – but not in relation to William. After his arrest, and after he'd been interviewed about the alleged abuse, I questioned him, again, about the missing three-year-old.

Perhaps he might say something different this time, I thought. His world had shifted beneath him. I wasn't sympathetic. I was tough. It was an unpleasant conversation but there was a good reason to have it. There was a chance, however small, that William might still be alive and I was prepared to be unpleasant if it meant that we might find him. I had given my word to William's foster parents. I was doing police work.

It all came to nothing. In the end, the white goods repairman spent 58 days in custody, during which we conducted a covert operation that convinced me he had nothing to do with William's disappearance. The sexual assault charges were taken to court by the State's Director of Public Prosecutions but were dismissed. Sometimes, that's how the justice system works.

Since then, the repairman has gone back to court to sue the New South Wales Police Force, claiming malicious prosecution, false imprisonment and abuse of process. He claims we used the child sex charges as a way of pursuing the unrelated investigation into William's disappearance, that we were out to punish him and that we coaxed witnesses into giving evidence against him. He's named me as being at the centre of these allegations. The case is now dragging its way through the court system at the same time as the inquest into William's disappearance. As much as I try to put this past behind me, I am still tied up.

I'm tired of having to justify my actions. Of being attacked for doing police work. Sometimes, I just want to give up. I wake up, thinking, *I don't want to face the morning.* I don't want to build a new career, I don't want to do a podcast. I don't want to do anything.

I feel worn down but it might be years before the white goods repairman's legal action is resolved, the lawyers tell me. Until then, I have to keep going.

* * *

On Tuesday, 16 June 1987, the five men found guilty of murdering Anita Cobby returned to court so that they could be sentenced, all of them snickering together behind their hands. They were so young – Michael Murdoch was still in his teens, while John Travers had by then turned 20. Les Murphy was 24 and his elder brothers Gary and Michael were 29 and 34. A couple of them still had moronic smiles on their faces as the judge began to pass sentence.

The judge said he'd never seen a worse crime, not during almost 40 years in the court system. What made it so bad was the killers' absence of humanity.

'Wild animals are given to pack assaults and killings,' he said, staring down from his raised bench at the front of the courtroom. 'However, they do so for the purpose of survival, and not as a result of a degrading animal passion.' These men, then, were less than animals. They had attacked Anita to satisfy their lust and killed to prevent her from identifying them. 'The victim almost certainly was made aware, in the end, of her pending death.'

The five rose to their feet and each was given a life sentence. In most cases, in Australia, a life sentence doesn't mean a lifetime. Often, a prisoner serving a life sentence may one day be released on parole from prison; it might take years, or decades, but it happens. In this way, the system allows for forgiveness.

Not here.

Instead, the judge ordered that their sentences be as harsh, as tough, as violent as he could make them, saying, 'The circumstances of the murder of Mrs Anita Lorraine Cobby prompt me to recommend that the official files of each prisoner should be clearly marked, "NEVER TO BE RELEASED".' He also added an instruction to any future government that might one day consider releasing these five monsters, perhaps once the details of their actions had faded from memory, that they 'should grant the prisoners the same degree of mercy that they bestowed on Anita Lorraine Cobby in the Boiler Paddock'.

In doing so, the judge was taking away their freedom, their hope and their chance of redemption.

Those watching in the courtroom broke into applause.

A White Button in the Darkness

Ian and I both need a drink after finishing his interview for the podcast. Just like when I used to question killers as a Homicide detective, I feel drained after listening to all that evil. We go for lunch and have a schooner, then a few more. Over our beers, Ian tells me another story, about one time when he was going after an armed robber, who the cops called 'Bondi Bill' and who was wanted for holding up three banks in Sydney's eastern suburbs.

On the morning of 7 August 1979, Ian says, Bondi Bill went after a fourth bank, taking a sawn-off shotgun with him during the hold-up before fleeing in a hijacked taxi. The police tracked him to a unit block in Rose Bay and laid siege to the building. Ian tells me how a detective sergeant went inside and ended up wrestling with Bondi Bill before getting shot in the stomach. I wince, imagining the pain and the bravery of this detective.

The ambos couldn't get the stretcher up the stairs to get him, says Ian, so instead he went up there and told the sergeant, 'This is going to hurt,' then picked him up, threw his wounded colleague over his broad shoulders and carried him down to the street, trailing blood behind them.

'What happened to Bondi Bill?' I ask Ian.

'He got wasted.' Ian doesn't say who it was who shot the crook, but a coroner later found the killing was justified, meaning it was legal.

Listening to Ian, I recognise the outline of this story. I've heard it before – or something like it. Bernie Matthews, the old armed robber I met over hot chocolate in a Sydney café told me a story about that same police shooting, it's just that his was from a different perspective.

***

Bernie's version starts with a bloke called Wobbles. Wobbles was born Gordon Thomas and, growing up, he was so skinny it looked like his stick-like legs were struggling to hold up his body. So, instead of walking, Gordon seemed to wobble along – hence his nickname.

Bernie was 15 when they first met. Wobbles was a year older. The two of them were both working at a Sydney auction house and, one day, decided to knock over their employer's payroll – this being back when companies paid their employees in cash, meaning they'd have thousands sitting there in the office on the night before payday, ready to be collected.

Only, when they ransacked the place the pair couldn't find the money.

'Listen, we're in a bit of strife here,' said Wobbles.
'Why?'
'Our fingerprints are all over the place.'
Oh, fuck.

With hindsight, they should have known having their fingerprints in the office wouldn't prove much, because they worked there, but, of course, the two of them were kids, not trained investigators. So they panicked. How could they get rid of those fingerprints? They'd never wipe clean every surface in the whole place. What if they missed one? Wobbles came up with a bright alternative: 'Listen, how about we burn the place down?'

They did it, using packing straw to make a fire, and it burned. As they left, Bernie took the empty cash box home with him – him being only a kid and not thinking clearly.

The next morning, both he and Wobbles turned up for work as normal. But their boss was suspicious. The cops searched Bernie's place and found the cash box. He and Wobbles were pinched and were facing time in juvenile detention. That's when they came up with another plan together, to escape. As they were being led through the big, iron gates to the Yasmar Children's Court at Ashfield in Sydney's inner west, they both belted the guards who were escorting them and bolted.

Bernie went over a wire fence and down the back lane. Wobbles took off down the front drive. The guards ran down the front drive, chasing Wobbles. No one went after Bernie.

Fourteen years later, in 1979, Bernie was watching the TV news about a crook the cops called Bondi Bill, who'd done a bank and tried to escape inside a hijacked taxi. He saw how it had ended in a police siege after Bondi Bill retreated to a flat in Rose Bay, and how the cops then stormed the building. He saw how a cop had gotten shot in the stomach. The crook had been shot also.

Bernie watched as a shrouded, lifeless body was carried from the unit building on Dumaresq Road and he felt a wave of sadness. He knew Bondi Bill as Wobbles.

Bernie thought back to the 16-year-old kid who'd shown no fear when they escaped from court together. Who was growing up in a boys' home when he met Bernie and had hated life there, so wanted the money from their failed payroll robbery to get away and make a fresh start. Who was loyal to his mates and never dobbed, even after their escape ended in recapture. After ending up back in juvenile detention, word was that Wobbles picked up a heroin addiction, Bernie told me, and it was his need to feed this that got him into the bank robberies, which led to his shooting.

To Bernie, the lesson was that criminals can be victims also.

***

I drive out early, heading northwest from Sydney to visit Bernie at home, following the highway as it climbs into the Blue Mountains. It's early November 2020 and on the car radio, the presenter is talking about William Tyrrell's disappearance. The coroner has said she'll hand down her findings in seven months, in June 2021, meaning the hearings will, by then, have taken more than two years to come to a conclusion.

The longer this goes on, the less likely it seems that anyone will find him. That makes me sick. I think about William's sister, who is the last person known to have seen him alive. She was five back then, a foster child like he was, and remembers that the two of them were playing a game of tigers on the lawn beneath the house, out of sight of the adults. She was six, I think, the first time I met her, running around under our feet during a visit to the foster parents' home during the investigation. We said hello and I made kid talk, like I used to with my daughter when she was about the same age. The last time I saw her, she had grown up and was sitting at the table with the family when we met at a yum cha place in Sydney. We'd barely started eating before she was asking, 'Can we go now?'

She was strong-willed, just like my own daughter had been. Maybe a little hard to manage but, then, who could blame her? She'd been through so much already; being taken from her birth family, being in State care, a foster child, then her brother's disappearance. But she was definitely determined. Before the end of its public hearings, the inquest had heard someone read out a prepared statement from the then 10-year-old, saying:

'I hope this speech makes you solve the case. If it doesn't, when I am officially adult, I will be in the police force, a detective specifically, and I will find my brother and not give up until he is found.'

Outside the car, the trees on either side give way to golden fields and sun-burned cattle country as the road heads down the far side of the mountains, towards Bathurst. I pull up by an old building on the main street, where the morning sunlight is only starting to warm up the cold, stone shopfronts on either side of the doorway to Bernie's small apartment. It's quiet enough to hear the birds.

Inside, he leads me through the hallway into a little living room where his TV is set up facing a comfy, two-seater lounge with a clear indent in one of the two cushions. The room's cluttered with books and papers piled up on different shelves and on a little table, but I don't see any family photos.

'Mate, it's luxury for me,' Bernie says, seeing me looking the place over. 'You sit in a cell with nothing long enough and anything is luxury.'

He makes a cup of tea and offers me the lounge to sit on, then sits beside me. We're knee to knee, too close for any barrier between us to last long. We both relax. Making conversation, Bernie mentions a few names of guys he knew inside and I nod to say I knew them. Men like Graham Henry, who Bernie says he did time with and who grew up in North Epping, on the northern edge of Sydney, in a broken-down house on Grayson Road, less than 10 minutes' walk from my childhood house.

Graham and I went to the same school, though he was about a decade older. He grew up to become one of the few men at the very top of Sydney's underworld throughout the 1970s, 1980s and 1990s, along with his close mate, Arthur 'Neddy' Smith, who would later go down for two murders as well as being charged – and cleared – of several other killings.

Graham was a feared man. He bashed a cop over the head with a rock once, leaving him to have his face redone with wire and plastic surgery. Another time, he stabbed a police prosecutor during a drunken confrontation. Eventually, Graham fell out with Neddy and laid an ambush for him, planning to shoot the other man dead, only for some police to turn up and spoil the show.

Bernie tries to colour in the picture. Try to understand where that violence came from, he says. The story was that

Graham's father was a soldier who came back from World War II and turned to drinking. He used to flog Graham's mother until her clothes were stained with blood and, growing up, Graham would sleep on the streets to avoid him.

That anger had to come out somehow. For Graham that was fighting. According to another story, he left school at 13 after belting a teacher. Years later, I had my own run-ins with that teacher, I tell Bernie. He used to put me on detention, day after day, in a classroom on my own at the back of the school where he just stood there staring at me. I walked out.

Out on the streets, Graham formed a gang of toughs, who became known as the Sharpies because of the sharp way they dressed, with short-cropped hair and in the latest fashions. They carried knives. My cousin Russell used to run with the Sharpies, but he didn't deal in Graham's kind of badness. Graham had a way of making trouble, getting into prostitution and protection rackets while still a teenager and, later, armed hold-ups like Bernie.

Bernie says that he, too, grew up watching his mum get bashed, only for him it was by his stepdad. And, like Graham, he spent time in boys' homes. These were brutal places, he says, with kids living in fear, sleeping in brick-walled cells and beaten or starved as punishment. As well as himself and Graham and Neddy, there's a long list of other killers and vicious crooks to come out of those institutions, including the serial killer Archibald McCafferty, James Finch, who was jailed over the 1973 Whiskey Au Go Go firebombing that killed 15 people, Peter Schneidas, who beat a Long Bay prison guard to death, and Billy Munday, who committed a string of rapes that earned him a 58-year prison sentence. Billy later murdered another prisoner.

The pale sunlight filters through Bernie's lounge room window. It shows how thin his skin is. His face looks gaunt, older and thinner than I'd realised the last time we met up. Bernie is in his 70s, he tells me. His voice is hoarse. It echoes like it's never left his prison cell.

***

Bernie tells me his life story: born in Sydney, like I was, raised by his mum after his parents separated, who then married a violent drunk. My parents stayed together, but they fought. After Bernie got in a fight with another schoolboy, his mum signed him up to learn boxing at the local Police Boys Club. My grandad, my mum's dad, taught me how to box as a young boy. It was a way of helping a kid to stand up for himself and also those around him.

Aged 12, Bernie's family moved to a house on the southern edge of Sydney where he got in with a bunch of kids who introduced him to petty crime, like breaking into local shops. It was a game, he says. A heart-pumping adventure. Aged 12, living in Sydney's northern suburbs, I fell in with a mob of kids who got me into shoplifting. I felt the same thrill Bernie did. The excitement. The racing heart.

Looking back, it was like I didn't have a conscience; I just didn't think that much about it. The poor bloke in the corner store might be working 18 hours a day to make ends meet but we'd go in there and distract him and take everything we could and never wonder if it was right or wrong to do so.

Bernie says his first break-in was a hairdresser's. One Sunday he and his mates were arsing around when he climbed on to its roof, got down inside and found the cash register was open. That was all there was to it. The one difference between us is that Bernie got caught.

He was put in juvenile detention. Afterwards, he met Wobbles and they tried to rob the auction house together, got caught, escaped, then Bernie got caught again riding in a stolen car and was sent to the Mount Penang Training School for Boys. The place was built on an old naval training base on the Central Coast of New South Wales, he says, and they worked the kids ploughing the fields and paddocks until they dropped from exhaustion. In Mount Penang, Bernie met some of the people with whom he'd later carry out armed hold-ups, which would in turn lead to him being sent to adult prisons.

The worst I ever got for acting up was some harsh treatment from my dad.

Bernie's first proper stick-up was at an all-night garage on Woodford Road in western Sydney, which was rumoured to hold the night takings for local taxis. He teamed up with a kid he'd met at Mount Penang and together they cleaned it out. Success. They decided to roll the dice again; next up was the payroll at an ice-cream depot. It was a bust. They missed the payroll but made money instead off their next job, $30,000 from robbing a factory. Bernie was on the up.

Then he got sent down.

On 13 October 1969, he was arrested.

'And how old were you?' I ask.

'Twenty,' he says. 'I guess young and stupid, young and ignorant, call it what you want.' He takes a swig of tea. 'I don't use my age as an excuse.'

'Twenty,' I repeat, thinking, *We're all pretty bloody stupid when we're twenty.* Bernie got sent to Parramatta Gaol on remand, while waiting for his trial to take place.

'I didn't like Parramatta,' he says. 'So I decided, if I could get out of here I was going to get out of here. Simple as that.'

But it was not that simple. I've been in that prison as a policeman. I remember the heavy doors, tall sandstone walls and gun towers.

'You see those gun towers and you know if you try and escape they are going to shoot you,' I say.

'Of course.'

'OK,' I say. I'm starting to admire Bernie's toughness. His first escape attempt didn't involve being shot at but, listening to him tell it, I think he was no less brave than if he had.

Bernie swallowed razor blades and told the guards – who he calls screws – what he had done. He figured they would think he was trying to kill himself and so transfer him to the psychiatric centre, which would be easier to escape from. But what the screws wouldn't expect was that Bernie had wrapped the blades in cellophane, so they'd show up on an x-ray but wouldn't shred his insides.

It seemed as if the plan worked. An ambulance was called, which drove Bernie out of Parramatta. But, instead of the psych centre, he was taken to another prison, Long Bay, in Sydney's eastern suburbs. Here he was met by two new guards, who must have worked out what he was trying because they flogged him with their batons, then left him alone in a cell with a rubber shit tub for three days until he'd shitted out all the razor blades and cellophane. He lost that dice game, but didn't let it stop him.

His next escape attempt involved scratching away at his cell wall with a metal bed leg and ended in another beating after the screws spotted the flecks of mortar on the prison floor. As well as being beaten, this time he got four weeks locked in cold, dank, solitary confinement.

'It was pitch-black in the solitary cells,' he tells me. 'Like you'd imagine being blinded. And you had a coir mat, you know, like an office mat with bristles. You had two of them. You put one on top of the other and that was your bed for the night. And you had a shit tub.' No light. No sight. No noise. Few sounds reached that deep into the prison.

Try sitting with your eyes closed in silence. The seconds seem to stretch out into hours. The hours are never ending. One day, feeling his way around the cell on hands and knees, Bernie found a button. By touch, he could tell that it was plastic and he guessed that it was white, just like a pearl is. To him it was a treasure, more valuable than anything that he possessed – which wasn't much – because it could save him from the mind-numbing ordeal of solitary confinement.

'I flicked the button into the dark and I started searching for it,' he says. 'And I found it, then I flicked it, then I found it.' He did this for entire days, hands stretched out on the cell floor, checking every centimetre of the darkness. Sometimes, it might take minutes to find the button, sometimes it might take hours, or longer, it was impossible to know how long

A White Button in the Darkness

he kept at this, but it gave him purpose. 'I've got to find that button, where's that button? It's here somewhere, I know it's here because I flicked it.'

His four weeks passed. They let him out. When the sunlight hit Bernie's eyes, it felt like somebody had stabbed him. Another man might have given up at this point. Stopped bucking against the prison system and done his time. But getting out of solitary only strengthened Bernie's conviction: he wasn't staying. They could lock him up in darkness but they couldn't break him. His third escape attempt was made from the van taking him to the Queens Square District Court for sentencing, having by now been found guilty of robbing the all-night garage, ice-cream depot and factory payroll. Bernie managed to slip his handcuffs and, stepping out of the van, used them as a knuckleduster to belt the escorting cop. He bolted, just like he and Wobbles had from Yasmar. The cop chased him. Bernie ran like a hare. The cop just kept on coming.

They ran one city block, and then another, Bernie was going flat out, desperate. The cop wasn't as young as he was, but somehow Bernie could not outsprint him.

'I kept on going, I kept on going,' he says. Everything was right there, in front of him, if only he could run fast enough to get there. Freedom. Turning a corner, Bernie ran straight into a group of office workers, standing outside on the footpath. The cop behind him shouted 'Police!' and the office workers jumped on Bernie.

'Fucking heroes,' says Bernie in his lounge room, sighing. 'The cop ran up and pulled his gun and shouted, "Don't fucking move!"'

Bernie looks down at the floor. 'What I find out later was that this copper was some sort of marathon runner,' he says, looking cheated. That explains how he could keep up with Bernie.

I laugh. But Bernie isn't smiling.

'Well, it is pretty funny,' he says. Then Bernie starts to crack up too.

Bernie got ten years for the armed robberies, plus six months on top for the escape. That was in June 1970. After being sentenced, he went back to Long Bay.

He broke out that November.

A Foreign Body

This time, Bernie Matthews hid himself inside one of the prison's slop bags, which were filled with old, uneaten food and wheeled out on a trolley through the metal gates to feed the pigs outside it. A guard was supposed to run a metal spike through each of the bags on the way out but Bernie got two other convicts to distract him. Afterwards, when they'd dumped him in the slop bag, Bernie lay there, still and silent, hardly breathing, waiting until he couldn't wait any longer, before wriggling to freedom.

Hurrying away from Long Bay, Bernie thought, surely somebody would notice him, sound the alarm and he would hear the noise of running feet. But he heard nothing. This was his chance; he could leave his life of crime behind him. Get away and he could make sure of never doing anything again that risked going back to prison. Bernie says the silence was deafening.

Soon after, a friend gave him a .38 pistol and he handmade a balaclava out of some scrap material. Bernie hit the rent office at the Villawood Housing Commission, then the ANZ bank at Yagoona. By now, he says, armed robbery felt natural. Walking in through the bank doors, his adrenaline would be going and everything just flowed.

Inside, he ordered the customers onto the floor, threw a shopping bag at the teller and shouted, 'Fill it!'

Terrified, the teller did so. The only noise was the rustling of bank notes. Bernie could smell fear inside the room.

A week later, he did the same again, walking into a bank in Rozelle and jumping onto the counter with his pistol. This time, as the teller filled the shopping bag, Bernie thought he saw one of the customers lying on the bank floor looking up, as if about to challenge him.

'Don't try it, mate,' growled Bernie, swinging the barrel of the .38 around. A bullet from a gun like that could kill a man, no problem.

For a few, nervous, seconds, the two men looked at one another. Bernie had been in the army reserve for a few years after going to Mount Penang, and he knew the damage that would happen if he fired the weapon. The stand-off ended when another customer, a woman, pulled the man down, flat on the floor beside her. Bernie thought that was a smart move.

'Did you consider the consequences to the people you were pointing the weapon at?' I ask him.

The simple answer, Bernie says, is no. 'If you're going to rob a bank, the consequences don't come into play,' he says. 'Otherwise you wouldn't go in the first place.'

At least it is an honest answer. Bernie says he didn't stop to think about the badness of his actions. The way he saw it, other people went into banks and signed a withdrawal slip to get their money; he made his withdrawals with a pistol.

He's also honest when explaining why he did it: 'I was greedy. It's as simple as that.' But what he did scared people. I've worked armed robberies as a detective and spoken to the victims after. Some get recurring nightmares. Others become afraid to leave their homes or to walk down the road where the robbery took place, even years later. There might still be people out there, carrying the scars that Bernie left them, even after decades.

He sighs. It wasn't just that he didn't think about all this, he says, he *couldn't* have thought about it; post-traumatic stress disorder didn't exist back when he was holding guns in people's faces.

That's partly true. The diagnosis dates to the late 1970s, when doctors started treating US soldiers returning from the Vietnam War. But the history of the idea goes back much further, to the late nineteenth century at least, when doctors at the Hôpital de la Salpêtrière in Paris first wrote about how fragments of traumatic memories seemed to lodge themselves in the minds of their patients, wreaking havoc. Sigmund Freud, who worked at the Salpêtrière around this time as a young physician, later wrote that the memory of trauma 'acts like a foreign body' in the mind. Just like a bullet fragment.

Today, we understand it better. We know people who suffer trauma are changed by the experience. They have been found to suffer higher rates of depression, alcoholism, drug abuse and suicide.

'I never physically hurt anybody,' says Bernie. To his mind, he wasn't doing badness. He walked out of those banks as good a person as he walked in because he chose not to fire his pistol. In his mind, Bernie didn't hurt people until later. That was after December 1970, just a few weeks before Christmas, when he was dreaming of another payday, this time from the Villawood Textile Company. The upcoming holiday meant a bigger payroll and Bernie also had a bigger crew: a driver; a backup man; and two to run in. The job went well, just like in a movie, except that this time shots were fired. No one was hit, but that was down to luck more than a deliberate decision. A security guard was also assaulted.

This was another level, then, in terms of violence. 'That's when, from a police point of view, they're going to come after you,' I tell Bernie. 'You would understand that.'

'Yes, of course,' he says, unflinching.

***

Bernie didn't even make it to Christmas. On 18 December, six weeks after escaping inside the slop bag, he got caught. They took him back to Parramatta Gaol, where he was now facing another 10 to 15 years for robbing the banks and textile company, as well as his escape, all on top of the decade he was already serving. This time, Bernie knew what prison was like. It might mean beatings. Being put in solitary confinement. Three times, he tried to break out again and failed.

After almost a year, facing the prospect of another Christmas as a prisoner, Bernie used a metal jug to knock out one of the guards, then stole his keys and scrabbled to open the prison doors while the alarm echoed off the sandstone walls. Other guards poured in, surrounding him but, for a moment, says Bernie, he held them back with a shiv he'd sharpened out of a plastic toothbrush handle. They overwhelmed him. He was beaten semi-conscious, dragged into an empty cell and left there. At 6.30 am the next day, he was taken to another prison: Grafton.

I've heard the stories about Grafton. Even the worst crooks feared it. Bernie describes the journey there, a full day's drive from Sydney, as going so far away that it felt like a whole lifetime spent staring out the window at the blue sky and sunlight washing over trees and fields, the sea, the surf. It was like a dream between two days of waking, he says. Then the two-car convoy crossed the bridge over the wide, black Clarence River into Grafton and stopped.

Bernie was dragged out by the guards and made to walk through the front gate. This time, it was his own fear that he could smell.

'What's your name, you bastard?' one of the guards asked him.

Bernie looked up to answer. That was enough.

'Don't look at me, cunt!' the voice screamed. Another guard slammed his baton into Bernie's back. A fist smashed into his face and he could taste the blood. They beat him until his knees buckled and he fell onto the concrete floor.

'What's your name, cunt?' the voice repeated.

'Matthews, sir.'

'You won't fucking escape from here.'

The guards forced Bernie to strip naked and beat him with their batons until he was black and blue and traumatised and broken. Bernie knew he must not cry out. He didn't want the other prisoners, who would be listening, to think that he was weak. So he kept his mouth shut, as more blood welled up inside it. Blood has a thick, gluey taste, he says.

Eventually, the beating slowed, and the screams of anger from the pack of screws surrounding Bernie died down. He lay there in silence for a moment, before another baton slammed into his skull, sending him tumbling into darkness. He woke up in solitary confinement.

The next day, Bernie says, he was given a breakfast of oatmeal mush, the surface alive and crawling. Maggots or worms, he couldn't tell, but they wriggled off the spoon and he refused to eat it. Another screw unlocked the cell and Bernie stood there, eyes down, having learned this lesson from his beating.

'Are you on hunger strike, you bastard?'

'No sir.'

A baton smashed into the side of his head and sent him spinning. The cell door slammed. He crawled over to his plate of infested mush and ate it.

In that moment, Bernie says, he changed. Knowing what we do today about how the brain responds to trauma, we might talk about it differently but, back then, with that first spoonful, Bernie says only that he switched off. His mind became a void, without thought or feeling. It was a form of self-protection, he says. This way, all the batons, boots and fists over the coming days, weeks and months would never find a target. Because he wasn't there.

***

In Grafton, you were beaten for singing. Beaten for not facing the back door of your cell when the door was opened. Beaten for trying to use the gap beneath the heavy metal cell door to talk to another prisoner. The night before driving there to visit Bernie, I'd sat up late, reading the report of a Royal Commission into the State's prison service that took place years after Bernie's incarceration and which exposed these same abuses.

It found Grafton had been approved to serve as a special institution for the treatment of 'Intractable' prisoners, long before Bernie arrived there. That first beating, after walking through the prison gates, was standard. They called it the 'reception biff'. Some witnesses, including prison guards, claimed the beatings were 'departmental practice'.

'Such a defence is redolent of other debates concerning more sinister and more notorious happenings,' the commission's report concluded. That sounds to me like lawyer-speak for saying something similar happened under fascist regimes, such as in Nazi Germany, where those involved later tried to justify their actions by saying they were following orders.

According to this argument, those who carried out the bashings were not themselves acting out of any real badness. They were not motivated by hate or madness or a thirst for blood. At worst, it was a brainlessness committed by prison guards who could not think past their orders to see that beating prisoners was evil.

Anyone can follow orders and these guards might have been good people outside prison. Loving husbands. Fathers. Listening to Bernie talk, a part of me – the old part, the cop part – thinks that men like him deserved rough treatment. Grafton held the worst of the worst, the killers, armed robbers, men who had escaped or attacked guards, proving that they themselves weren't afraid to use violence. Another part of me – the part sitting here in Bernie's lounge room with him – sees things differently. He is human. In time, he says the screws managed to break through his defences. He started having violent dreams in which he saw the guards' decapitated heads impaled on the spiked fence surrounding the prison workshops. The violence done to him inside Grafton bred violence in his imagination. As Bernie slept, he dreamed of watching the guards being fed into an imaginary tree-chipper that ground through bone and human gristle. Blood saturated his subconscious. Having emptied his mind in order to protect it, revenge came flooding in.

Bernie's first chance for vengeance in real life came when he was transferred back to Parramatta Gaol.

An Attack Dog

Expecting another beating when two screws opened up his cell door in Parramatta, Bernie struck first, burying his fist into one of their faces. The man staggered and Bernie leapt, sinking his teeth into the guard's neck. He tasted blood and heard a scream of terror. It was as if his dreams had taken over. That screw was every screw who'd bashed Bernie in prison. Only, he was awake now. He was the monster they'd created. Crouched on top of the writhing prison guard, Bernie was going to kill him.

In his lounge room, Bernie breathes out. He's still holding his mug between both hands although we've been talking for so long now the tea inside it is finished.

'Bernie, that's really heavy stuff,' I say. 'You're describing trying to bite someone's throat out.'

'Well I had no other weapon, I only had myself,' he answers.

'Talk me through your mindset there.'

'I just attacked. Like an attack dog. I went for anything, you know?' He pauses. 'Yeah. I'm not proud of it, but that's the way I was,' he says. 'That's the way I was, and …' He stops. Looks back at me. 'And, yeah,' says Bernie. There is another silence.

Other guards piled into the cell, pulled Bernie off and beat him unconscious. As he fell back into that blackness, Bernie could hear them calling him an animal. He didn't care. From then on, they could do their worst, he realised. Beat him. Put him in solitary. It would just make him angry.

I notice my mug, too, is empty. Driving there this morning, I didn't expect to feel sympathy for Bernie, yet I do. He tried to kill a guard but he was driven to it. What I struggle to sympathise with, though, is how the guards could carry out those brutal, daily bashings.

I guess they told themselves crooks deserved it. I've said the same myself in court, as a detective, after seeing someone be sentenced to prison: 'He got what he deserved.'

In the 1960s, a US social psychologist called Melvin J. Lerner came up with a reason for this. He ran a series of experiments watching people's reactions when they saw someone else be punished and found a strange result; that people started to think less of the person who was suffering. Melvin tried to explain this by saying most of us have a deep need to believe the world we live in is fair and just. But that means if something bad is happening to someone, that person must deserve it.

This helps explain how the Grafton guards were happy to follow their orders, and maybe even to exceed them, by bashing crooks. They believed the prisoners deserved the beatings. Talking to Bernie, I think that you can also turn the idea round. That the people getting bashed might start to believe bad things were being done to them because they were bad people.

'I watched what went on around me,' he says, still cradling his tea mug. 'And what I found was something that scared me.' Prisoners changed inside Grafton, says Bernie. Being in solitary changed them. So did the floggings. Something boiled up inside these crooks, which the guards could control only with more beatings.

Then things got worse. In November 1975, Bernie was transferred to Katingal, the State's brand-new, super-maximum security block, which had opened to take the intractables from Grafton. In Katingal, Bernie says, prisoners couldn't see the daylight.

You couldn't tell if it was night or day there, he says. There were no windows, though each cell door had a peephole through which the prisoner could see a clock ticking away the seconds of his sentence. Bernie did two years and eight months in Katingal, time marked by other prisoners' suicide attempts and violence. He took part in prison riots where, he says, the years of swelling anger and frustration came spewing out of the cell-blocks. It was in Katingal, in September 1977, that Bernie barricaded himself inside a prison workshop, tying the door shut with cables he'd ripped from a television set, and torched the place, turning it into a suicidal pyre, then fought wildly with the guards who came to save him carrying riot shields and batons.

Soon after, the State Government closed Katingal and Bernie was sent back into the regular prison population, where he saw out his sentence. Released after more than half a lifetime in prison, in 1991 the cops came for him again, this time over another armed robbery in Queensland.

Bernie swears he didn't do it. He says he was verballed by a cop, who gave false evidence against him. No one listened. Bernie was sent back inside until two other men, arrested over a different series of robberies, also pleaded guilty to the crime that Bernie had been charged with. He was released but was now unable to stop his anger boiling over. In 1996, a month after his claim for compensation over wrongful imprisonment was rejected, Bernie held up the National Australia Bank on Eagle Street in Brisbane.

This was his way of saying, 'Fuck you', Bernie tells me. He ended up back in prison, serving another four years. Looking back, 'I put it down to the pressure cooker syndrome,' he says. He was like other prisoners he'd seen in Grafton and Katingal. Put them back on the street and they were like little pressure cookers when the lid was taken off. Whether it was that they'd started to believe they really were bad people, or out of rage at the way they had been treated, Bernie couldn't tell you. But something had caused him to explode.

***

Outside, the sun is high in the sky now, casting few shadows across the main street. Sitting together, Bernie and I no longer feel like ex-cop and ex-robber. Instead, there is a friendship growing.

He says, 'You know, some people are saying, "Why are you hanging out with Jubelin?"' He means some people he's done time with. People with reasons not to trust a policeman. 'I tell them, "Well, from what I see he is a good fella and he's not hiding anything."'

I could say the same thing about Bernie. The things he's seen, his life experiences, they feel important, I tell him. Something people can learn from.

'They are, yes.'

'That must give you some satisfaction to be able to tell those stories.'

'You see, that is the trouble, Gary,' he says, taking our empty mugs over to the sink to wash them. 'People don't really want to hear about crims. They want to hear about the nuts and bolts – *How many banks did you rob? What did you do when you walked in there? How did you escape then?* That's all they want to know.' People want to know what the crook did but not why they did it.

Maybe that would be too confronting. Because the answer isn't just that bad things happen to bad people. Most of us don't want to know that, Bernie says. 'They don't want to know about the person who's behind those actions.'

But I'm starting to think of crooks as people.

Champion

I'm lost. It's late November 2020, almost summer, just a few weeks since visiting Bernie Matthews. I've started taking long walks through the city, at first just to get out of my unit. Even with the new job, I often work from home, on the kitchen table, which means waking up alone, watching the day pass in the strip of sky visible above the wall of my little courtyard outside the lounge room window, then falling asleep, only to wake up and repeat this. Walking, I can feel the sunlight on my face and see the blue sky all above me and soon I am heading out like this daily, alone, for hours, 20 kilometres or more, sometimes following roads that take me to parts of Sydney that are strange and where no one seems to know me.

Finding my way back to the city centre, I pick a road that leads down to Sydney Harbour, where I stand looking out over that empty space of sky reflected in the water's surface, before turning round and walking back in the opposite direction.

I don't have any end in sight. If this road leads me to another stretch of the city's shore line, I might turn again and walk off in a new direction. Like Forrest Gump running across America.

I see a face I recognise among the figures on the footpath. I know those eyes, behind thick glasses. That slight frame, reduced by age. It's Johnny Lewis walking towards me. I've seen that man countless times inside a boxing ring, when he was training champions.

I remember watching Johnny, live on Channel 9 in 1985 – the year I became a cop – when his fighter Jeff Fenech fought for the bantamweight world title in Sydney. Jeff was a tough kid, a streetfighter, who walked off the streets into the gym where Johnny met him. At home, he had a dad who was often absent, laid up in the hospital with a busted heart, and a mum working two or three jobs at one time to keep the family above water. What I remember is the way Johnny gave his man a kiss on the cheek before stepping through the ropes and leaving Jeff alone to face the bell.

Four years later, I remember watching the TV broadcast at the end of the 11th round in Atlantic City, where Johnny was in the corner of another world champion, Jeff Harding. This time, his fighter was cut and bleeding over both eyes and behind on all three judges' scorecards. Somehow Johnny found the words to send his man out to fight and win.

He did it again five years later, in 1994, by which time I was a Homicide detective, watching on TV as Johnny led another boxer, Kostya Tszyu, into the ring in Tampa, Florida, with the fighter's gloves raised up on Johnny's shoulders. By the ninth round, Kostya's face was swollen. In the tenth round, he looked tired. Johnny must have worried he might lose it. As Kostya sat down in his corner Johnny spoke to him softly, but insistent, 'One round. You've got to win this round, son.'

'You feeling good?' he asked Kostya. 'You feeling like a champion? You've got to win this round. You're a champion, understand? That's what you are, a champion.'

Kostya went out and gave it everything. He took the fight on his way to a world title the next year.

That's one reason I like boxing: redemption stories. Another is the way no one judges you in boxing. Cops box. Crooks box. I used to train in a boxing gym built in the old cells at Surry Hills Police Station in central Sydney. The only thing that matters is whether you can hold your hands up when you step through the ropes into the ring.

I keep my eyes down as I walk towards Johnny. He's half my size, but I'm intimidated by him. The first time I had anything to do with him in person, I was boxing at a charity event, raising money for injured cops or the families of those who are hurt on duty, and Johnny was working my opponent's corner. All evening, before the fight, people were saying, 'Jesus, he's got Johnny Lewis'. Or they would look at Johnny, look at me and say, 'Good luck', like I would need it.

The only thing that kept me calm as I stepped through the ropes that evening was that I had another serious boxer, Dave Letizia, working my corner. Dave and I were mates. We'd trained together at his gym in Perth. He's a hard man, a former State champion and Golden Gloves winner, but even so, after the bell went, I kept thinking, *Wow, that's Johnny Lewis*. It was like being a child who'd fallen asleep and was dreaming of being grown up and in a boxing ring, with the crowds screaming and Johnny standing there.

We met again, briefly, in a pub after I left the cops. My

trial was underway at the time, so my name and face were all across the media. I was drinking at the Rose of Australia Hotel in Erskineville, the inner-city Sydney suburb where Johnny grew up, when I walked up to the bar and saw him there. He frowned, as if he couldn't place my face, but stuck out his hand and said, 'Hello, mate, how you doing?'

I stumbled through an answer. 'I love the work you do,' I said, meaning the way he helped his fighters find something inside themselves. I was thinking, mostly, of Jeff Fenech and how Johnny saw potential in him that no one else had noticed. He took Jeff in, believed in him, helped to guide and shape him, and made him into a world champion. Without Johnny, Jeff has said, he'd probably have been in prison.

Johnny smiled and nodded. It was a short conversation. But when I got a drink and walked back to my table, all that I could think was, *I've just met Johnny Lewis.*

Now I am lost for words again to see him walking the other way on the footpath towards me.

***

He stops, and I can see the frown lines above his eyes crowding together. I'm getting used to this reaction now; people who recognise my face because they've seen me in the newspaper or on TV coverage from my trial but can't place me.

'G'day,' he says.

'Hey, Johnny,' I say, thinking, *I'd love to stop and talk to Johnny Lewis,* only I choke and keep on walking.

Two weeks later, I'm walking along an empty stretch of road in Erskineville between an empty building site on one side and a deserted car park on the other, when I notice Johnny, just up ahead of me and walking in the same direction. I say, 'Excuse me,' as I overtake him.

'G'day, mate.' He stops again and looks at me. I stop. I can see it clicking over in his mind: Who is this bloke?

This time I put out a hand and introduce myself.

He's still frowning, as if he's wondering how he knows me. 'I'm that ex-cop,' I say.

'Oh, yeah.' The lines around his eyes reorganise themselves as he smiles. 'The William Tyrrell case,' he says.

And that's enough. We stand there for maybe half an hour, alone together on the footpath, talking.

* * *

Like many people, Johnny asks if I miss being a detective. The honest answer is I do. I miss the work. I miss the chase. I miss having that one reason above all others to get up and face the day ahead; that you were trying to solve a murder.

Sometimes, I hear other old cops saying that they don't miss the work — the stress, the sleepless nights, being a witness to fatal accidents and suicides, the first called to crime scenes, or watching autopsies being carried out then going to meet that person's family. Often, those old coppers say what they miss is the people.

I don't miss the people.

I remember sitting at my computer on 2 January 2019, my first day back at work in what would be my last year in the police force. I was typing up an email in an attempt to hold my team in Homicide together. I started out acknowledging the good work of the year before: cases like the murders of Qin Wu, who was shot at a Sydney house being used as a Buddhist temple; or Clint Starkey, who was bashed to death by bikies; or Teah Luckwell, a 22-year-old murdered inside her home. Teah's body was found with her toddler beside her.

Sometimes, as a detective, you come across cases that just need to be solved, I wrote. Then there was William's disappearance. That case was tough, I wrote, it had gone on for years, was still unsolved and had broken many of the staff who worked on it, but I wanted to thank those who'd hung on, regardless of whether the wider police force understood or supported us.

That was the way I felt then: undermined by some of those around me and abandoned by the ranks above. I poured it all out in that email. I'd seen too many detectives in my team adopting an attitude of why should I help others? I would like this to change, I wrote. Homicide investigation was meant to be a team sport. I also wrote that I was being bypassed on decisions. This was not to occur in future. Finally, I'd heard rumours that some of those on the team wanted to leave it. For the sake of team harmony, if anybody wanted out, for whatever reason, I would help them leave.

'Mate, you've no idea how much support you've got out here,' says Johnny, as we stand together on the footpath.

I don't know what to say in reply, so I put up my defences.

'It's all right. I'm still busy,' I tell him, saying how I'm working for the paper now and doing the podcast. I tell him about meeting Bernie Matthews and Johnny says he knows him.

He mentions Graham Henry, who Bernie did time with in Parramatta.

I say I'd like to get Graham to come on the podcast. I've been thinking of opening it up, so it isn't just me interviewing old cops but also trying to hear from those, like Bernie, who can tell the crook's side of those stories.

Since catching up with Bernie, I've been reading about Graham, who has confessed to multiple stabbings, a shooting and a bashing with a baseball bat, though none of them were fatal. Graham's made millions from crime, by his own count. His gang mate Neddy Smith was in the pocket of corrupt police, who gave him a green light to commit crimes in return for a percentage of the profits. I've read how Graham claimed the green light meant they could do anything, even commit murder, and get away with it – though he didn't say this actually happened. There is a whole world of badness there I'd like to understand better.

Johnny nods. He asks if I do any boxing.

I say yes.

He asks if I want to come down to the Erskineville Oval to hit some pads and do a bit of training?

I do, but at the same time, I'm nervous. Life would be easier if I just went for my walks. I've got so used to being on my own now that the prospect of opening up defeats me.

Graham comes down every so often, Johnny tells me.

I nod. OK.

'Done,' says Johnny. 'See you there. It's 5.45 every morning.'

You Do the Crime

I arrive as the sun's cascading up the concrete tiers of the grandstand. Johnny's standing beneath it with six other shadowed figures and, walking over, I can hear the murmur of their voices and a faint outbreak of laughter. Johnny introduces me. They nod a welcome.

He pairs us up and we stand in two lines, facing one another. Johnny tells us to start punching each other's gloves, either straight-arm shots or uppercuts. I notice that he doesn't raise his voice or have to repeat an instruction. After a while, he sends us off, in turn, sprinting up the steps of the grandstand and back down, then it's back into the line and punching. The first time, we run up those steps once, then twice, then three times. I'm running hard, sucking in air, blood pulsing louder in my ears until all that I can hear above it is the slap of gloves, footsteps and my own ragged breathing.

Moving along the line, for a time I'm standing opposite Johnny. He holds two pads, telling me to keep my elbows in, to move my hips more and to slightly change the angle of my punches. I'm thinking, *This is great. I'm being trained by Johnny Lewis.*

'Oh, Graham said to say hello,' says Johnny. The sun rises clear above the trees on the far side of the oval, banishing the shadows. The next person sprints out of the line and we each move up, on to a new partner. I'm head down, punching. After we've each run up the grandstand steps five times, Johnny leads us into the old gym beneath it. The sweat is soaking through my shirt now. I try to guess at who the other people here are, piecing identities together from scraps of conversation.

'Well, fuck, he's got twenty years,' a man says.

'That's a long time at his age,' Johnny replies.

'You do the crime, you do the time.' The man shrugs. Listening to others talk, I get the sense that they themselves have done some time in prison.

Johnny takes us through a set of stretches. I'm on my back, one leg crossed over the other, when he comes and gently pushes my foot higher, beyond what I would have believed I could manage. The session stops and I feel great, like everything today will be better for it. I am at peace. *I want more of this,* I think. I want this tomorrow.

As I head off, the others grin and wave. The next morning, I am back at the oval.

This time, I feel more comfortable among the group. Again, Johnny forms us up in pairs. We run the steps. I'm coming down when I notice the blue light flashing in the shadows on the roadside, beyond the silhouettes of trees on the far side of the oval. I recognise the blue-and-white checks and the red strip beneath them. Highway Patrol.

'What do they want?' someone asks.

'Fucking cops,' someone jokes. Everybody's stopped now and we're all looking over.

'They're probably after me,' I offer. It gets a laugh but I mean it. I've been pulled over more times in the two years since leaving the police force than in my entire life before it, so every time I see a cop car now I'm thinking, *Here we go. Now what are they after?*

Not this time. They've pulled another driver over. Johnny walks across the grass and I watch him talking to the uniforms. Somehow, he gets between them and the man they've stopped, then walks back with the driver. The man gloves up. At Johnny's word, we line up and I'm head down again, punching. When I look up, the cops have gone. No one asks any questions.

I start turning up for training every morning. Johnny never asks for any money. The other fighters treat me like they treat each other. There is a lot of laughter.

I get called The Sprinkler because I sweat. A lot. But I sweat because I'm working hard and that's something to be respected. I start going to bed early, knowing that I'll be up early the next morning. I watch how Johnny sets us little tests. I might be out on my feet, head spinning with the effort, but whenever he calls for more, I find it.

After one session ends, Johnny calls me over, along with a bloke I know as Dave. I don't know his background, he doesn't know mine and neither of us has asked the other for details. Johnny leads us to a stretch of gravel pathway, tells us to take off the handwraps we wear to protect our wrists and knuckles, then says to Dave that he should get down on two closed fists and do push-ups. Dave does it without complaining. It must be painful, having those spikes of stone sticking into your unprotected fingers but there is nothing on his face to show that he is hurting.

'OK, Gary, your turn,' says Johnny. I get down and set my knuckles in the gravel. It grinds into my fingers, deeper with every push-up. I tell my mind to leave the pain alone and find myself thinking back, instead, to meeting Bernie. I wonder what he'd make of me now, just one crook among others and all of us hurting. Most likely, he would laugh and tell me to go harder. The stones mash into my skin and scrunch the bones, yet I feel a kind of comfort in it.

'OK, that's it.' Johnny's face is impassive. I finish up. Dave and I look at each other. Johnny asks if I'm coming for a coffee with the other fighters after training. We walk back towards the grandstand and I'm happy.

If that was a test, I passed it.

Round Two

Psycho

I start with a warning to the listeners: 'We are going to be discussing some dark subjects.' It sounds like a confident introduction though, really, I am nervous. Like I am every time we record one of these podcast interviews, sick at the thought those people listening will think I am an imposter or that I'll trip over my words, mumble or even bang into the microphone. Though the man sitting opposite seems confident enough for both of us. He's also older than I remember, from when his work first made him famous and the newspapers ran photographs of him standing broad-shouldered in a sombre suit outside the Victorian Supreme Court. Back then, he looked troubled. His face is lined with age and lessons learned now. It is softer.

'I hope I don't disappoint.' He smiles.

The interview begins.

***

Tim Watson-Munro has seen badness from the inside. As one of the country's leading criminal psychologists, he started out working in Parramatta Gaol – the same western Sydney institution that once held Bernie Matthews – then built a career outside it, often giving evidence for the defence of some of Australia's worst criminals, including terrorists, gangsters and mass killers.

'As you would know,' he says, looking at me over the rim of his glasses, 'behind every crime there is a story. People counselled me against taking this job when I was fortunate enough to be offered it. They said it's going to destroy you; you will change.'

I'm still trying to make sense of what I've learned so far, from Kathy Nowland and Sarah Yule, Dennis O'Toole, Ian Kennedy and Bernie Matthews. That evil people can seem ordinary and that even monsters can be understood, if not forgiven; that we all have badness in us, but that criminals can also be victims. They are strange, contradictory lessons and I don't pretend to fully understand them, but they have started to make me look at the world differently. It's not all angels and demons, the way I used to think it was when I was a detective. Tim, I hope, can help me understand where to go from here.

He talks about walking into his job as a resident psychologist in Parramatta Gaol and being overpowered by the smell of Lysol and wolf whistles ringing out among the heavy, metal doors and stairways. He was 25, Tim says, this being in August 1978, and about half his current body weight. He guessed some of those wolf whistles must be from the prison rapists, who thought that he was cute.

'Welcome aboard son,' said the prison governor, Harry Duff, when Tim first went to meet him. 'I've just got one message for you. Remember this – if you can be conned, you can be fucked. The last psycho lasted three months.' Harry dismissed him with the instruction, 'God speed.'

I can't help laughing at the story. Tim says he later found out the prison staff were running a book on how long he'd last before quitting. Two months was the longest anybody gave him.

But he survived, though those warnings had been right; the job changed him. It changed the way he looked at people. His job at Parramatta was to care for the prisoners and he got used to seeing hard men, killers and some of those rapists among them, carrying a crumpled *Dear John* letter in their hand, sent by a wife or girlfriend to announce that they were leaving. Sometimes, they were close to tears.

After more than two years in the prison, Tim left and went into private practice, building up a reputation, particularly for his work on behalf of an alleged crook's defence lawyers, giving evidence about their client's mind. Among these jobs, there was one that changed him more deeply than anything he'd seen in Parramatta, leading Tim to spiral into darkness. He was shamed, publicly exposed and had his career taken from him, just like I was. Tim says he has since had to accept that and find a way back upwards.

That one job was working with Julian Knight, who carried out the 1987 Hoddle Street massacre, killing seven and leaving 19 injured. Tim spent hours talking to Julian in prison, over several months.

* * *

It was a pale, cold morning, Tim says, when he arrived at Pentridge prison in Coburg, north Melbourne, only a few suburbs over from where the massacre happened. The dull bluestone walls and turrets seemed much starker than the warm sandstone Tim remembered from Parramatta and, beyond the heavy gate, was a maze of gates and checkpoints leading him deeper into the shadows. Tim says he was uncertain, following the prison guard through these. At the time, he was a young husband and father, unsure how much he really wanted to speak with, and possibly help defend, the killer who'd destroyed so many families.

Something made him keep on walking, listening to the echo of his footsteps in the prison corridors. Maybe it was the way the killings grabbed international attention, Tim says. The bare facts are that on a Sunday night, 9 August 1987, Julian armed himself with a shotgun and two rifles at his mother's home in the quiet suburb of Clifton Hill, not far from the centre of Melbourne. One of those rifles was a high-powered M14, similar to those used by the US military. Then Julian walked out of the house and opened fire.

At the time, I too was newly married, thinking about starting a family and renting an apartment behind a pub in another quiet suburb, in northern Sydney. My wife Debbie and I watched the television news reports from Melbourne, describing how Julian had fired more than 100 times, raking cars as they passed him without mercy, then surrendered. Neither of us could understand it. No one could. It felt like the whole country was left wounded, our sense of security and safety in our ordinary, daily lives had been punctured. Inside Pentridge, Tim's job, having been engaged by Julian's lawyers, was to establish why the 19-year-old did it. Was he insane? Was there something in his life – maybe his childhood or upbringing – that could help to explain it? Or was he born a killer?

The prison guard who walked with Tim through the corridors that morning didn't want to understand the killer. To him, the teenager was a fucking mongrel. Just give me five minutes alone with the cunt, he told Tim. There'd be no need for a fucking trial then. Julian might not even make it into court, the guard said. When they got to the cell door, the guard swung it open and Tim took a step forward. He says he could understand the man's anger. It felt like everyone knew somebody, or had a friend who knew someone, who'd been killed or injured. Before coming to the prison, Tim says, he'd sat down to look at all the photographs Julian's lawyers had provided, taken at the scene of the shooting and the autopsies that were conducted after. In those photos, he had seen what Julian had done.

How his guns shattered the victims' bodies, their flesh torn and bone slivered into fragments. Tim had insisted that he look at these photos, he says, because he felt a need to understand the killings.

'I was over-enthusiastic,' he says now. He was 34 then, 'so still comparatively young'.

The door clanged shut behind him. Inside the cell, Julian sat on the rubber mat he used as a bed.

He looked up. Tim introduced himself and they began talking. Julian was quiet, polite and deferential.

'I was expecting a green-headed monster,' Tim says. 'What I actually found was a 19-year-old kid, bewildered.'

AWOL

Julian Knight was mouse-like, with a pinched face, narrow moustache and thin, untidy hair. He seemed out of his depth, Tim says, like a child might on his first day of high school. For a moment, Tim even felt compassion for him. Then reality snapped back and he remembered what he'd seen in those photos.

The horror Julian had committed.

At first, the two of them talked often as the year passed before Julian's trial was due to take place, and even as their talks became less frequent they still took place every month. The teenager described how he had been adopted and found out about this at an early age. His adoptive father was an army officer and, as a child, Julian grew up wanting to become a soldier, just like he was. He liked playing with toy soldiers and Tim wondered if these fantasies might be a way of compensating for the loss of control over his own life when he was put up for adoption.

In his mock battles, Julian could be the general. He would have been all-powerful. Everything those toy soldiers did was because Julian controlled them.

He wasn't stupid, Tim thought, but he'd been an underachiever. Julian's time at school was also troubled; the family had moved overseas, which meant upheaval. Returning to Australia, he was suspended from one school after a playground fight and left his next school after a year. His adoptive parents separated when Julian was about 12, which meant the home life he'd grown used to changed again. Julian's adoptive father encouraged him to join the army cadets and there, finally, he found something stable. A sense that he belonged.

Finishing his HSC, Julian's grades were good enough to get into university but he dropped out after a few weeks. He said that he was lonely. The same year, 1986, Julian enlisted in the army reserve and later wrote about his first parade night, when he got involved in a brawl with some young guys in a street outside the barracks. When one of their brothers came back, looking for revenge, everyone in the barracks' mess came piling out to defend Julian.

'As it was my first parade night, no one in the unit knew me personally; the fact that I was a member of the unit was reason enough to come to my aid,' wrote Julian. Just like in the cadets, here was something he could be a part of. As the year ended, Julian was accepted into Duntroon Military College, the army's elite officer training establishment, housed on a sprawling estate at the foot of Mount Pleasant in Canberra. Arriving in January 1987, Julian would be living in the heart of the nation's capital. From Duntroon, you could walk along the shores of Lake Burley Griffin and up towards the Australian War Memorial along Anzac Parade, which was lined by monuments to those who had given their lives in different conflicts. There was a sense of history, of being part of something bigger than yourself.

But Julian had come from a different world from most of the others who arrived there with him, Tim says. Unlike them, he hadn't gone to one of the country's leading private schools. He hadn't had his path smoothed by family connections. While Julian was the adoptive son of a career army officer, his father was not a general or a colonel. And, by his own admission, Julian was immature. He said that he was constantly tormented.

Duntroon has a history of bastardisation. Junior cadets were expected to obey their seniors without question. Julian claimed he was made to fetch food with a plate in his mouth, before crawling back over the mess room chairs. His money and belongings were regularly stolen. He was pushed and shoved, confined to barracks then reported as being absent without leave, or AWOL.

Sitting in the prison cell together, Tim listened to Julian's stories. The challenge for him was separating the facts of Julian's humiliations from his perception of them.

The young man seemed unwilling to accept responsibility for his own actions, Tim thought.

'In one AWOL incident I was blamed for convincing two other junior staff cadets to accompany me to McDonald's,' Julian wrote later. 'It was actually their idea and I offered to drive them there after they initially asked to borrow my car.'

Julian said he got a reputation as a troublemaker, an uncouth lout who got into fights, which was also unfair to him.

'Most of the fights I was involved in off duty with civilians were either stepping in to protect a fellow cadet or finishing fights a fellow cadet had initiated,' he wrote later. Tim says he thought Julian had a seething anger, and that the young man might himself have been unaware of how deep this ran.

***

Listening to Tim, it's like a light switches on in my mind and I can now see where Julian was heading. Since starting to learn more about badness, I've read how, two decades after this mass shooting, a group of US psychologists led by Professor Mark Leary looked at the relationship between aggression and what they called 'interpersonal rejection'. They found that rejection – which seems to run through Julian's descriptions of being adopted, his parent's separation, his failed attempts to make a success of himself at school and university, and then again at Duntroon – was 'the most significant risk factor for adolescent violence'. That meant there was a stronger link between violence and rejection than gang membership, poverty or drug use.

Rejection has also been linked to a whole range of other badness, from domestic violence to school shootings. Feeling rejected was one of the most common causes in criminal cases where husbands killed their wives. One study of 551 such murders found almost half took place in response to a real or imminent separation – where you can imagine the male partner feeling rejected and lashing out in fury or using violence to reassert control. Knowing this does not excuse these killers, but it might help to understand them.

Julian was a kid who didn't fit in, I think. Who was crying out to be part of something. I almost feel sorry for him.

Almost.

Not everyone reacts to rejection with violence. I know that. But it's a normal, human feeling to get angry. I felt rejected when I left the cops. I'd given them my all in every case I worked on and got nothing in return. Afterwards, I'd stood on stage at the Crown Casino, giving that speech to the News Corp executives and privately imagining how I, too, might hurt the senior police officers who forced me out. *Imagine what that feeling is like if you're too young to understand it, or control it.* 'The link between rejection and aggression in childhood is as incontrovertible as any in psychology,' the scientists wrote in that research paper. They also described another study which showed that, out of 15 well-documented school shootings, in 13 there was evidence of the perpetrators previously being rejected or mistreated by others.

In July 1987, six months after starting at Duntroon, Julian got into a confrontation with a group of senior cadets in the barracks hallway. Julian claimed that they struck first but only he ended up being confined to the barracks. The next day, a Saturday, he snuck out and went to a Canberra nightclub. He got into another fight with some other cadets and drew a knife, stabbing one of the men and also getting injured himself. Afterwards, Julian was told to leave Duntroon.

In disgrace, he would now face a military court martial.

Going back to his mother's home in Clifton Hill, near Melbourne's centre, Julian found his old bedroom had been packed up in his absence. His clothes were in boxes. He struggled to pick up the threads of his old friendships, including with a former girlfriend. Around this time, Julian tried to make contact with his biological mother, without success. Two days before the shooting, Julian found out his old girlfriend was having a party, but he was not invited.

On 9 August 1987, Tim says, Julian had lunch with his mother, his siblings and his grandmother, before driving home in his old Holden Torana. The car was playing up, its clutch went and it kangaroo-hopped along the road.

'It probably represented to him, metaphorically, another failure,' Tim says. And Julian already had that seething anger in him. I imagine him, inside the car, smashing his fists against the steering wheel in sheer, violent frustration.

'It's definitely a build-up,' says Tim. Julian's idea that he was being persecuted at Duntroon; the trouble he got into with the stabbing; having no bedroom at home to go back to; the rejection from his friends, his ex-girlfriend and his biological mother. His broken car. Julian would have known that he still faced court martial and, most likely, discharge from the army, Tim says. He was never going to be a real soldier now.

That evening, Julian went to a local hotel and got drunk. Tim says the teenager tried to engage strangers in the bar in conversation. He tried speaking to a barmaid. She ignored him.

'It was that sliding door moment,' Tim says. 'What if there'd been people at the pub that he'd had a drink with? If he hadn't drunk so much? If the car hadn't broken down? All these what ifs.' The lesson is that evil is not inevitable; at all these what if moments, somebody might have been able to intervene and stop it. Things might have ended differently. But none of these what ifs happened.

Inside the pub, Julian later claimed, he became convinced the darkened streets outside it had been occupied by a camouflaged militia. They needed to be ambushed. He left the hotel and headed home to get his guns. By that point, he'd been overwhelmed by badness.

Inside his mother's house, Julian had a .22 semi-automatic Ruger rifle, the M14 carbine and a 12-gauge shotgun, all three of them were registered and legally owned. His mum was watching TV elsewhere in the building. Collecting his guns and ammunition, Julian left the house and crossed over Hoddle Street, the main road leading through Clifton Hill.

'So he's just walking out, this angry man?' I ask.

Tim nods. 'Walks out with three high-powered weapons and lots of rounds and he just pulled the trigger.'

During their conversations in the prison, Julian told Tim he believed that he was in a war zone. One thing that he was good at in the army was target shooting. Julian took up position in a park on the far side of Hoddle Street and began to fire on passing cars.

After the first shot, Julian said he couldn't reload fast enough. He was excited. It was unreal, like he was dreaming. He talked about his victims being pop-up targets and dark figures, rather than being people. One victim was a faceless mannequin with a plastic appearance. Another was a silhouette.

Tim says the different experts who assessed Julian disagreed about whether this was a kind of temporary insanity. One said he was suffering from a personality disorder with hysterical features and could be described as crazy. Another that reality and fantasy were mixed up in his mind. One said it was as if Julian's military training had taken over. A judge said that he 'never grew out of playing soldiers. Instead, he developed a fantasy life.'

'But, you know, he managed to shoot down a police helicopter,' Tim says. Armed cops had flooded the streets in response to the shooting. 'It didn't crash but he hit the tank and they had to come down quickly.' Julian was still a good marksman, Tim says. That, at least, suggests clear thinking.

In the end, he ran low on ammunition. Tim tells me Julian later claimed that he'd planned to keep one round for himself rather than be captured. 'It's better to die on your feet than live on your knees,' he told police.

The fucking hypocrite, I think. I have the same words tattooed on my ribcage. I live by them. But, when the end came, Julian surrendered meekly. I'd been expecting more, like Tim had when they first met in prison. I'd been expecting something evil. All there is in Julian is weakness.

Yes, he got rejected. We all get rejected sometimes. But, even after the massacre, Julian went on making the easy decisions – either to give up or to lash out.

The High Life

Ten days after the Hoddle Street massacre, on 19 August 1987, 16 people were shot dead in Hungerford, a town in southern England. The gunman also shot himself. Four months later, on 8 December, there was another massacre in Melbourne, this time at the Australia Post offices on Queen Street in the city centre. Eight people were shot dead and five more injured. The gunman fell from an 11th-floor window, apparently while trying to escape.

Despite it taking place on the far side of the world from Melbourne, the police working the Hungerford massacre established that the killer had followed the news reports of Julian Knight's killings. A search of the Queen Street killer's bedroom also found newspaper clippings about the shootings on Hoddle Street, underlined in red pen.

Afterwards, when Tim Watson-Munro visited Julian in Pentridge prison, the teenager seemed to be revelling in the attention. Julian even wrote an open letter to *The Age* newspaper, offering his expertise on mass murder to a State Government now reeling from a second brutal attack.

In the end, Julian pleaded guilty to seven counts of murder

and 46 counts of attempted murder. That meant there would be no trial and no need for the lawyers to argue publicly over whether he was sane or infected by madness when he carried out the shooting. At his sentencing in the Supreme Court of Victoria, judge George Hampel said it was, in fact, unnecessary to determine the exact nature of what he called Julian's 'mental aberration.'

'You were not medically or legally insane,' the judge said. Instead, 'you had a diagnosable serious personality disorder, a mental condition'. That difference was important. If all the experts who'd looked at Julian found him to be insane, it would have meant his mind was broken. Julian would not have been responsible for his own actions but instead a prisoner of his fractured thoughts, without free will.

Instead, the judge said, he was sane but with a mental condition. Tim can see me unsure of how to understand this, so simplifies it for me: 'It was decided Knight was bad not mad.'

'Could he justify it in his own mind, his actions?' I ask Tim, wondering about all the conversations he and Julian had together in prison. Surely, Julian must have said something to suggest where he thought the blame lied.

Tim looks straight at me for a moment.

'He never directly said, "I'm sorry",' Tim says.

***

On 10 November 1988, Julian was given a life sentence, with the judge ordering that he spend at least 27 years in prison; after serving this time he could apply for release on parole. In effect, it was a way of making Julian an offer: repent and you might be allowed back into the world outside your cell walls. Any longer a minimum term, the judge said, 'would defeat the main purpose for which it is fixed, namely your rehabilitation and possible release at a time when you would still be able to adjust to life in the community'. But to get out, Julian would have to show the parole board that he was a changed man. That meant accepting responsibility for his actions.

During the years he's since spent in prison, Julian has published a slew of things he's written about himself and his killings online, using a website linked to a charity that allows prisoners some limited communication with the outside world. In these, he seems to dodge the question of whether he is at fault. He seems to want to blame the army, writing that if he had not been bastardised at Duntroon, then he would not have ended up stabbing another cadet in the nightclub, then he would not have been forced to leave the military college, then he would not have committed the shootings that took place just over two weeks later.

'At 9.30 pm on Sunday, 9 August 1987, I would have been in my room in my barracks at Duntroon in Canberra polishing my boots and ironing my uniform, not committing a mass shooting on the streets of Melbourne.'

It is uncomfortable to read this. I ask Tim how it feels to have spent so much time with Julian.

He says he's still haunted by those photos of the victims, either lying opened up by the power of the gunshots or during their autopsies. Tim frowns, as if he can see those pictures again now before him.

The High Life

I ask him, why expose yourself to that badness in the first place? 'At the time, I was much younger,' he says. 'I just wanted to do the best job I could and so became over-involved.' I can understand that impulse. At the same age Tim was then, 34, I'd just started as a Homicide detective and been assigned to work on the murders of the three children in Bowraville, on the Mid North Coast of New South Wales. Two of their bodies had been recovered from the forest outside the town years earlier but I'd seen the photographs of their remains. I studied those photos also, then spent the next two decades working on that case, unable to let it go, or resolve it.

'My peers at the time, they had normal lives,' Tim continues. But after Hoddle Street, he wasn't like them. Those images were lodged in his mind, like bullet fragments. Tim says he had a choice: keep working in forensic psychology or find something less corrosive.

He kept going. The work was interesting, he thought, it paid well and it was high profile. As his reputation grew, partly as a result of his work with Julian, he found more work: a parade of liars, gangsters and other killers. That then fed his reputation. Called on to give evidence in court, the judges would listen to his opinion. The newspapers started running photos of him walking out of the Supreme Court building. He kept working. Around this time, both he and I would put in 60-, 70-, sometimes even 100-hour weeks.

At work, as a psychologist, Tim began to assess and counsel some of Julian's victims who'd survived the massacre and realised he was suffering from their symptoms. Like them, his sleep had become restless, he'd lost his appetite, had less energy, and sometimes felt like he was being pulled down beneath the surface, drifting deeper into depression.

At first, his work itself felt like a lifeline, Tim says, like each new case he was asked to look at was something he could grab hold of. So he tried to ignore what was happening – after all, professionally, he was still successful – only to find he couldn't pull himself up and the water all around him was getting deeper. The scenes in the Hoddle Street photos were reappearing like flashbacks. At home, like my own marriage to Debbie, Tim's relationship with his wife fractured.

At the same time, 'I was also living the high life,' he says. There were boozy lunches in exclusive restaurants along with some of the lawyers, doctors and judges Tim knew through working in the courts. He was self-medicating with expensive wine, Tim says. All told, it took almost a decade for Hoddle Street to pull him under. At one lunch in 1997, he was offered cocaine.

'I made a silly decision,' he says. The drug made him feel as if nothing could hurt him, so he could carry on ignoring his problems. Within two years, Tim was spending $2000 a week on his cocaine addiction. At the same time, his ex-wife, Susan, was gravely ill with cancer. His second wife, Carla, suffered a miscarriage. He spent his days dealing with death and hurt at home and at work, and in the evenings he turned to drugs and booze in an attempt to hold back the rising tide of fear and exhaustion, telling himself another high would lift him out of the dark water.

Really, he was sinking deeper. By June 1999, Tim was getting chest pains. His pulse would start racing and he couldn't stop it. Some nights, he'd sit in his chair at home for hours, fearing that if he moved, his heart would burst into a thousand pieces.

'Inevitably, it was going to be a train wreck,' Tim says.

I nod. Working in Homicide, I often spent my days and nights confronting death, like Tim did, either at crime scenes, in the morgue, or reading through the pathologists' reports and witness statements I took home with me. By working hard, I also built a reputation and a public profile. I was given bigger cases. I started picking arguments at work. I wasn't above telling my bosses to get fucked or if someone I didn't respect disagreed with my approach to an investigation, I ignored them.

That didn't help me. No senior police officer welcomes being challenged by someone who ranks below them and I had few allies in the force. At home, after my first marriage failed, I dated a Homicide detective. We broke up and I remarried, then got divorced again. There were fewer people around me who might reach out in those what if moments. I got used to living my life my own way and found that it worked well enough.

Until it didn't any longer, when the police charged me with recording those conversations with a witness.

In Tim's case, he says, 'eventually, one of the guys who was supplying me with drugs was arrested'. He was told the cops had also intercepted phone calls in which he was recorded discussing his drug habit. It was make-or-break time, Tim says. 'I made the decision to make full admission of what was going on in my life, because you can't tell half-truths.' He went to court and was fined, as well as being placed on a good behaviour bond. The case was adjourned without conviction.

'Was it very public?' I ask him.

'It was front-page news.' Tim remembers walking out of the courthouse with reporters and television cameras standing three-deep on the pavement. Later, the Victorian Psychologists Registration Board held their own hearing into his cocaine use. They found him guilty, saying his character was flawed, and stripped Tim of his professional title.

'I went from making a lot of money to earning nothing,' he says. 'It was very hard, but if that is not a wake-up call nothing was ever going to be.'

I realise this is the real reason I wanted to talk to Tim for the podcast. He's faced up to his failings.

'People say you have a choice,' he continues, 'you could just wallow in it, but I was never going to do that. It's not in my personality to do that. I recognised my wrongdoing, I apologised for it and resolved to turn my life around and get back.'

He still had kids to support, for one thing. He needed to be earning. 'It was a long process.'

'How long did that take you?' I ask him.

He takes a breath. 'It was near enough to three and a half, four years.'

I say nothing. It's now December 2020, eight months since my conviction. If I'm anything like Tim is, that means I've got another two and three quarter years to go before I get my life back.

* * *

In time, Tim beat his addiction. He reapplied to practise as a psychologist and was accepted. Looking to rebuild his career, it felt like he was shunned at first by the judges and the lawyers he'd once lunched with but, slowly, the work came in.

He seems more comfortable in himself now, I think, looking over the microphones recording our conversation. Decades ago, when I first saw his photo in the papers, he seemed haunted.

'Do you look back and think, well I had to have that experience to become the person I am now?' I ask.

'I think I could have done it differently, but I would have been a different person.'

I wait for him to continue.

'I think what it taught me was that I am not invincible. I am vulnerable, I am human. We all have a break point.'

We do. I just don't like to admit it.

***

Talking about rehabilitation, I ask Tim where Julian is now.

Still in his prison cell, Tim tells me. In April 2014, seven months before the end of Julian's 27-year minimum prison term, the Victorian State Parliament passed a new law, created for a single person.

It prevented his release from prison. It said the State parole board could now allow Julian to be released only if he 'is in imminent danger or dying, or is seriously incapacitated, and as a result he no longer has the physical ability to do harm to any person and he has demonstrated that he does not pose a risk to the community'.

The State's Minister for Police, Kim Wells, told parliament this was a public duty. The Premier, Denis Napthine, said the law was a response to the threat Julian posed to others: 'This is guaranteeing that he remains in jail until he's dead, or so seriously incapacitated he's no risk to other people.'

The new law did not mention rehabilitation.

Julian went to court, trying to challenge the legislation, but failed. The end of his 27-year minimum prison term came and went without release.

I ask Tim if he believes some people should be kept in prison. For a man who started his career getting called a do-gooder, he's less forgiving than I expect.

'A lot of people that are in jail, they really are beyond redemption,' he says. 'People who abduct and kill children, for example. People who break into houses and rape women. Contract killers. People who import drugs, those who are profiting on the lives of others.'

Shortly before the 30th anniversary of his killings in 2017, Julian published online what he called an 'open letter to my victims'. Unlike his other online essays, which are typed, this was in neat, rounded, childlike handwriting.

'I offer my sincerest apologies,' Julian wrote. His remorse, he said, was real: 'I wept during my initial police interviews and this is recorded on audio tapes never released by Victoria Police. I also wept for my victims during my committal hearing.'

His killings were 'despicable, cowardly and senseless. I am the first to say so.' His only explanation was that, 'they were committed in a dream-like state, a war fantasy of my own making because my dream of being a real war hero was dashed when I was forced out of Duntroon'.

In the letter, Julian says he is a changed man now, 'far from being the immature, disturbed, desperate teenager' who committed his killings. Over the page, he raged at the Victorian Government's decision to change the law, preventing his release.

* * *

Many times since he was sent to prison, Julian has gone back to different courts, taking legal action against the parole board, the prison service, the State's Attorney General and its Department of Justice.

Just like he used to lash out in the army cadets when challenged, Julian is fighting the decision to reject him, either by challenging his conviction, the conditions of his imprisonment or the new law preventing his release. He's launched so many legal salvoes like this that in 2016 a judge declared him a vexatious litigant for life, meaning he would have to get a court's permission before pressing the button on another legal challenge. His lawsuits were 'frequently baseless', the judge said, or else 'foredoomed to fail' and 'hopeless'. In 2017, the Australian High Court ruled on Julian's final attempt to overturn the Victorian Government's decision to change the law and prevent his release on parole. He lost the case.

On the last page of his 'open letter' Julian wrote that, if he had been released after his 27 years were over, he would have faded into obscurity, ending his days 'leading a quiet life devoted to community service.' Instead, his future holds nothing but endless legal battles. 'I didn't want this. If the blame lies anywhere, it lies with Corrections Victoria and successive Victorian State Governments.' It is as if he is always at war. Still playing with toy soldiers.

Is that his fault? Or the result of his upbringing? Is he provoked solely by his own bad temper, or by his feelings of rejection? I think Julian would argue it is the result of the treatment he suffered at school, at university, in the cadets, at Duntroon and at the hands of the parole board, the prison service and successive State Governments. But that is his weakness.

Unlike Tim, he will not admit that he and he alone did wrong. Without that, I do not see how he can be rehabilitated. Instead, Julian Knight is always trying to blame someone else.

Stolen From Me

Normally, I like these mornings. Getting up at ten to five, with my boxing gear laid out ready. Eating a piece of toast with a banana in the light of my tiny kitchen while darkness pours in through the apartment windows, then heading out into those pre-dawn shadows and walking through the empty streets to train with Johnny Lewis.

It's autumn now, March 2021, and the days are growing shorter as the night advances. Normally, I'm happy walking alone under the streetlights but today I cannot shrug off a grim feeling. My thoughts, again, are with William Tyrrell's family. His foster grandmother has died, the woman in whose house William was staying at the time that he went missing. I talk to her daughter, William's foster mother, often these days. Sometimes she calls me to check on how I'm doing. Sometimes I call to check on her.

Her voice breaks as she talks about what's happening to the family. Despite criticising the police force, she and her husband still hang on what the cops are telling them; that they are looking at Frank Abbott, or they are searching for the LandCruiser someone claims they saw speed past with a little boy dressed up as Spider-Man inside it.

'Let's hope you're right,' I tell her. Surely, we would know by now if either of these leads meant anything, but I say nothing. I don't want to take away hope from her.

I cross the road, out of the bright pool beneath the last streetlight, and walk through the open doorway in the brick wall of the Erskineville Oval. On one side, the grandstand rears up, more felt than seen among the darkness. Up there, I notice that the sky is growing paler. A small crowd of people are waiting at the bottom of the grandstand stairs.

Quiet greetings are exchanged in the shadows. After turning up most days for a few months now, I'm starting to recognise the different voices. There's Dave, a tough guy and hard trainer who always pushes me to my limit, but who has a gentle way of dealing with his young son, who he sometimes brings to training with him. There's Stan, who's old enough to remember Sydney's gangland wars of the 1980s and 1990s and who is mates with that old gangster, Graham Henry. Almost always, somebody among the group is laughing. There's a sense of shared sacrifice, as if everyone here has gone without sleep and got up early to be here, so we are going to make the most of it together.

I do my handwraps, weaving them around my wrist and knuckles, and take off my jacket. It's cold but I know that I will soon be sweating. Johnny walks out from somewhere inside the grandstand with his mate Jack, who's worked here as a groundsman longer than anyone remembers. As they approach the group, the first real sunlight of the morning also seems to reach us.

But this morning, something's different. There's someone else, standing in the half-light. Someone I don't recognise. He's a big guy, must be six foot four, maybe six foot five, and he's out there doing kicks and shadow boxing. From the way he's moving, you can see that if one of those kicks landed, it could hurt you. I hear someone call him Adam. Johnny pairs me up with him and we line up facing each other and touch gloves, ready to get started.

We start punching. He's powerful. So good, I think he must have been a real fighter. I lean into the work, head down, punching hard, the way that Johnny tells us. When I look up, now the two of us are closer, I recognise the face. I'm thinking, *Adam?*

'Are you Adam Watt?' I ask him.

'Yeah.' He answers slowly. Adam will later tell me he suspects that I might be a plant, sent in undercover by the police to strike up a relationship and try to get him talking.

For my part, I'm still paranoid that the police are watching me, ready to jump on me if I make a mistake, and take me back to court again. *What if they see me here with Adam Watt*, I ask myself. *After everything that happened to him?*

I try to ignore my suspicions, telling him, 'Mate, I'm a big fan. I loved your fights.'

He laughs but doesn't drop his gloves. Johnny sends me to run the steps. The line rotates. I run up, my breathing ragged. When I get back to the line, there's silence.

Later, I will come to think of Adam as another of Johnny's redemption stories, though he'll tell me he doesn't like that description because, for him, the fight still hasn't ended. During the 1990s, Adam was living in Japan and won four world titles in kickboxing before moving back to Sydney and getting into boxing. I'd watch his fights in the pub or read about him in the fight mags, where they called him Lights Out because of his punching power. In 2000, he won a Commonwealth title on the undercard of a Mike Tyson bout in Glasgow and, later that year, he fought for a world title. Then he seemed to disappear.

In September 2008, Adam was arrested by the Australian Federal Police and charged with being part of a conspiracy to import pseudoephedrine, one of the chemicals used to make crystal methamphetamine, the drug people call ice. I remember thinking at the time that it was sad, but that the police must have something on Adam for them to charge him. As he and I get to know each other through these morning training sessions, Adam will open up and tell me that he, too, trusted the system at first. He thought it would clear him.

'I believed the mistake would become as obvious to all as it was to me.'

Instead, Adam was in for a fight.

He spent two years on remand in maximum security, meaning he was held in a jail block with a Who's Who of Australia's worst criminals while waiting for a court trial. Inside, Adam discovered the charges against him were tied up with another, bigger, criminal investigation. A few months before his arrest, in June 2008, one of the bosses of the New South Wales Crime Commission had been charged over his role in an international conspiracy to import drug precursors. It was among the biggest scandals in the history of Australian law enforcement, with one of those at the very top revealed to be as crooked as the drug dealers they were supposed to police.

Adam tried telling people the charges against him were also crooked but they didn't seem to listen. He said he'd been wrongly accused and it was all tangled up with the badness in the Crime Commission. As the months passed, Adam learned one of his jail-mates had been cooperating with the commission as an informant. Talking to this other prisoner, Adam started to suspect the corruption went much deeper than anyone admitted.

On the morning of 1 October 2009, Adam was sitting at a table in the Metropolitan Remand and Reception Centre at Silverwater when one of the other inmates crept down the stairs behind him, carrying a green prison pillowcase containing a metal sandwich press. One blow put Adam on the floor. A second crunched into his skull while he lay there helpless. His attacker, a convicted killer called Django O'Hara, shaped up to swing again until another prisoner ran up and grabbed a plastic chair, holding it out in front of him like a lion tamer. Django retreated and Adam lay there. He was unconscious and bleeding.

He was picked up by the prison guards and taken to the hospital, then back to Silverwater overnight, then back to hospital two days later. During this time, Adam lay in jail, feeling his body shutting down and thinking he was dying. Even after the doctors operated on his head injury, he was in a bad condition. Kept in custody, vital scans the doctors said he needed did not happen. In August 2010, a magistrate ordered Adam's release on bail, saying he had no faith in the State Government's Justice Health System. Adam needed to be treated outside the jail walls, the magistrate decided. Without this, there was a risk that he might not survive.

Within days of this decision, Adam was assessed at Gosford Hospital and found to have brain damage. His recovery was painful. For years, he fought headaches, dizziness and seizures. He couldn't think; what might take him weeks, others managed in minutes. Later, he went back to the Supreme Court, suing the State of New South Wales for failing to protect him.

The court heard Django was a dangerous, unstable offender who was known by authorities to hear voices telling him to kill someone and had a long history of violent attacks in prison. A judge found the State had failed by placing Django in the communal block with no plan to ensure the safety of the other inmates, by not providing the guards with any details of his violent history and by not stopping him from getting his hands on the metal sandwich press used to attack Adam. He ordered the State Government pay Adam compensation for his pain and suffering, as well as for the time when he had been unable to work during the years of slow rehabilitation.

'I don't feel as if those years have been stolen from me,' Adam says now. 'If I did, I would have gone mad or worse.' Adam does feel that he was stolen from his friends and family, though, and he says that hurts him. As he and I keep training together, he will tell me he is still only half the man he was before the prison bashing. And his fight wasn't over. While he might have been released from jail, Adam still had to face the drug charges.

***

During one morning's session, Johnny pulls me out of the line and tells Adam to come with us. Adam follows, grinning, the grey stubble on his chin the same colour as the pale sky behind him. They're both in the mood for something fierce. I can feel it. Johnny stands the two of us at arm's-length, facing one another.

We trade blows, punching glove to glove.

'Come on, give it,' Adam tells me.

'Punch it out. That's it, that's it,' growls Johnny.

I'm thinking, *Surely this will stop soon*, but it doesn't.

'Watch those elbows,' Adam says. He wants me to keep them in. It generates more power and doesn't telegraph your punches.

Then Johnny says to run the grandstand. I take off.

'Go on Adam, catch him!' I hear Johnny call behind me. Adam chases after me, running faster, and soon he is behind me, shouting, 'Come on! Come on! Don't do one step, do two at a time!'

I lift my feet up and we're sprinting up the steps together. At the top, we turn and race down the steps to the strip of concrete where the others are training and, afterwards, I'm broken.

'That was really good,' Adam says, his broad shoulders blocking out the low sun behind him. 'I enjoyed that.'

* * *

After being released on bail over the drug charges, Adam kept working to prove his innocence, visiting different prisons to speak with others who'd been charged in relation to Crime Commission investigations. He spoke to lawyers, journalists, politicians and the Australian Human Rights

Commission; to anyone who would listen. By chance, one of his lawyers went on to become the magistrate who oversaw my conviction.

As his trial approached, Adam planned to point at the corruption in the Crime Commission and say he'd been wrongly accused. But the doctors were divided as to whether his brain injury meant Adam was fit to take part in what would be a long, complicated court process. That meant the judge could rule Adam was unfit to stand trial and he would escape a conviction, his lawyers told him. All he had to do first was concede the prosecution had what they called a 'prima facie' case against him.

Adam refused to concede this. He insisted he was fit enough for the trial to go ahead. The judge disagreed. In December 2012, Johnny stood with Adam in court as the judge said his injuries were too severe. As they walked away from the court together, Adam said to Johnny that for him it wasn't over. He was never going to concede the cops had a case against him.

Johnny told him that was like someone who'd just escaped from a lion's cage deciding to go back into it because they'd left their hat behind.

Adam didn't listen. He stopped working with his lawyers.

A year later, in December 2013, five years after Adam was arrested on the drug charges, a judge ruled there was a prima facie case against him, although this was a formal process, not a finding of guilt and meant the police evidence was never tested in court. Johnny stood by Adam then as well. By now, Adam was talking to the New South Wales Police

Integrity Commission and the Australian Commission for Law Enforcement Integrity, calling for an inquiry into the corruption surrounding his charges. He started working with journalists, hoping they would tell his story.

At 11.35 am on 2 July 2014, Adam answered a knock on his door. There were three men standing there in suits. One introduced them as detectives from the New South Wales police. Adam was charged again, this time over a murder.

The journalists stopped calling Adam. He found he had been silenced.

***

The weeks pass, punctuated by these early-morning training sessions. In May, Graham Henry texts me, saying he's heard I'm hanging out with Johnny Lewis. Johnny says I should tell Graham to come down and box with us one morning and I keep hoping he'll show up at the oval, but he doesn't.

Instead, Johnny often pairs me up with Adam. He tells me about the murder. The cops claimed Adam became friendly with his cellmate, a gangster called Luke 'Fatboy' Sparos, while in jail awaiting trial over the drug charges. Luke was doing time for his part in a separate multi-million-dollar drug ring and was alleged to have ordered the shooting of a witness. The cops claimed Adam said that he could get a gun.

But the cops only had one witness, Adam tells me, the same former jail-mate he'd been talking to about corruption at the Crime Commission. The one who'd previously agreed to roll-over and become an informant for the Crime Commission itself.

According to this witness, Adam had told Luke in jail that he could get a .22 for $5000, though Luke told him he needed something bigger. That was all. There was no recording of the conversation, no mention of what the gun was for, nor any proof of money being paid or a gun handed over. Adam says the conversation never happened.

But that didn't stop the headlines saying a former kickboxing champion had been arrested in connection to a murder. The newspapers loved it.

'I hate being the bad guy,' he tells me. 'I know it's used against me. So when you go online now, that's all you see: Adam Watt arrested. In the eyes of the public, I'm now forever tainted.'

I understand, I tell him. It's like you're screaming, trying to shout out that you've been wronged and no one's listening. We're talking while trading punches at one of Johnny's training sessions and any one of those in the line next to us can listen in, but no one says a word. Adam says he refused to concede that he'd done wrong this time as well. The case dragged through the courts – and eventually collapsed. The State Director of Public Prosecutions decided not to pursue the charges against Adam, and Luke Sparos was found not guilty.

'You're still cocking your elbows when you punch,' Johnny tells me, calling me out of the line again with Adam. This time, he takes us over to a corner by the grandstand, telling me to back into the corner until I'm jammed in between it and the brick wall. He tells Adam to go hard at me. The brickwork forces me to keep my elbows in.

Trapped in there, I'm thinking about my own case. How I could have gone into court with an excuse. Said I was under stress. That I made a mistake when I recorded those conversations. Had I done that, I might still be a cop now. But that's not me. Nor is it Adam, either. Neither of us are ever going to take a backwards step. We're fighters.

'That's good,' Johnny says to stop us. The sweat is soaking through my shirt now. Adam drops his fists.

'The only way to look at it,' says Adam, 'is that I was chosen for this fight. The only way to think about it is to ask, why was I chosen?

'I was chosen because others would quit. I was chosen because I'd never give up. I was chosen because I'd spent a lifetime preparing for this fight. This experience is not a negative, it is a positive. It is making me stronger.'

I feel close to him in that moment. After everything he's been through, Adam is still standing. Today, he runs a media company hosting boxing, mixed martial arts and other sports events online. He's still hoping to tell his story. And he still turns up in the mornings before dawn to train. His fight hasn't ended, he tells me. As he sees it, right now, he's facing the championship rounds, those few rounds at the end of a title match when both fighters are in pain, bleeding and exhausted and only the best boxers have enough in them to keep going.

'They didn't win,' he says, of the authorities that pursued him. 'They thought they might have but they didn't.'

Johnny sends us off to run a lap of the oval and I do so, shaking my arms to get some feeling back, enjoying the sensation of movement after being trapped in the corner.

***

It's June, the month by which the coroner had said she would hand down her findings into William's disappearance, but nothing happens. No one I speak to seems to understand the delay. The inquest has been running for more than two years now and it is a full year since I last heard from anyone official about it. Despite still not wanting to call me as a witness, the State Government's Director of Inquests wrote, asking me to set out on paper what I knew about the case.

I wrote back saying I was concerned 'potential evidence … has been lost'. Evidence we'd gathered when I led the investigation had not been put to witnesses, I wrote, because we had understood they would be questioned about it during the inquest hearings. After I was taken off the case, this had not happened. Over more than a dozen pages, I also tried to explain what we'd learned about some of these people.

Two, the neighbour Paul and the white goods repairman, both seem to have been publicly ruled out as potential suspects since I left the investigation. Of the others, there were a few locals I'd expected to be questioned at the inquest, although I hadn't seen that happen. There was Frank Abbott, who'd chosen not to give evidence at the inquest and – as far as I knew – could not be linked to the location where William went missing. Beyond that, there was William's family.

I wrote how we had investigated both William's biological and foster parents. We looked at whether they might have done something to him deliberately or by accident, then tried to cover it up. We even looked at whether William's foster grandmother might have done something to him, given the family were staying at her house when he disappeared. Inevitably, you look at the family in a case like this one, given they were the closest to William at the time he was last seen. But there was no actual evidence of their involvement, I wrote.

I never heard back from the coroner. A year on and still with no word of what she is thinking, this starts to worry me.

Do the Right Thing

Bernie Matthews steps from the crowd hurrying off the country trains at Sydney's Central railway station alongside another man who looks stiff-backed, solidly built and with a sense of menace to him.

Walking over to the café where I'm sitting, Bernie introduces the man as John.

'G'day,' says John and Bernie smiles.

I reach out an open hand in welcome.

We sit facing each other across the table. Like Bernie, I figure John is an old crook. He nods at the phone beside my cup and smiles, saying, 'Anything I say will be taken down and used in evidence.' The words of the old police caution.

'I don't think I can caution people anymore,' I say and then I place him – John Killick. He, too, was on the front page of the papers once, a long time ago, for breaking out of the Silverwater prison complex in a helicopter that his girlfriend had hijacked at gunpoint. It landed in the prison yard, John jumped on board and she handed him a machine gun. They flew out to the sound of gunfire from the prison watchtower and cheering from the prisoners beneath them.

Bernie pulls his chair up and I notice that he's carrying a tote bag, which he puts on the table.

Jesus, I think. *This feels wrong.* These are heavyweight crooks. Is there a gun in there? Am I overseeing a drug deal?

I can see cops patrolling the station. *If this is something crooked and I am caught with this pair, then we're all going to go down together.*

Bernie reaches into the bag. Time slows right down. He pulls out a stack of comics, saying there must be one in here that John hasn't read yet. The two men start going through the comics, laughing, and talking about their favourites that they used to read in prison.

I breathe out, not wanting to let them know what I was thinking.

* * *

John did 30 years, all told, at different times, for different crimes and inside different prisons. Long enough to have been among those watching from their cell windows when the hangman arrived at Pentridge prison on Friday, 3 February 1967 and Ronald Ryan was led out to the gallows, becoming the last Australian prisoner to be executed.

'He was like me,' John says of Ronald. They both started robbing banks at around the same age. Both men also were fathers, both loved to gamble, both tried to escape and it cost them.

Just before eight that morning, Ronald was led out of his cell and walked to a point in the long cell block where a white beam running between the prison gantries was used as a gallows. Around a dozen newspaper reporters had been invited to watch and more than one later described Ronald as childlike, hardly seeming to be a man at all, more like a boy waiting to be punished. He was to be hanged for killing a prison warder during an escape attempt from Pentridge. The police said he confessed to the shooting, but Ronald never signed his typed confession and, in court, he denied it.

On either side, the prison walls stood silent. According to one newspaper report, Ronald gestured at the gallows. 'That,' he said, 'or thirty years of this?'

* * *

John counts up the different prisons he's been kept in. There's Adelaide and Bathurst, Goulburn, Maitland, Brisbane's Boggo Road – that was where he met Bernie – 13 or 14 of them in total, across South Australia, Victoria, New South Wales and Queensland

'You could do the travel guide to jails on the east coast of Australia,' I say, laughing.

'One of the judges said that,' John says. 'He said we've got the east coast covered.' His smile fades. 'I mean it's not funny really.'

I wait for him to continue.

'It's the tragic loss of all of it,' John says.

I tell him how I'm trying to work out what causes people to end up where he was.

'A lot of crooks just go down because of their bad background,' John says. 'They never have a great chance.' He starts talking about his childhood, growing up in inner-city Sydney. Born in 1942, he was given up for adoption – like Julian Knight – and taken in by the Killicks, Reg and Lorrie. Reg was an alcoholic, 'a truck driver, an ex-fighter, a tough guy who terrorised the whole neighbourhood', John says. Lorrie was a nervous wreck beside him.

John says Reg would whack Lorrie and call her a slut. There were times when she and John would walk the streets at two in the morning, rather than go home to face Reg. John loved his mum. Only, she took an overdose when he was 17 and died, leaving him with his adoptive father.

After her death, John was dirty on himself, and on Reg and on the whole world. He blamed the banks who'd threatened to foreclose on the family. He started committing petty crimes, like shoplifting or stealing bank books and using false signatures to withdraw money. When he got caught, they sent him to the Albion Street Shelter, where juvenile suspects were held until their families bailed them out. John says he lay in bed there, crying for his mother.

Reg bailed John out and they argued. John graduated to robbery, was arrested on a break-and-enter and got three months in Long Bay.

'That was real jail,' he says. An adult prison. 'It's almost like you are on another planet. You were right out of the system, you were right out of society.' Prison was also a criminal university. 'That's all prisoners ever talk about, what jobs are best' – and, on release, he graduated.

John tells me how he robbed a department store in Bathurst, made a mint, then got busted. Back in prison, he got solitary confinement, like Bernie. They stripped his clothes and left him there in total darkness. Listening, it seems to me as if John's life was chaos growing up and chaos as a grown-up.

Every time John got out, the same cycle was repeated: he'd have a go at going straight then end up back in prison. One time, he worked as a grocer. Another time, he installed security peepholes. He became a manager at Coles. Each time, I'm thinking, *Go on, John. This time just do the right thing.* The more I learn of him, the more I like him and the more I find myself hoping, this time, he could make a go of being a civilian. But, every time, I am disappointed. John always returned to crime, as if gambling that the higher risks would bring in more money.

His risk-taking continued at home. During the 1970s, John was married with a son but he started having an affair with a younger woman, Jacqueline Hawes, who was also living with them. When she found out, John's wife, Gloria, kicked the two of them out, then he got charged over a swag of bank jobs and sent to Boggo Road in Brisbane. John got Jackie to smuggle him a replica pistol. He used it to escape and later to rob a bank. They went on the run together. But, after five months on the run, Jackie turned herself in, leaving him to his hold-ups.

John was recaptured, jailed and served out his sentence. On his release, Gloria took him back in. Once again, John gambled with her affections, taking up with their married neighbour, then leaving her for Lucy Dudko, a Russian former librarian who he met at a party. Lucy also had a husband and a daughter but staked everything on John. After a night together at the casino in 1999, they walked out with John having lost and owing $10,000 to a drug dealer.

'What will we do now?' Lucy asked him.

'A bank on Monday,' John said.

He tried it and got caught. They put him in Silverwater. That was when he got Lucy to hijack the helicopter.

It worked. They got away. The plan was to head for Europe and, from there, South America, but instead the fugitives ended up trailing around Australia in a ragged circle: from Sydney to Goulburn, Wagga Wagga, Wangaratta, Melbourne, Ballarat and Bendigo, before coming back and hiding out at the Bass Hill Tourist Park, about 10 kilometres from Silverwater.

John's face was everywhere by then, on the TV news and newspaper front pages where I first saw it. The cops came for him and Lucy in the early hours of one morning, he says. This time, John decided not to roll the dice again on one last escape attempt and, instead, he surrendered.

I sit there at the café table, thinking, *What a waste.* Not just of John's life, but of Jackie's and Lucy's. Both of them were caught up in John's crimes and suffered for it. Lucy's daughter was taken from her, while John sat out a lifetime in his prison cell, reading comics.

He isn't looking for excuses.

'You know you have hurt people,' John says. 'You know you've done damage. But you can't take back the things you've done. It's my story, it's my life. I'm getting old, I want the truth out there.'

Besides, prison wasn't easy. After his recapture following the escape by helicopter, the authorities put John in the High Security Unit at Goulburn prison, in southern New South Wales. John tells me how he used to say to Lucy when they were on the run that, if they got caught, the authorities would want to punish him for breaking out in such spectacular fashion. They'd put him with the worst offenders, he'd say. He'd probably be sharing a cell with Ivan Milat, Australia's most notorious serial killer.

Well, that's what happened, John tells me.

Across the table, Bernie watches us in silence.

How You Going, Ivan?

They weren't exactly cellmates because every prisoner in the High Security Unit was kept in segregation, but John Killick knew Ivan Milat was in there because he could hear him. Everybody held in there would sing out from inside their lockup. Ivan didn't say much, John says. Unlike some of the others, he was quiet and didn't argue. But from the way the other prisoners spoke to him, you could tell he had charisma. Sometimes the guards would come and ask him for an autograph.

John would listen to their conversations:

'How you going, Ivan?'

'I'm going well. Just working.'

He was working on getting out of prison, John says. It was three years since Ivan had been convicted, in 1996, of murdering seven people, two men and five women. The victims were aged between 19 and 22 and disappeared after setting out to hitchhike along the Hume Highway near Liverpool, in southwest Sydney. Their bodies were discovered an hour's drive outside the city, in the Belanglo State Forest, covered with branches and leaf litter. Their murders were so brutal it made you wonder what must have been twisted deep inside their killer to enable him to do it.

Of the seven, two had been shot more than once in the head and one had been decapitated. Three others had stab wounds that would have caused paralysis, with two of these having their spinal cords completely severed. All but one appeared to have been sexually molested, either before or after death. Already, Ivan had made one failed attempt to appeal his conviction and was now working on taking his case to the High Court.

Before his arrival in Goulburn, John had never doubted that Ivan was guilty. From the moment he heard the news of Ivan's arrest, when around 50 cops surrounded his home in Eagle Vale, on Sydney's southwestern edge, John thought, 'That's it. they've got the bastard.'. He'd hated Ivan for what was done to those people. But after several months in that strange place, listening to the voices of the men locked in the cells around him, Ivan became the person to whom John was closest.

It happened when the guards moved some prisoners to the Multi-Purpose Unit. In there, John spent a few more months in segregation before they asked if he wanted to go outside twice a week into the prison yard and walk round with another inmate.

Yeah, John said. Because naturally you'd want to after months inside with nobody to talk to. But the guards said the only inmate he could walk round with was Ivan. All the others were on strict protection; men like Robert 'Dolly' Dunn, a paedophile who had abused boys as young as seven, meaning he was seen as the lowest of the low inside the prison and couldn't be allowed to mix with other prisoners in case they killed him as a punishment for his crimes.

So it was Ivan or nothing. John told himself that he needed to talk to someone.

OK, then. He'd do it. He would talk to Ivan.

* * *

'In jail, you learn,' John tells me now, as we sit facing each other, the sky falling away from us outside the café windows. Sunlight is reflecting on the water. This is the second time I've met John, after our first meeting with Bernie Matthews at Central railway station, and I've come to visit him near his home in Milsons Point, an arm of land reaching out into Sydney Harbour.

We walked together beneath the Harbour Bridge and John brought me to this café where he knows the owners. He introduced me to them as his friend. I realise that I don't mind people knowing that I am now friends with old crooks like him and Bernie. Talking about Ivan, John says, 'Over the years I've come across so many murderers who did horrific things. You come to accept them.'

That first day, when the guards opened up his cell door and led John out into the daylight, Ivan was standing, waiting. John says he had narrow eyes and was smiling a thin, mean smile. John stuck out his hand and Ivan took it.

John told Ivan, 'I just want you to know that what you did was a horrific crime.'

'I agree,' Ivan replied. 'If I'd have done it, John, I'd be a monster.' The smile again, just like a knife's edge. 'Only, I didn't do it.' They started walking round the yard together.

For months, the two men met up often. It's hard to know how long this went on for, John says, inside a place where days and weeks had little meaning. Maybe six months, he thinks. Or maybe nine. Ivan could hold his own when they were talking. He was charming. Both knew the other was facing a long stretch inside prison, so there was little to gain from trying to protest their innocence but, still, Ivan insisted.

'He said, "Look, I didn't do it",' John says. But John already knew enough about the murders from reading about them in the papers to have his doubts. He asked Ivan about the evidence the cops found when they raided his home in Eagle Vale: the gun parts, including a firing pin that matched the bullet casings recovered from the Belanglo State Forest; the silencer; the tent that once belonged to one of the murdered backpackers, 21-year-old Simone Schmidl.

'That was planted, John. All that stuff was planted', Ivan told him.

John looked at him and didn't think that Ivan looked like he was evil. Nor did he look like he was innocent.

'Look, I'll prove it to you,' said Ivan and told John about the court transcripts from his trial, which he had access to in prison because he'd been working to challenge his conviction. There were pages where the prosecution had a witness, Paul Onions, who'd been hitchhiking on the Hume Highway around the time of the murders. Paul's evidence in court was that a man had offered him a lift. He took it and, just short of the turnoff to the Belanglo State Forest, the man pulled out a revolver and told Paul he was going to rob him.

Paul fled, leaving his rucksack behind. Asked in court to describe his attacker, Paul said he had a moustache like the cricketer Merv Hughes and was driving a white or silver four-wheel drive, maybe a Nissan or Toyota. Ivan had a moustache like Merv Hughes and drove a Nissan Patrol, the court heard. Paul had also said the car that picked him up had chrome wheel trims and a spare wheel attached to the back door. During the trial, Paul was shown a photo of Ivan's four-by-four, which had chrome trims and a spare wheel. It matched his description.

Then Ivan's lawyer told the court those trims and that spare wheel had been added only *after* the date Paul claimed he was hitchhiking on the Hume Highway. Paul's memory must be mistaken, Ivan told John. It couldn't have been Ivan's truck that picked him up. It could not have been Ivan.

'He nearly swung me. He nearly swung me,' John says, looking out the café window. 'Because of what he showed me, he started to put doubts in my mind.'

* * *

On their walks round the yard together, John learned more about Ivan. He was one of 14 children. His mum, Margaret, had been 14 when she met his dad, Stijphan, a Croat who was more than twice her age and himself one of 22 children, only four of whom survived through infancy. Stijphan emigrated to Australia in 1926 and found work labouring on the ships that docked along the Hungry Mile, a stretch of waterfront on the far side of the harbour from where John and I are sitting. Ivan was his parents' fifth child, born two years after John was.

I find myself thinking about their two lives. How John had got caught up in badness but Ivan was so much worse. What was different? By the time of Ivan's birth, in late 1944, his father had changed his name to Stephen. A year later, the Milats had their sixth child. They lived in Bossley Park in far-west Sydney, where the family home was little more than a shed with a dirt floor, divided down the middle by a curtain. By child seven, they'd moved – they moved a lot – to Rossmore on the southwestern edge of Liverpool. Stephen bought a few acres of land there and scrabbled to grow cabbages and tomatoes for market. It was hard work. And, as well as working, the Milats were often fighting.

By child eight, Stephen was drinking heavily and often. He'd whack Margaret and call her angry names. She would threaten to leave him. To their neighbours, the kids seemed sombre, scowling and closed-minded. If they acted up, their parents flogged them.

Stephen and Margaret had more children. The family moved again, finding a place near the army reserve at nearby Holsworthy where they all slept in a two-room shack with a dirt floor and where meal times often descended into conflict. Stephen would lash out, saying that the food wasn't ready or that he didn't like it. More than once, he reached down and flipped the table over, sending plates, cups and frightened children spinning across the room around him.

One time, their neighbours watched as Stephen delivered a public beating to two of his boys, who lay on the ground beside the shack while he went at them with a length of timber. I wonder if this violence got passed down through the family. Whether it was something Ivan's father gave his boys, like their dark hair or black tempers. Or did the fact his father beat him mean something inside Ivan got broken? Is that enough to explain why he grew up to use violence against others?

But then, John Killick saw violence growing up with his alcoholic stepfather. So did Bernie Matthews. Neither of them became killers.

By the age of seven or eight, Ivan was working long, grinding hours alongside his brothers and his father, growing tomatoes. One summer, soon after the birth of the Milat's 11th child, their tomato crop was stolen. That meant financial disaster. Stephen went back to labouring, this time at a concrete manufacturer. With their dad gone all day, the kids ran wild in the ruin of the tomato sheds. Ivan started to play truant from school and, around the time he turned a teenager, one of his teachers recommended to his parents that their son be sent to Boys Town.

Run by the Salesian Order of Catholic priests, Boys Town was meant to provide a safe home for wayward boys. It was only decades later that the reports of children being beaten and raped by the adults who ran it began to be told in public. Ivan always claimed to have enjoyed his time there but his offending got worse after. He did burglaries and armed robberies, getting caught and later sent to the Mount Penang Training School for Boys near Gosford on the Central Coast, where Bernie Matthews also spent time as a young man.

Decades later, just like Boys Town, people started telling stories about Mount Penang. Of children being stripped and beaten. Of children being raped by the officers who ran it. Neither Ivan nor Bernie told these stories but, even without them, Mount Penang sounded rough. Ivan had his 18th birthday inside the place and, when he got out in early 1963, he and his brothers started causing trouble again, only this time they were wilder.

By now, the brothers were doing smash-and-grabs and packing guns. The Milats were tight; they shared crimes. If one brother got caught, another might take the blame to save him. But, all the same, Ivan got caught often, like John Killick, and spent time in and out of prison.

Like John, Ivan might come out and go straight, finding some work labouring or with the Water Board, until the money didn't fit his lifestyle. Crime paid. Ivan spent time in Parramatta Gaol, in Long Bay, and out at Emu Plains, a prison farm at the foot of the Blue Mountains. When he got out, he did another job – a vehicle theft – got arrested and sent back to Parramatta. He spent the Christmas of 1965 and his 21st birthday on remand and was later sent to Grafton, just like Bernie Matthews. Like Bernie, Ivan endured the reception biff, where three or four guards went at him with rubber batons. So it continued: release, reoffend, get sent back to prison. John had gone through the same cycle.

On their walks around the prison yard together, John started thinking, maybe Ivan was right. Maybe he had been fitted up by some bent coppers. John had seen it happen. Just think of Ronald Ryan, who'd been sent to the gallows despite every prisoner in Pentridge believing he wasn't guilty.

Maybe Ivan didn't do those murders. They were both facing decades in prison, so why would Ivan lie to John? And Ivan was insistent.

Ivan Had a Day Off

In all, Ivan Milat went to court seven times to challenge his conviction, calling for an inquiry into the court's handling of his case. Each time, he repeated what he said to John Killick in the yard at Goulburn; that he couldn't have been the killer. At different times he said that he could not have been the man identified by the surviving witness, Paul Onions, because his truck didn't have chrome trims or a spare wheel on the back door. He argued about DNA evidence taken from hairs found in the hand of one of the victims, which did not match his own. In court, his barrister argued that, while the prosecution had established that the murders were carried out by someone who was part of or close to the Milat family, it wasn't Ivan. Perhaps it was one of Ivan's brothers, his barrister suggested.

No judge was convinced by Ivan's claims of innocence, or his claim that his brothers may instead be guilty. There was no basis for his claims, the courts ruled, again and again: every one of Ivan's applications for an inquiry was rejected.

As for that evidence about the chrome wheel trims and the spare tyre, it remains unexplained. Possibly a trick of memory. But it was not enough to overturn the other mass of evidence linking Ivan to the attack on Paul, which one judge described as 'remarkable in its breadth and detail'. Among this was a shirt belonging to Paul which he left behind in his rucksack when he fled on the Hume Highway. Police found the shirt in Ivan's mum's house when they raided it. It was next to a shirt of Ivan's.

John, too, now accepts Ivan was guilty. For him, the moment of realisation came in prison, after he and Ivan had been moved to different facilities, and John used the prison library to get hold of a transcript of Ivan's evidence in court.

'I went through it and what I found was a glaring omission in our conversations,' John tells me. 'Every day one of those victims went missing, Ivan had a day off.'

He laughs. 'The odds of that,' he says. 'I'm a gambler and I know odds.' By then, he says, he trusted Ivan. The two of them were writing to each other from their separate prisons, with Ivan offering to help challenge John's conviction. 'I cut it off and I wrote him a letter saying, "Look, don't write to me again."'

'Do you see him as evil?' I ask John.

'Yes, I do. Definitely,' he answers. 'I think, on the inside, there are just some people who are beyond redemption. It's not just their childhoods, their upbringing, whether they found themselves rejected. Ivan was mistreated as a child, but so were his brothers and sisters, and not all of them grew up to become serial killers.'

This is my sixth lesson about badness. That different people might have the same life stories, but not all of them will go on to do evil.

'If someone is bent on being a criminal, then they'll do it,' John says. Which makes me wonder how many more people like this there are out there. Take serial killers, like Ivan. We do have some idea of the numbers. Two US universities – Radford University and Florida Gulf Coast University – keep a record, the Serial Killer Database. It relies on information gathered from prison records, court transcripts and media reports and uses a definition of 'serial killing' put forward by the FBI at the 2005 Serial Murder Symposium in San Antonio, Texas: 'The unlawful killing of two or more victims by the same offender(s) in separate events.'

That database suggests there was an average of 54 serial killers operating *every year* inside the US between 2010 and 2015. If that's alarming, that figure is *down* from a high of 145 on average every year between 1980 and 1989.

Most were men (roughly 90 per cent), most were white (around 52 per cent) and most were organised rather than disorganised killers. The single most common motive given for their killings was enjoyment; either thrill, lust or power (just under 37 per cent). Other motives were financial gain and anger (roughly 30 and 16 per cent respectively). Some had multiple motives.

I doubt any of these numbers are perfect, because catching serial killers and getting them to admit their crimes or explain why they did them is not a perfect science. But, looking at the figures, the main thing I take from the database is that serial killers are much more common, you could even say more normal, than I had imagined. The database lists over 5000 whose crimes have been recorded. Probably, the number is much higher.

One last thought: the database focuses on crimes committed in North America but does include some information on serial killers elsewhere, including Australia. Here, it lists 81 known serial killers. When compared to the size of its population, this means the Lucky Country has the second highest ratio of serial killers anywhere in the world, after the US.

* * *

I sit back and look across the café table at John Killick, the white-haired ex-crim I first met trading comic books with Bernie. I feel more comfortable with the pair of them now than I ever expected. To be honest, I feel more comfortable sitting here than I would with some of my old colleagues in the police force, who I'd thought were friends.

Some of those friends failed to speak up when the organisation turned on me, or failed to reach out, even with a phone call, after I left the police. The few who did were ostracised by others. What frustrates me is that I can see senior officers right across the police force enjoying their rank and reputation, when I know from working with them that they're hiding other, human failings. That they are lazy or blindly ambitious. That they're only taking what they can from the job rather than treating it as a duty. There's one senior officer in Homicide who we used to see through the glass wall of his office watching repeats of old TV shows while the rest of us were working. And a junior detective on the William Tyrrell investigation who snuck off to the movies when he should have been monitoring telephone intercepts.

Elsewhere, I've seen resources poured into police investigations because politicians are being lobbied by people with wealth and connections, while other cases have too few staff to run them. In contrast, here you have someone like Bernie, who puts his hands up and says, 'Yes, I am an armed robber. This is why I did it. I make no excuses.' Or John, who admits that he hurt those who loved him but just wants the truth told.

John asks for the bill and pays it. We agree to meet up again. Next time, he says, we'll get some beers.

I stand to leave, we shake hands and I walk out, heading home to my apartment. I think about the people who I'm meeting in my new life. Bernie and John and Dave and Stan and Adam Watts and Johnny Lewis. All of them who I would likely have never met if I'd stayed in the police force. *I know where I stand with them,* I think. Johnny is only ever going to judge me on what I put into his morning training sessions. But is it a mistake to put these people on a pedestal? What if they don't deserve it? What if I try to get up there with them? They might make me welcome, or they could turn around and rip me to pieces.

Did You Solve That One, Gary?

Bob Gibbs is one of the good cops. I remember the first murder we both worked on, of a local councillor who was stabbed at home by his girlfriend. Bob was also there for one of the worst jobs I remember, where the victim's body had been left inside the boot of a car for so long during a hot summer that it was liquefying, leaking out as an oily trail that ran beneath it.

The smell got into your skin, working that job. Hoping to wash it off, you'd try a shower, only your pores would open up in the hot water, releasing the death-smell. Or the next day, you'd go running, start to sweat and that same stench would trickle down your forehead.

'Did you solve that one, Gary?' Bob asks, as we sit at his dining table. It's July 2021, and I've driven up from the city centre to his home on a hill looking out over Sydney's northern beaches, where Bob has spent the past week renovating the kitchen. There's exposed brickwork and gyprock boards all around us. The cupboards are up but the oven's not in place yet. Exposed electrical wires are sticking out of the walls.

'No, we didn't,' I say. 'Although I've got a good idea who did it.' Bob smiles in understanding. That happens, sometimes. You think you know who the killer is but haven't got the evidence to arrest them. We'd interviewed this man after learning that he owed the victim money, but he denied playing any part in the killing. Afterwards, he moved away from Sydney.

Bob shakes his head. The stench from that car was so bad, he says, that after they were done with the forensic examination one of the bosses made them move it out of the car park underneath the police station. They couldn't get rid of the car because it was evidence. The stench hung around it for years.

Bob stands and picks a path through the devastation in his kitchen to the backyard, where he pours us both a beer from a tap set up on the verandah.

'What a place,' I say, looking at his set-up; the wide verandah, the open sky beyond it, Bob bending over the beer tap.

Bob says he brewed the beer himself.

'It's good,' I tell him. It's very good. *Bob hasn't changed*, I think. Good company. Hard working. Never one to whinge, 'Oh me, oh my,' at how tough the job was. His wife and her sister are elsewhere in the house and, ever since I arrived this morning, the place has been full of laughter. *This is more like the retirement I'd imagined for myself after leaving the police force.*

Instead, I'm still struggling to work out who I am now. When people ask me what I do, I don't know how to answer. I'm an ex-cop? A crook? A reporter? Bob sits back down at the table, stretches out, kicking a piece of loose plaster out of the way, and raises his glass. I get the sense he doesn't regret being a detective, though it took a lot out of him.

Bob worked in forensics, meaning it was his job to gather evidence from crime scenes, including plotting the detail of blood spatter and calculating bullet trajectories from the damage they did on impact. And there were a lot of crime scenes. He never added up the figures but reckons he would have seen several thousand dead bodies during his career. Many of them were grossly disfigured by violence, maggot-infested, or green and purple with decomposition. He's dealt with child murders, mutilations and, more than once, the killings of whole families. I wonder how he made sense of all this horror – and if that is what has brought me here.

Out of all that badness, Bob says, one case that had a profound effect on him was the 1996 Port Arthur massacre. He was one of the first police officers sent in after a lone gunman drove himself to the remote, colonial-era prison in Tasmania and began firing.

Bob got the call at home, late on a Sunday, telling him to join a team of Sydney cops who were flying down the next morning to help the Tasmanian police. He'd been following the news all afternoon, he tells me. Every time you switched it on, the list of casualties grew higher: three people dead; then five; then 10.

Something evil had clearly happened, but no one seemed to understand it. The deaths kept on climbing, into the 20s. Bob got what sleep he could then woke up five hours later and drove into the city to catch a commercial flight to Hobart, the State capital. All the other passengers on board were reading about the shooting in the morning newspapers.

In Hobart, they had a briefing from the Tassie cops. The death toll was even higher by now; somewhere in the 30s. The gunman had holed up overnight in a guesthouse a few kilometres from the old penitentiary at Port Arthur and been surrounded. Earlier that morning, the place had been set alight and the heavily armed cops watched as a tall man, with bleach-blond hair had staggered out, his shirt on fire, before disappearing then reappearing amid the smoke, this time with the burning clothes torn from his body.

They had got him. The man was now in hospital, Bob learned. His team drove down the Arthur Highway, to Port Arthur, past the smoking ruin of the guesthouse.

On any other morning, that road would have been busy with tourist traffic as hundreds of cars and buses made the same short drive through the thick forest, scattered with pastel-coloured houses, to visit the ruins of the colonial prison complex. On that day, the road was closed and empty. It was eerie, Bob says, knowing what was waiting for them. When they arrived, he'd never seen so many TV crews and reporters. The Sydney cops drove past them in silence. Inside, the lawns of the old penal settlement were neat and green and the crumbling, pink brick of the prison building itself was lit by the warm morning sunlight. For a moment, no one spoke. Nothing moved. It was so quiet.

'It was just weird,' says Bob, 'because it was a beautiful area and you knew what had happened there.'

People Don't Realise

Bob Gibbs's job was to gather and process evidence from the Broad Arrow Café where the gunman shot most of his victims. It was a small building, he says, around 20 metres by 20 metres, with maybe half of that space for seating, along with an adjoining gift shop. Piecing the accounts given by the surviving witnesses together with the physical remains, including the trail of toppled chairs and unmoving bodies, the police worked out that the gunman had eaten a meal on the balcony outside, walked back into the café and placed the sports bag carrying his guns on an unoccupied table. Then he took out a semi-automatic rifle and began firing.

In the first 15 seconds, the gunman killed 12 people. In total, Bob counted 20 murdered bodies in the café. Some were draped in Port Arthur Historic Site souvenir tea towels. Bob guessed that the survivors must have found the tea towels in the first moments following the shooting and laid them on their loved ones, to hide the horror of the gunshots.

'People don't realise what those injuries can do to a person,' he says. 'It's not like TV and the movies.' Among the sights that got stuck in Bob's memory that morning was one of the

Thirteen-year-old Michelle Pogmore, whose death remains unsolved. *Courtesy of Kathy Nowland*

Kathy Nowland at her daughter's graveside, on what would have been Michelle's birthday. *Courtesy of Kathy Nowland*

Bernie Matthews, a hard man and a good friend. *John Grainger / Newspix*

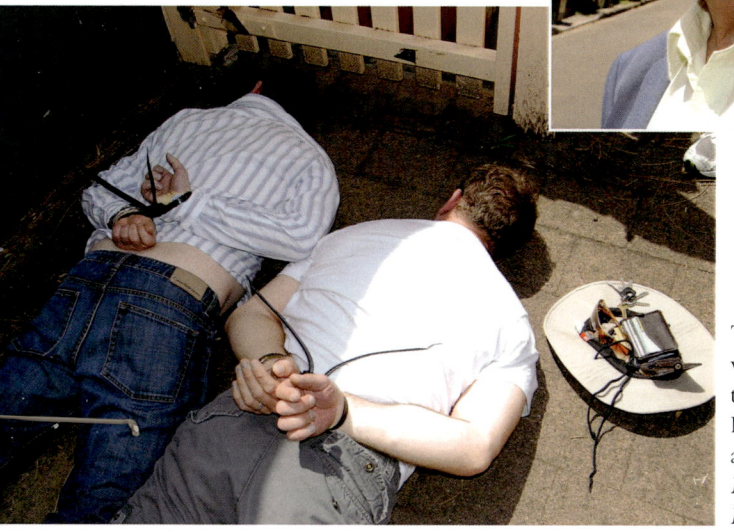

Two of the people we arrested over the murder of Terry Falconer, who was a friend of Bernie's. *NSW Police / AAP Image*

Lytiah Stadhams and Michelle Jarrett, the sister and aunt of four-year-old Evelyn Greenup, one of three children murdered in Bowraville in the early 1990s. *Nathan Edwards / Newspix*

Handprints left on the glass wall of the NSW Law Courts in September 2018, in protest at the ongoing failure to jail the Bowraville killer. *Dan Himbrechts / AAP Image*

The Granny Killer, John Wayne Glover, in prison. Some people should never be released. *Anthony Moran / Newspix*

Garry Lynch holds a photo of his daughter, Anita Cobby. *Kylie Melinda Smith / SMH*

One of Anita's killers, Gary Murphy, is led away. It looks like he lost control of himself while being arrested. *Steve Moorhouse / Newspix*

Imagine the terror of being on Hoddle Street in Melbourne on 9 August 1987, when Julian Knight began shooting. *The Age*

Julian Knight is led out of court by police. A judge said he lived a 'fantasy life'. *John Lamb / SMH*

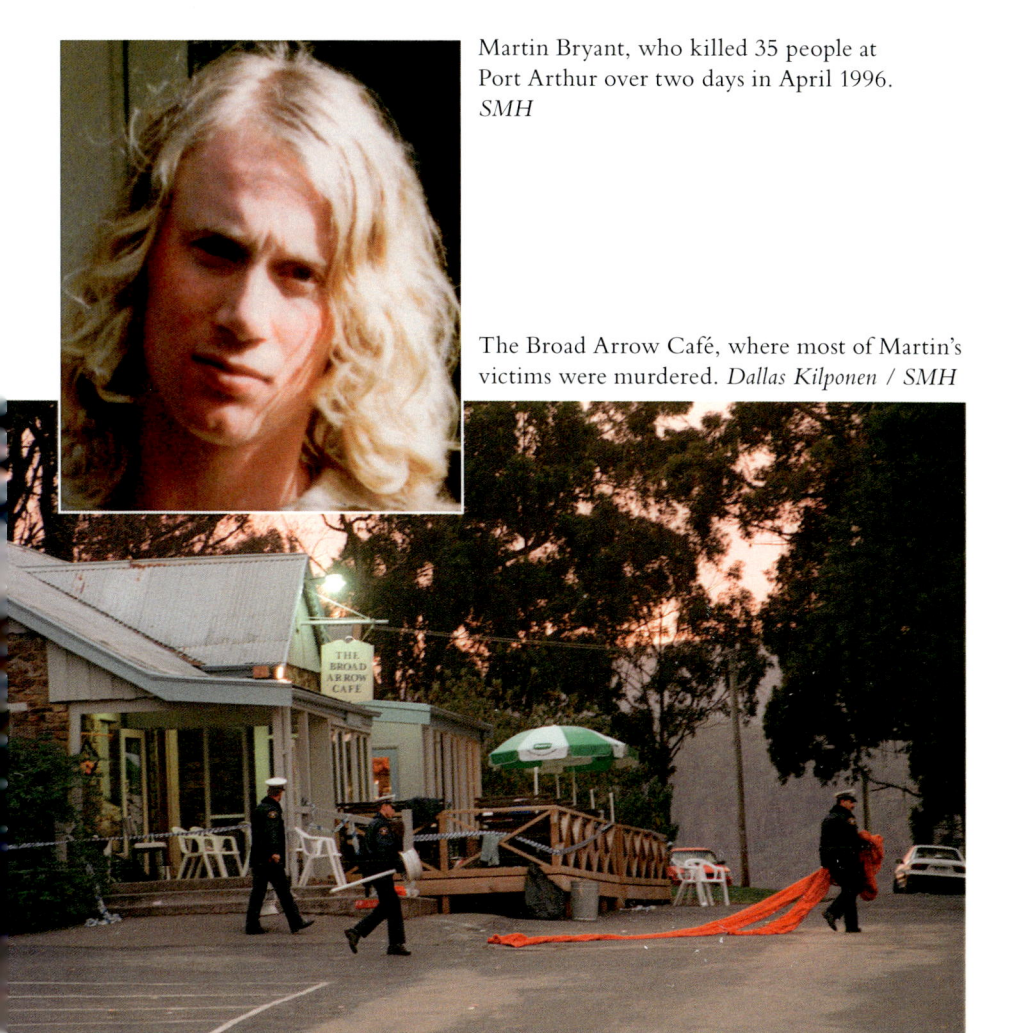

Martin Bryant, who killed 35 people at Port Arthur over two days in April 1996. *SMH*

The Broad Arrow Café, where most of Martin's victims were murdered. *Dallas Kilponen / SMH*

One of the good guys: Bob Gibbs worked the crime scene after the Port Arthur massacre. *Richard Dobson / Newspix*

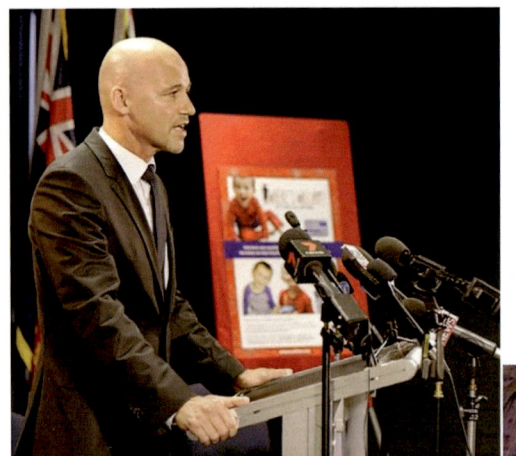

Speaking during the investigation into William Tyrrell's disappearance, a case I led for four years. *NSW Police*

Police search for possible traces of blood outside the house where William went missing, in November 2021. *Mick Tsikas / AAP Image*

Stan, Johnny Lewis and Jack: three men at the heart of the Erko boxing crew and who I know will always be in my corner. *Nathan Lowe*

With Adam Watt, a hard man with a big heart, who taught me to ask, 'Why was I chosen?'

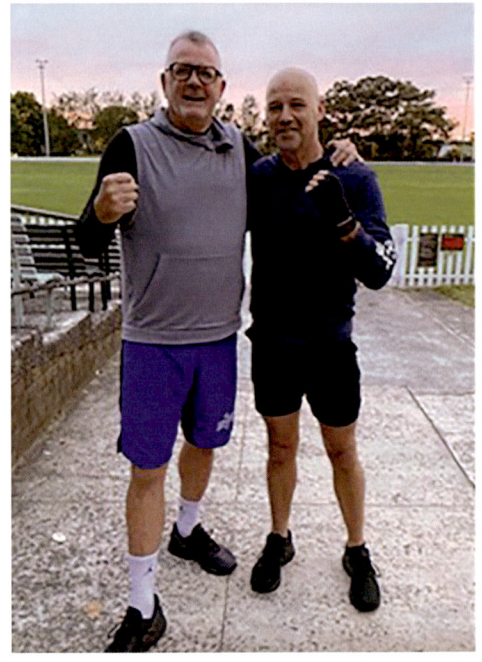

Ivan Milat smiles from inside a police car while being driven from a court hearing. He murdered seven people.
Rick Rycroft / AAP Image

The painstaking and awful search for evidence of Ivan's killings in the Belanglo State Forest.
Peter Rae / AAP Image

With John Killick, who broke out of prison in a helicopter and ended up serving time with Ivan.
Julian Andrews / Newspix

It's like the goodness shines out of Wilma Robb, despite the horror of what was done to her. *Rohan Kelly / Newspix*

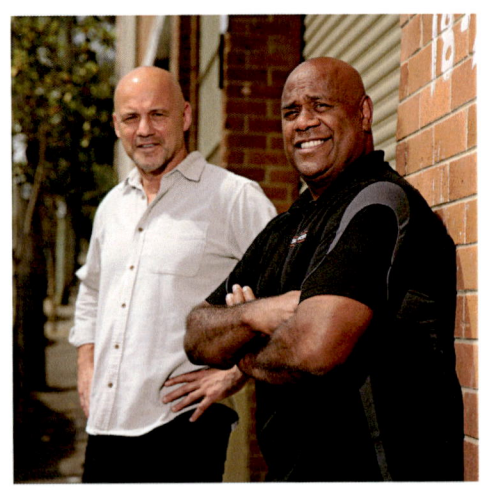

Another of the good guys, Shane Phillips, who taught me a different way of fighting crime. *Adam Yip Photography / Newspix*

After his son Michael was killed in 1994, Ken Marslew founded anti-violence support group Enough is Enough. *Richard Milnes / Alamy Stock Photo*

Graham Henry shows me how the cops shot him, during his arrest. *Tim Hunter / Newspix*

gunman's victims whose brain had been ejected from its skull on impact and landed in a soup bowl on the table. Another was the sight of a man who seemed to have been trying to protect his wife and child and had been shot dead through his outstretched hands.

Other of the victims suffered deep bloody gashes after being hit by bone fragments flying out of the person who'd been standing beside them. Bob says you could feel the fear, still hanging heavy in the café, along with the metallic smell of blood and the scent of gun smoke, which he recognised from the police firing range. The Sydney cops split into two teams, each with 10 bodies to examine. Recording injuries and physical evidence, they moved quickly, finishing up that same night, less than 24 hours after Bob got the call at home in Sydney. The official death toll eventually reached 35 men, women and children. More than 20 were injured. It was the worst massacre by a lone gunman anywhere in the world.

Near the toll booth at the entrance to the Port Arthur settlement, the police found an abandoned yellow Volvo with a surfboard strapped to its roof racks. Witnesses described the driver as tall and blond; the same man who had been arrested that morning after the siege at the guesthouse. His name, the police discovered, was Martin Bryant. The next day, detectives stood at his bedside in the Royal Hobart Hospital, where Martin was being treated for burns, and charged him with murder.

The same day, inside the Broad Arrow Café, Bob kept working long after the victims' bodies had been removed and taken for autopsy, recording the different types of bullets that were fired and exactly where they struck the shattered walls or bodies of their targets. He could see the damage done but nobody could understand why Martin did it.

* * *

Trying to work that out means following the thread of Martin's life story. Since sitting down with John Killick, I've been thinking about how some people will go on to do badness while others will not. What makes the difference? Is it something that they're born with, something that's passed down in their DNA? As it turns out, Martin's DNA is twisted up with the place he carried out his murders.

Port Arthur was built in the middle of the nineteenth century, when Australia was being used as a penal colony by Britain. Within the colony, Tasmania was run as a prison within a prison; an island physically isolated from the mainland. And Port Arthur was a prison within that prison, notorious around the entire country as the worst place you could end up in, a grinding-mill for those convicts who committed further crimes after their arrival.

In Port Arthur, prisoners were whipped, starved and served their sentences in enforced silence. They endured solitary confinement in special cells a little over two metres by one metre, where the stone walls were so thick they shut out both light and sound. The place was named after the man who founded it, the Tasmanian Lieutenant Governor Sir George Arthur, who would himself meet new convicts on their arrival in Hobart, telling them that their conduct would be narrowly watched and their names, crimes, and their actions all recorded in official files. Misbehave and the threat of Port Arthur hung over the entire island.

This was the world to which an Englishman called Richard Cordwell was committed. His name, physical description, crime, details of transportation and assignment were noted down on his arrival at the docks in Hobart. Those files record that Richard was a young man, 19 at the time of his arrest in London, a gardener by trade, tall for a man of his time, with pock-marked skin, light brown hair and grey eyes. Convicted of theft with violence and highway robbery over a fight in which he was accused of attacking a woman and stealing her shawl, he was given a death sentence. He was lucky. Rather than being hanged, Richard's sentence was commuted and, after ten months in the filth of Newgate Prison, he was instead loaded aboard a convict ship in April 1825 for the long, one-way journey to Hobart.

There, Richard was assigned to work for a wealthy landowner. Almost a decade later, in March 1835, another convict arrived in the city, a woman called Eliza Fitzgerald. Her age is uncertain, though she was likely in her early 20s. Found guilty of pickpocketing on the streets of London, she too had been sentenced to transportation for life.

How Richard and Eliza met is unrecorded but in October 1837 they sought permission to marry and, four years later, their first child was born. A boy, he was named after his father, Richard. The child grew up, married a local girl and had a son called Albert. Albert had a son called Martin. Martin, in turn, had a daughter, Carleen. Carleen married a man called Maurice Bryant and they, too, settled down in Hobart.

In October 1975, Carleen and Maurice left the city and drove down the Arthur Highway – also named after the former lieutenant governor – towards the ruins of the prison he had founded, which had by then become a tourist attraction. Just beyond the entrance to the historic site, the Bryants chanced upon a little fibro cottage overlooking a white sandy beach that stretched out in an almost perfect crescent with the iron-coloured water of the Southern Ocean beyond it. They bought it as somewhere to take their son and daughter for weekends and holidays. Growing up, the kids would spend days, weeks and months in the cottage near Port Arthur. One day, the couple's son would return there as an adult.

Isolated

It feels too easy to look at Martin Bryant's criminal ancestors and ask if he received some dangerous genetic inheritance. This is the territory of Cesare Lombroso, the founder of criminology, who argued some people were born criminals. But modern Australia was populated by British convicts, meaning many of us have criminals in our families, yet we do not commit crimes. And, if Martin did inherit some badness, then it was not obvious, like Cesare argued it would be. Or, at least, it was not obvious at first.

His mother Carleen's pregnancy was uneventful. Martin's delivery, in May 1967 at Hobart's Queen Alexandra Hospital, was straight-forward. Like every new arrival, the baby was checked during the hours after his birth for any disability and the staff took special care to look for signs of a congenital heart condition that Carleen had lived with all her life. Nobody was worried. When the new family got home, in the seemingly peaceful and contented first few weeks of their baby's life, it seemed like everything was fine.

Soon, though, Carleen noticed he rejected cuddles. Martin disliked physical affection and didn't want to breastfeed, either.

It didn't seem to hold him back, though, and by 16 months, he was up on his feet, not just walking but running, and escaping. As a toddler, he'd disappear and his desperate parents would eventually find him on top of the chook pen next door, or playing on a swing on the other side of the railway line that ran along the city foreshore.

For his parents, it was exhausting. Martin was blue-eyed and blond-haired, the picture of a perfect Aussie child, but something in him was different. His speech was slow to develop. As he played, or ran and climbed around the neighbourhood, his parents could see that his fine motor skills – the smaller, carefully controlled movements of the fingers and hands that children use to hold a crayon or pick up a toy – weren't as coordinated as they expected. He did not seem to be maturing like other children.

Carleen loved her son, that was only natural. But showing him that affection did not come as naturally to her. Her own childhood had been tough and her parents' marriage was unhappy. For Carleen, coping with her son as he grew older was a day-to-day struggle. She washed, she cleaned, she cooked. Martin needed space so his parents bought a new home, a sprawling place with a big backyard for him to play in. They took him for long walks, trying to burn up some of his endless energy. Mum and boy became a common sight on the quiet streets around their house, either on foot together or her pushing a stroller containing the pretty child with the blonde curls.

At pre-school, aged four, the staff could barely understand him. Martin's parents tried another school but he was disruptive and they were called to meet the headmistress, who suggested another school might be better suited for their son.

After another move, Martin's baby-like speech meant that he still stood out. He'd wander the playground on the fringes of the other kids' games or conversations. His school reports said he enjoyed writing nasty stories about other children, while his handwriting was littered with capital letters and difficult to read. In maths, Martin was a year behind his classmates. Sometimes he kicked, or spat, trying, it seemed, to get attention. One teacher later described him as the most isolated person they had ever seen.

***

Looking back at Martin's childhood, I still struggle with the magnitude of what he grew into. It's hard to think beyond the sheer horror of what his victims would have experienced. This wasn't badness done out of any human feeling, like lust, which drove Anita Cobby's killers, or led to the death of Michelle Pogmore. To walk into the café at Port Arthur took unfeeling. Because anyone who thinks or feels like I do, could not do that.

If there is a lesson here, maybe it is that evil isn't always done because people want to do it but because they see no reason not to. Today, scientists in the US and the UK have done studies on twins as young as seven, identifying what they call 'early warning signs of life-long psychopathy', such as seeming callous and unemotional. These children are at great risk of becoming criminals in adulthood. They start offending at a young age, and their acts are often predatory in nature. By studying twins, who share their genes but may have different life experiences, the scientists argue that environmental factors do not explain the emergence of some of these early warning signs. Instead, callous, unemotional behaviour may be something you inherit from your family.

If so, few of those who dealt with Martin growing up seemed to understand this. When he threw objects around the classroom, he got sent out, extending his isolation and meaning he drifted even further behind in his schoolwork. Outside school, he caused more trouble, setting fire to a large pile of wooden crates and sometimes treating animals without compassion. One schoolmate later told police how Martin caught a cat and seemed to be trying to pull it apart with his bare hands.

As Martin grew older, his father, Maurice, took him for long walks, trying to calm his son's nervous energy. They ranged out together around the city or into the foothills of Mount Wellington, which rises behind Hobart like a black storm cloud. Out there, father and son kept away from the main paths, pacing their way instead along a network of fire trails threaded through the forest, meaning they saw only a handful of other walkers. When Martin was eight, his parents bought the little fibro cottage at Port Arthur. Set well back on a big block overlooking the water, there was more space there, and more freedom, than in the city. That meant Martin could be wilder.

It did seem to calm him. He loved the sea, and would go swimming, fishing and later scuba diving. But onshore, Martin burned himself while playing with fireworks and was hospitalised. He got called 'Silly Marty' by the local kids.

On his 14th birthday, Martin's father gave him an air rifle. He took the gun out into the night with him, alone, hiding in a creek bed that ran alongside the little cottage and fired at passing traffic, or out into the darkness of the ocean. Sometimes, for fun, the kids would hide in the pitch-black, solitary confinement cells of the Port Arthur prison, waiting for the tour guides to bring in groups of nervous tourists they could frighten. Martin didn't get it. He started throwing rocks at the tour parties instead and got them all banned.

In May 1983, around the time of his 16th birthday, Martin left school and his parents later took him to a psychiatrist. Martin kept interrupting the doctor, asking questions. After a few consultations, the doctor said he was likely unemployable. 'Cannot read or write,' the doctor wrote in his case notes. Only his parents' efforts prevented further deterioration. Martin 'could be schizophrenic and his parents face a bleak future with him'.

By this time, in his late teens, Martin had grown up to be slim, well-muscled and good looking with long, curly bleach-blond hair and the broad grin of a surfie. Aged 19 or maybe 20, he met a woman called Helen Harvey who lived with her mother and dozens of cats in a house a few hundred metres from his own. They struck up a strange, mutually dependent friendship. Martin moved in. He would later call Helen his only real friend. She died five years later, in a road accident in October 1992.

The following year, Martin's father, Maurice, took his own life and was found lying face down in a dam, his body weighed down by Martin's diving belt, which was strung around his neck and across his torso.

The younger man had lost his only friend and his father. Like Julian Knight, I think, here was someone who had been rejected. Silly Marty. Someone who had been kept in check by different support structures — for Julian it was the army; for Martin it was Miss Harvey and Maurice Bryant — only for those structures to fall away. What did the world look like now through Martin's eyes? I cannot answer. From the outside, he still looked like an archetypal Australian. Except, maybe for his eyes, which seemed shadowed, as if they were looking out from the darkness. Like a prisoner who'd been locked in isolation peering out into the sunlight after the guards unlock his cell door. Those eyes would soon be seen in news reports around the world.

I'm Sure You'll Find the Person

Sitting in the shell of his kitchen, Bob Gibbs says he doesn't give much thought to Martin Bryant these days. Though he's not been able to forget him.

Bob stayed on at Port Arthur for almost a fortnight after the shooting, collecting the last of the forensic evidence.

'It was the most beautiful place,' he says, as if trying to make sense of the memory. The ivy-covered, gothic ruins. The jetty running out into the tranquil water and the long headland stretching out around Carnarvon Bay. Bob got to know some of the Tassie cops who worked alongside him and, every now and then, they would take a break and go for a walk outside to try and clear their heads. In the evenings, they'd go out on the piss together, and start crying. Then they would laugh and have another beer. It was like that for 12 days, Bob says, before he was sent home to Sydney.

Being back felt strange. Both weird and sad. It was like coming back from a war zone, Bob thought, as if the adrenaline that had sustained him had drained away, leaving him empty.

Not that the work was over. There were still the photos from the crime scene to process. Bob also had to write a formal statement describing each body they'd examined. The cops sent him to see a psych and there was a follow-up appointment a month later. But he wasn't having problems back then. It was only later, in restaurants and cafés, that Bob started sitting with his back to the wall, so no one could walk in without him seeing.

'Is that because of Port Arthur?' I ask.

'I'm not sure.'

* * *

When the police interviewed Martin Bryant about the shooting, he at first denied any involvement.

'Do you think people should take responsibility for their actions, Martin?' one of the detectives asked him. 'Accept the consequences of what they do?'

'Yeah, I do,' Martin said. 'I s'pose I should for a little while for what I've done.' His attention seemed to drift, as if he couldn't concentrate on their questions. 'Just a little while and let me out,' Martin said. 'Let me live my own life. I'm missing my mum. I really miss her actually, what she cooks up for me, her rabbit stews and everything.'

I can imagine the detectives being unsure of what to make of this. Had Martin just accepted his own guilt? It was as if he didn't understand what he'd been involved in. What did he mean by 'for a little while'? There was no way he was going to be let out any time soon.

Often, during the interview, Martin would smile. At times, it seemed that he was joking about something. When the detectives told him the ballistic evidence showed each of the dozens of dead and injured people had been shot by guns in his possession, he looked at them and said, 'Yeah ... I'm sure you'll find the person who caused all this.' He sat back and pointed at himself: 'Me.'

Was that a joke or a confession?

'I don't find that a very funny statement at all, Martin, to be quite honest,' replied one of the detectives.

Martin said he'd really like to help the police out, but he couldn't.

'Have you had other trouble like this, dramatic?' Martin asked the detectives.

'Not on this scale, no,' one told him.

'No,' said Martin. 'Suppose it happens, doesn't it?' he replied.

There was no empathy. No sense of grief. No understanding of the pain or loss that he had caused.

***

In court, Martin pleaded guilty. Sentencing him, the judge said that he was pathetic. A social misfit. But Justice William Cox also seemed to accept that Martin wasn't simply evil. It was more complicated: 'Without minimising the gravity of his conduct ... it would appear to me that the level of his culpability is accordingly reduced by reason of his intellectual impairment.' There was something wrong with Martin. Something, perhaps, that he was born with.

Martin suffered from a 'significant personality disorder', the judge said. That was combined with external factors beyond his control, including the death of Helen Harvey and his father's suicide. The result 'calls for understanding and pity, even though his actions demand condemnation'. Martin had a limited ability to feel empathy, or to imagine the feelings and responses of others. That 'left a terrible gap in his sensibilities which enabled him not only to contemplate mass destruction, but to carry it through'.

Seven months after his killings, in November 1996, Martin was sentenced to 35 life terms, with the judge ordering he never be released from prison. The word 'evil' was not mentioned once during the sentencing hearing. Instead, the judge said, 'I have no reason to hope, and every reason to fear, that he will remain indefinitely as disturbed and insensitive as he was when planning and executing the crimes of which he now stands convicted.'

You might try to understand him. You might agree with the judge that he is not simply evil. But he will always be a danger to other people.

* * *

A little over a decade after the massacre, in February 2008, a psychologist employed by the police force told Bob he might be suffering from post-traumatic stress disorder. Bob went to see his GP and was told to take four months off work. He did so, then returned. Two years later, while at work in the Crime Scene Section, Bob felt unwell again and was told to seek treatment from a psychologist as soon as possible. This time, he did not go back.

As a cop, the job worms its way inside you. It wasn't as if Port Arthur was the first, or only, horror Bob saw in the police force. On his first day working a crime scene, a man stabbed his ex-wife to death at her real estate office, fled in his car and tried to kill himself by driving head-on into a bus. It swerved, hit an embankment and rolled over, killing two elderly passengers. Bob worked that case.

Another time, he was called when the body of a newborn baby burst out of a green garbage bag caught in the jaws of a truck's rubbish compactor. He and I worked together on the murder of a three-year-old boy, beaten so badly his bowel had separated from the lining of his stomach. I still have an image of that child lodged in my memory, just like Bob does. The bruising around his neck. His smooth skin. His lifeless eyes. His innocence.

And there are other cases; killings that made little sense, or that no one could make sense of because the killer did not show remorse. A street robbery shortly before Christmas that turned into a murder, where the killer got away with a credit card and used it to buy a packet of cigarettes. Bob and I worked that one, also. I locked up the killer. Like he says now, it seemed a wicked waste of a life for a packet of smokes.

If Martin's lack of empathy helps to explain how he carried out his murders, I think Bob's ability to empathise with his victims may have been his weakness. More than once while we are sitting in the kitchen, he talks about cases involving the killing of children and, as a parent, I guess he found those particularly traumatic. The morning he flew down to Port Arthur was his daughter's fourth birthday, Bob says. I tell him how I missed my son's fifth birthday chasing another killer.

'I think of it like having a bucket,' Bob says. 'Slowly it gets filled up.' Eventually, it spills over. It's been more than a decade now since Bob worked as a cop.

Sitting in his half-built kitchen, he looks at our empty beer glasses and asks whether I want a refill. Standing up, he tells me how he plans to get on with the electrics. Get that oven finished. Do the tiling. He takes great pride in the fact that he's done the work himself, even if the bits are not perfect, saying how he didn't measure up one of those cupboards properly, meaning he'll have to take it down and try again. But Bob says he is learning. And he is enjoying the rebuilding process.

***

Driving home, it feels as if something is different. I feel at peace. Like I can take a breath for the first time since I left the police force. I remember how angry I was, just over a year earlier, after my conviction. Back then, I wanted to do violence. I could picture my fists smashing into the face of a stranger who abused me outside the courthouse. I imagined myself standing, wronged, facing those people in the cops who'd been involved in the decision to charge me. I would beat them. I would show them. I'd cause them pain, smash bone and cartilage. At the time, I'd been confused by this anger in me. By my own desire to do violence. More than anything, I felt bitter regret at those cases I had left behind, unsolved.

Heading back over the Harbour Bridge from North Sydney, I start to let these things go. On either side, the great steel uprights slice the sky into ribbons. Life outside the cops is more complicated in some ways – nothing is black and white out here

I'm Sure You'll Find the Person

for starters – but I am finding my way through it. Over the bridge, the road leads into the city and, as the street lights turn on against the darkening evening, I start to smile.

Back in my apartment, I see Sky News is showing a documentary about the disappearance of William Tyrrell. I don't want to watch it but feel I should. It's unresolved, so I sit, watching my replacement as the head of the police investigation, David Laidlaw, describe what the cops are now doing. At first, he seems to say the case is still wide open: 'Nobody has been excluded.'

That's interesting. We had excluded the families. Have they really reopened every part of the investigation?

The reporter, Peter Stefanovic, asks David, 'So, if anyone out there is thinking I might have gotten away with this, what's your message?'

'They haven't.'

'Do you believe you know who the person is?' Peter asks him.

'We believe we can identify who it may be, or the circumstances of him going missing, yes.'

I sit up. What?

'You know what happened, don't you?' Peter pushes for an answer.

'We have thoughts about what occurred to William.'

Peter asks if the policeman has thoughts about who did it.

'Yes.'

Hang on to That

Bernie Matthews' phone calls have become less frequent. Since first meeting up, we've been speaking to each other often. Bernie will call and the two of us will end up talking long into the evening. Of all the people I've met since leaving the police, Bernie is the one I share the closest bond with. When I look at him now, I see a hard man who made decisions in his lifetime that few could understand unless they'd lived it with him. Yes, he broke the law but he followed a code: you don't back down, you stand by your mates without question, and you don't dog, meaning you don't cooperate with the police.

To my mind, that's more than many people live by. Bernie has also been punished for his crimes and I think he's tried to make good some of the damage done, by helping other people. Among other things, he has become a journalist, writing about conditions in the State children's homes, or prisons, and what that did to people. He's even won a couple of awards for his reporting.

Often, when he's called in the past, it was to talk about ideas for my own journalism, or help put me in touch with crooks who might do interviews for the podcast. Bernie's told me how he started out by editing the prison magazine in Parramatta and sent copies out to politicians, journalists and the trade unions, hoping it might break the perception that all criminals were six-foot sinners with broken noses and tattoos of topless women if he could just show them how many gifted people there were inside.

But now he doesn't call so often and, when he does, his voice sounds more hollow, as if there isn't as much of him on the end of the phone. He's always got a new idea, though, and he's always busy. He's working on a book and says he and I should write something together. This time when he calls me, he asks, 'Do you want to catch up? I've got a mate here that I reckon you'd be interested in meeting.'

I tell him, sure. Any mate of Bernie's will be interesting.

He says we'll go for lunch, and to meet him at the old Covent Garden Hotel at the bottom of Chinatown. When I get there, Bernie's sitting outside having beers with a pale, stocky bloke who looks like he must be in his 60s. He has still got hard man written all over him. Bernie introduces him as The Pom.

I get a beer and join them. The Pom's telling a story about running around London as a kid when the Kray twins were the city's leading gangsters. Later, he moved out here and did some armed robberies with Bernie. The two of them start arguing about a stick-up; one saying to the other, 'You told me you could steal that car and we jumped in and you couldn't start it.'

'You shouldn't have been so fucking slow running down the road.'

Bernie asks me if I've managed to catch up with Graham Henry, who was starting out in organised crime around the same time as the Krays went down. Graham served the first of several prison sentences in 1969, the same year the twins were jailed for life. He went on to dominate Sydney's underworld like the Krays had in London. No, I tell Bernie, I've tried but I'm not sure that Graham trusts me.

Bernie shrugs and says, 'Let's get a bite.' I know a place, a nearby Chinese restaurant where I used to eat with other cops when I was in the Armed Hold-Up Squad. We'd go there when we'd had a good arrest and wanted to celebrate. The staff would let us have the whole top floor to ourselves, to drink and blow off some of the excitement of the chase. Later, when I was working as a manager at Chatswood Police Station in northern Sydney, I'd take the junior detectives there after a successful case. When Bernie, The Pom and I walk up, one of the waitresses standing outside seems to recognise me and leads us upstairs to a quiet table on the top floor. The three of us keep drinking. The conversation isn't that different from when I was here as a detective; telling stories, talking about crooks and cops we've known through work, laughing at the funny things we've seen and commiserating the sad ones.

As the afternoon stretches on, I'm feeling pretty comfortable. Bernie mentions he's been feeling a bit rough.

'I thought you were a bit off,' I say, thinking about his phone calls.

'Ah, I'll be fine.'

'You'll be too tough to say whether you are or aren't,' I tell him.

Bernie stands up to take a piss and his eyes look glassy with the beer now. While he is gone, The Pom leans forward across the table and speaks softly. 'Look, I don't know if you're aware of this but Bernie's pretty crook,' he tells me.

'What's wrong?'

'He won't talk about it, but he gave me his watch and said, "Here, you hang on to that",' The Pom says. 'I don't think that bodes well. Just keep an eye out for him.'

Bernie comes back and we change the subject.

Looking across the table at him, deep in conversation, I feel a great weight inside me. It makes sense now why he always seems so busy. Always in a hurry. It's because he doesn't have much time left.

Poison

John Killick later tells me that it's cancer. A couple of weeks pass and, in early August 2021, Bernie calls me, saying he's in the hospital. He's had the operation but, after the doctors went in, he says they told him that it wasn't worth it to continue. They couldn't cut it all out.

'Do you want to come out and see me?' he asks. He's at the St George at Kogarah in southern Sydney.

'I'll be there,' I promise Bernie.

***

A nurse behind the ward desk gives a little smile and almost half a laugh when I ask her, 'Is Bernie Matthews here?' *He must have charmed them already*, I tell myself. She points to a side room with six beds in it and Bernie sits up when I enter, leaning back against a pillow with a frown.

He still has that same old toughness to him but his hair seems thinner than it used to and his skin looks like its hanging off his shoulders and cheekbones.

'Right-oh, mate,' he says, carrying on as if nothing is different from any of our other meetings. I lean forward to hear what he is saying and ask if I can record the conversation. This time, the recording is not for my protection, nor is it for the podcast, it's because I don't know if this might be the last time we talk to each other.

He understands.

'We are recording now, so if you are happy with that,' I tell him.

'Yeah.'

'This can go anywhere you want,' I say.

'Yeah, that makes sense.'

There is so much to ask him. 'I just want to get your thoughts now you've had this diagnosis from the doctors.' There's no point ducking around it. Bernie told me on the phone his life would soon be over. 'Looking back at your life and how you went in a direction, what do you put that down to?'

He shifts, saying, 'I don't really know,' and drawing the white sheet closer around him. 'I guess it's just my way of going through life. Like I wasn't going to let anyone stand over me.'

When he was young, Bernie continues, he came to a fork in the road. He wanted to join the army but they didn't make it easy for him. He'd been in the army reserve and wanted a straight transfer but they said he had to discharge and re-enlist. 'So I said, "Ah, well, fuck that," and I grabbed a couple of submachine guns and got into armed robbery.'

He and I both know it's not a proper explanation.

'Do you reckon you were born bad?' I ask him. 'I don't get the sense that you were.'

'No,' Bernie replies. 'I don't know where it came from but I had a resentment for authority.'

'Yeah, I wondered where that came from. When did you identify that you didn't like being told what to do?'

'I guess it was in Mount Penang,' Bernie says. Or in one of the other boys' homes he was sent to.

I tell him about the first time I stood up to my old man, who used to beat me with the wooden handle of a feather duster. 'I think I might have been six or seven and I burned the feather duster that he was going to belt me with by throwing it on the barbecue.' I remember watching the thing burn and the feeling of satisfaction that it gave me. 'Do you remember a time when you sort of thought, "Fuck it, I don't get told what to do"?'

'I think it was when Mum met up with a bloke called Baxter and she ended up marrying him,' Bernie says. He grew up calling this man, Roy Baxter, 'Dad', not knowing that his real father left when he was two years old. 'She kept it from me,' he says.

'So you thought this Baxter was your biological father?'

'Yeah. He used to say, "You are no son of mine", and I couldn't understand why he said that.' After all, Bernie shared his surname. 'Anyway, when I was about 10 or 11, like any kid I went rummaging through Mum's room and I came across a cash box. I opened it up and there was a birth certificate in it. I looked at it and it said *Bernard Thomas Matthews*, and I thought, Who the fuck is that?' Bernie realised he'd been lied to. 'As it turned out, it was me.'

Eventually, Bernie's mum sat him down and told him the whole story.

'It crushed me.' He felt a sour resentment. He'd been let down by those in charge and that feeling curdled further every weekend when his mum and Baxter would get on the grog and end up in a punch-up. 'That used to piss me off no end, because you couldn't do nothing about it. Because I was too young, too small, and so I sort of sat on that for years.'

Later, when his mum walked out on his stepdad, she left Bernie behind.

'He tried to con me, you know, we have to face the world together. The usual shit. I said, "Fuck you, I'm off." I left. And I guess that was the start of everything.'

Criminals can be victims, even if only of their childhoods. That was one of the first lessons I learned about badness – one that Bernie taught me. I think about how many of those people that I've met or learned about over the past year had rough childhoods or grew up in fractured families.

'I'm not blaming that,' Bernie says. 'I'm not saying that's the cause of why I turned bad. I'm just saying that was a set of events that sort of pointed me in a direction. I thought I had a safe home. I thought I had a father and a mother. I had fuck all.'

'Did you make a conscious decision to be a crook?' I ask him.

'No. I made a conscious decision that I'd left home and I was living by myself and I was going to make the best way that I could.'

'You were doing what you needed to do to survive at that stage?'

'That's exactly right, yes.'

I think about what Tim Watson-Munro said about Julian Knight and the Hoddle Street massacre, how it just might have been prevented in any of those what if moments – if Julian's car hadn't broken down, if he hadn't drunk so much, if there'd been someone at the pub for him to talk to. What if Bernie had met someone else at that moment, who could have showed him there was another way?

Instead, Bernie starts to describe the first time he was sent to an adult prison and how the gates shut behind you with a clang, clang, bang, then you hear the turning of the locks. 'It's the most eerie fucking sound you will ever hear because you know your life is being locked away.'

'Do you think if someone had put some effort into you at that moment, if someone had got hold of you and said, "Bernie, you are at the crossroads. This is your life for the next thirty years if you don't pull your head in," could that have made a difference?'

He sinks back into the hospital pillow and stares at the ward ceiling.

'I don't know. I don't know Gary,' he says. 'Because I was very obstinate. It's a hard question to answer.' He pauses. 'Maybe, maybe not. I just can't answer that one.'

Around us, the ward is silent. There are a couple of other patients lying silent in their beds. I guess that they are listening.

'Prison changes you,' says Bernie. He talks about the beatings he received from the prison guards.

I tell him, 'My instinct is, if someone's flogging me, I'm going to hate them for the rest of my life. Is that the feeling you had?'

'Yes,' he says. 'I've still got it.'

'Talk me through that anger.'

'The sound of a baton hitting bare skin is a distinctive sound. It's like a staccato and you never forget it,' Bernie says.

'I've heard it, yes.' As a cop, you are issued with a baton.

'They didn't give a fuck whether you were big, small or whatever, they were just determined to fucking bash you.'

I ask him about the prison guard who Bernie leapt on, biting at his throat until he could taste blood.

'I just had to let it out,' he says. He was going to kill him. 'I look back at it and think to myself, yeah, that's weird. I think could I have done any different? I think no, not with the anger and hostility I had in me.'

For the first time, I fully understand him. Looking at Bernie, lying back on his pillow, I can see the young kid who grew up being lied to, who witnessed his mum being beaten, who was then abandoned, shut in boys' homes, then got locked up and flogged into submission. I can see how he would wind up capable of murder.

That's the lesson, I think. *It all goes back to childhood*. Once you know about his childhood you can understand who Bernie is now.

Bernie says he's sorry. Sorry that he hurt people. Sorry that he ran into banks carrying a loaded gun. 'I'm sorry I scared people to such an extent that they probably had bad nightmares for the rest of their life.' He's had his own nightmares, he says. Like the bloody things that swam into his head after being beaten in Grafton, when he dreamed of feeding the prison guards into an imaginary tree-chipper.

'But I can't change it,' he says. Words are cheap. He could try telling those people in the banks he robbed that he is sorry but would that change things?

Bernie looks down. I can hear the hospital machines beeping. There is another way of looking at it, I say. 'The victims at the banks you robbed, if they'd sat down with you when you were in prison and said, "Hey, I haven't been able to sleep since. I've been sick since. I haven't been able to go to work. I lost my job." Would that have made a difference to you?'

I mean, would that have stopped him committing more bank jobs?

'That would have,' Bernie says. Because, honestly, he didn't understand the hurt he was doing to those people. Not knowing about that harm made doing badness easy.

He looks up. There's still that old defiance in him. 'I'm not going to minimise it,' he says. 'I did it. It's my fault. But I paid for it, there is no debt owing.'

'Yes.'

'People ask me, "Well are you sorry for your crimes?" I tell them, "Listen, I served twenty-eight fucking years for me crimes, how fucking sorry do you want me to be?"'

'Fair call.'

We fall silent.

'Looking back at your life,' I say, 'how would you change it?' I mean, how would he change the world itself; what one thing would he do to stop people committing the kind of badness he did? No one ever asks the crooks this question. 'You know, if you got called into a parliamentary committee who were asking what can we change, what would you say?'

'It's so fucking easy,' Bernie tells me. There's something fierce in his voice now. 'Use your head; what are you going to change? Where it begins, not where it fucking ends.' Not here in this hospital ward. 'You can't change me,' he continues. 'I'm too old.'

You've got to look at the next generation. 'You've got to start with the kids,' he says. Stop sending them to juvenile detention. Stop letting them grow up with violence. Find a way to change the direction they're heading, so when they come to the fork in the road that Bernie came to, between doing the right thing and doing badness, they will make the right choice.

To do that, you're going to have to talk to them, says Bernie. Explain what it's all about in kids' terms. Not all the kids will listen, but some will.

'Doing that will make a difference?' I ask him.

'Yes.' He sinks back, looking paler, his skin colour closer to the white of the bedsheets than anything living. 'I think to myself, can I change it? Of course I can change it,' he says.

Bernie tells me how, one time, he was running a halfway house in Sydney for prisoners who'd been released on parole. The place offered ex-cons somewhere to stay and helped them find work, in the hope they'd make something of themselves and not end up going back to badness. Bernie found out a young girl, Holly, was using heroin and threw her out. Better that than have her lead the others astray, he reckoned. Holly had nowhere to go. She was sleeping in bus shelters. She came back and told Bernie she was sorry.

'Yeah, yeah,' he said, his heart hard in that moment. Holly told him she needed help. Bernie softened. 'Listen, this is the deal,' he told her. He knew another ex-crim running a rehab centre in Griffith, in country New South Wales, about seven hours' drive from Sydney. 'If I can get you in there, get you out of the city, will you take it?'

She said yeah.

'Now, don't tell me yes and I go to all the trouble to get you down there and you fuck up on me,' Bernie told her.

She said, 'No, I'll do it.'

Bernie drove Holly there himself. He also took her last wrap of heroin, meaning she did the long drive cold turkey.

'She was sick,' he says. 'Oh she was fucking sick. She spewed. I was the worst bastard in the world to her. I said, "You fucking spew in this car, you'll be cleaning it."'

Bernie told her that he wasn't stopping. She could spew out the window. By the time they got to Griffith, Holly downright hated Bernie, he says. Hated him like poison.

That was the last he heard from Holly. He drove back, got on with his work. A few years later, his partner came back from the mall one Saturday and walked into their place, laughing.

'You'll never guess who I just ran into,' she said. 'Do you remember Holly?'

'Yeah.'

'Bernie, she's cleaned up her act. She's looking a million dollars. She's married, she's got a kid. She reckons you are the worst cunt she's ever met. And she loves you.'

Bernie laughs.

And I laugh. Our laughter fills the ward. An hour and a half has passed since I arrived and he's tired, so I tell him that I've taken up enough of his time today.

Before I leave, he asks me if I've caught up with someone he's been telling me I should talk to. Another one of his friends, a woman called Wilma Robb.

I haven't had a chance to, I tell Bernie.

'Mate, you've got to meet her,' he says, his voice weak and rasping now, but insistent.

I promise to do it. Bernie doesn't explain why it's important. He closes his eyes and, for a moment, they don't reopen.

I want to listen to the recording of our conversation, I tell Bernie. After that, I'll come back to him with more questions.

'Let's have a chat again,' I promise. 'I'll come back and see you.'

I'm Struggling

John Killick calls again a week or so later, just as I'm sitting down to dinner.

'Bad news, mate,' he says. 'It's Bernie. He won't make it through the night.'

We speak a little. John says he'll let me know what happens.

The next morning, I get a text message from The Pom, saying Bernie passed away overnight.

'How are you going?' I text back.

'I'm struggling.'

* * *

I feel lost without Bernie. If I look back at myself when I was younger, when I'd just joined the cops, I never would have thought I'd be in such a fog because a bank robber had passed on. It's like my compass is spinning. I sit at home, alone and everything seems upside down. What's wrong is right. What's right is wrong. And I no longer have him with me to help find the way through this.

* * *

The days pass. A week. Then two weeks. In early September 2021, the *Daily Telegraph* newspaper publishes a story on its front page.

It says the police have 'zeroed in on a new person of interest' in the William Tyrrell investigation, someone 'they believe is responsible for the death and disappearance' of the three-year-old.

The newspaper says the police are now confident they will solve the mystery of what happened to him.

It says the cops have uncovered clues previously not explored. It quotes an unnamed, senior police officer, saying this 'shines a totally new complexion on what investigators believe happened to William'.

Even though I work in the same newsroom, for the Sunday edition of the paper, I got no warning this was coming. I later learn that those leading the investigation into William's disappearance claim they did not know about it until late the night before. Nor did the police force's media unit.

Reading the story a second time, I notice how it changes, from the first paragraph, where the unnamed individual who's now at the centre of the investigation is described as a 'person of interest', to the sixth paragraph, where they are a 'suspect'.

The police had better be certain they have the right person, I think. Call somebody a suspect in the death of a child and you risk ruining their life if you are wrong. Some people will believe they are a killer. They may never be forgiven. The paper says it cannot name this suspect but word soon filters out. Journalists talk and the police are talking to the journalists.

I hear the name from a reporter working for a different media organisation. The police say they are looking at William's foster mother herself.

Round Three

How Did You Get It So Wrong?

All day, my phone will not stop ringing. Family, friends and journalists are calling to ask for my reaction. What do I think about the news that the cops have a suspect over the disappearance of William Tyrrell? Do I know who the suspect is? Can I explain it?

No, I tell them, I can't explain it. Like everybody, I want to see this case solved and whoever is responsible in prison. But as a cop, this makes no sense. Imagine that you have a suspect; why go to the newspaper? You risk warning your suspect the cops are coming for them. You risk them destroying evidence or preparing a false story. If you ever manage to get them into court, you risk their lawyer pointing to this newspaper article and arguing the scandal it created means your suspect can never get a fair trial.

I say that I always worry when I see unnamed police sources leaking to the media. There has to be a reason why they do it. In my mind, I'm turning the pieces of this puzzle over, trying to fit them together. The police could be leaking information to provoke a reaction in their suspect. As a cop, I saw that happen. They could be doing it to distract attention after spending years going after Frank Abbott, the paedophile who lived in a caravan near where William went missing. I can't count how many times I've been contacted by journalists telling me the police were saying Frank is the person who did it. With this announcement now, the cops are admitting they got that wrong, but nobody is talking about that. Instead, everyone is focused on this new suspect.

Trying to figure the problem out, I think about what's changed between me leaving the strike force having cleared William's foster parents and this announcement. During that time, the foster mother has gone public, saying that her family's relationship with the police has changed, from empathetic to cold. She's criticised senior police, including those at the top of the organisation, demanding more be done to find William. She has demanded more resources be given to the investigation and that it not be shut down and sent off to Unsolved Homicide.

In all my 34 years as a cop, I've never seen a suspect do that.

I know that many senior cops do not respond well to public criticism, and it sometimes seems like the higher people reach within the police force, the thinner their skin gets.

Calling her a suspect silences a critic, I say, during these telephone conversations.

Have you got any evidence, they ask me.

No, I say. I haven't.

So why else would they do it?

Unless whoever leaked that story just wanted to make the cops look good.

I can tell from their silence on the phone that most people do not agree with my reaction. Even my close family are thinking that if the cops say they've got a suspect, then they must have the evidence to back it up. I imagine them asking themselves another, unspoken, question: Gary, you led this investigation for four years without finding who took William. If the police have got it right now, how did you get it so wrong?

***

Later the same day, 7 September, a journalist calls, saying William's foster parents have put out a written statement that describes the *Daily Telegraph* story as 'fake news'.

As the foster parents still cannot be named in public, this statement is published anonymously on the Facebook page of the Where's William? campaign, originally set up by the family and the police to keep attention on his case. The journalist reads from it over the phone.

'It's almost 7 years of grief and loss since William went missing,' the statement says. 'Imagine waking up to an unsubstantiated article published by a large NSW media outlet claiming that a senior officer within NSW Police has shared that they have a NEW person of interest, whilst inferring that this heinous crime is on the brink of being solved.

'Once again we are forced to watch others objectify William for personal gain,' the statement continues. 'William was a precious, innocent boy and the family are heartbroken.

'To publish unverified claims, without consideration to the hurt that articles of this nature cause is disrespectful and devastating to everyone who knows and loves William.'

The statement ends by saying there is still a million-dollar reward waiting for the person who can lead police to William.

'Make the call and help bring precious William home to the arms of those he loves and who love him ...'

The journalist asks for my reaction but I'm silent. I think how, less than three years ago, the news leaked that I was under police investigation. That was not part of any careful strategy, I am certain. Having been through a court trial and seen all the documents from the police investigation that were tendered in evidence, I know that I was not under surveillance at the time of the leak.

Some senior officer must have been behind this. From experience, I know that kind of information doesn't get released to the press without those in power being aware.

The journalist asks again for my reaction to the foster parents' statement. I tell her that I don't want to say anything publicly.

I can almost hear her thinking, *What if you got this wrong, Gary?*

That evening, I call William's foster mother.

She breaks down in tears.

You're Not Going to Like Me

William Tyrrell had been missing for five months when I took over the investigation in February 2015. The cops had already looked at his foster parents and found no evidence suggesting they were involved in his disappearance but I'd wanted to go in with my eyes open, so we took another look. Within the strike force, we asked ourselves if they could have murdered William. Or had him abducted. Or whether William might have died in an accident and his foster parents somehow covered that up.

We looked at how that might have happened. Could William have fallen from the balcony at his foster grandmother's house where the family were staying? Maybe his foster mother, who was in the house that morning, panicked. Maybe she decided to hide his body. I watched the couple closely during our first meeting, when the previous lead investigator took me with him to meet them as part of the handover, and kept watching them over the weeks and months that followed. Again, I could see no evidence of their involvement. But I did see the couple's grief. I did see their pain.

More than a year later, in May 2016, another detective

working on the strike force told me she still had doubts about the foster parents. I listened, partly because I thought she was a good detective, someone I had worked with years before on a murder in southern Sydney and been impressed.

Look, she told me, we both know most child murders are carried out by someone who is close to the victim. Also, William's foster mother says she was there when he went missing. Her husband says he'd driven into nearby Lakewood, looking for a decent internet signal to make an online video presentation for work, and we'd checked that story out, but he drove back soon after. So we know both of them were at the house that morning.

The detective told me she'd also found inconsistencies in the foster mother's evidence. Like how she said William was wearing shoes at the time he disappeared. In the last photo of him, taken an hour and a half before the 000 call saying William was missing, he is pictured playing on the front deck, without shoes.

There were also the cars William's foster mother claimed to have seen outside the house that morning, the detective told me. She'd told police there were two cars parked there, but the cops had found no evidence to back that up.

I wasn't sure. There were no CCTV cameras anywhere on that road, or near it, to show what cars were there or not there that morning. Memories are often unreliable. To me, these didn't seem to be inconsistencies but more like unanswered questions. Still, we wanted to be certain. I decided we would call the couple back in and told the detective to prepare interview plans; she and I would go at them once more in the interview room. Like with everything on that investigation, I reported the decision up the chain of command to my bosses, meaning some of the most senior officers in the police force knew what we were doing, and would know the result.

Four months later, in September 2016, we were ready. The plan was to ambush William's foster parents. To see what they might let slip if they were unprepared and exposed. I invited the couple to the police headquarters in Parramatta, western Sydney, letting them believe they were coming in only to meet some of the detectives for an update on the investigation, as they had done before.

William's foster mother smiled at me when they got there. We shook hands, then my demeanour changed.

'You're not going to like me today,' I told them. I was hard, professional. 'I don't want you talking to each other,' I said. 'We're going straight to Parramatta Police Station.' I looked at her: 'I'm going to interview you first.'

Turning to him: 'I'm going to interview you second. You're not going to get an opportunity to talk between the interviews. You are not going to like me, but maybe you will understand what I am doing. And, at the end of the day, we'll see where the cards fall.'

We drove them to the police station and I made sure that someone was always with the couple so they couldn't talk to each other. Once there, we split them up, showing each to separate rooms. You could see the shock and upset on their faces. They felt hurt but that's just smart policing. You don't give a potential suspect time to prepare for your questions. It didn't matter if they hated me in that moment. Not if it meant that we found William.

Inside the windowless interview room, I told the foster mother that everything she said would be recorded. She was fierce and disbelieving as I started asking questions, tears running down her cheeks, sometimes pale and sometimes flushed with anger. She wept. I didn't care.

If we broke either of the couple or made one turn on the other, I'd be happy, but, instead, she had answers. William could put his own shoes on, she said, when I asked about the photo. She'd told him to put his shoes on when he went out to play in the garden because there might be bindis or dog shit out there. She didn't know if it was bindi season during that visit to her mother's house or how many of the neighbours kept a dog but all the properties around there were unfenced, so any dog could roam around if it wanted. William knew to put on his shoes.

That sounded plausible, I thought, although I was not finished. The foster mother was led out of the room and her husband brought in. If either of them had done anything to William, I thought he was most likely to crack under this pressure. His wife had always seemed the tougher of the couple and if he himself wasn't at the house at the moment William was last seen there, then he might have the least to lose.

He repeated what he'd told the police before now; that he got back there around 10.30 that morning. His wife ran out with one of the neighbours, asking him, 'Is William with you?'

'No,' he said, confused. 'I just got home, I just got here.' So why would he have William?

'Well, where is he?' his wife asked him.

'I don't know,' he answered. Then he bailed out of the car, leaving everything behind him and started looking, yelling, 'William? Come out, William. William, where are you?'

From that moment, everything played out in public. Neighbours helped the couple search. William's foster mother called the cops at 10.57 am, who arrived nine minutes later. That meant if either of them had done anything to William, they had very little time to do it. And, if either the foster mother or her mother, who was also at the house that morning, had done anything criminal, they had very little opportunity to convince her husband to play a part in it.

It's possible, I thought during that interview with William's foster father. *Maybe your wife and her mother did that.*

'You know, it has been suggested to me that he might have hurt himself accidentally when they were looking after him, and they have panicked and covered it up,' I told him.

'Never likely. No way. They'd never do that, even if he hurt himself. You'd go straight to the ambulance. Police. They'd never do anything like that.'

'What about ... that you came home in the car, and William ran out to see you, and it's a classic case of a driveway tragedy?'

'Ran him over?' He was in tears.

'Yeah.' I pushed him.

'No.' He looked offended. He and his wife had thought they could trust me.

I kept asking questions. 'And another theory, there's a few of them, that [the foster grandmother] is an elderly lady and she might have done something to accidentally injure William, and [the foster mother] is covering up for her.'

'No, could not hurt a fly.' He didn't crack.

When the interview was over, we stayed with the couple, making sure they still could not talk in private. Both looked wounded. We led them back to their car, which we'd fitted with a listening device while they were being questioned. Inside it, alone and believing they could speak freely for the first time since arriving at police headquarters, they called me all kinds of names. They hated me in that moment. But then they started to calm down. They said, maybe it was a good thing. That at least I was trying to find their foster son.

***

The seventh anniversary of William's disappearance is on 12 September 2021, less than a week after that newspaper front page saying the police have a new suspect. My replacement as the head of the investigation, David Laidlaw, marks the date by taking some of the detectives on the case to visit the house where the three-year-old went missing. They walk around like they have never seen the building, looking at the front deck where William was last photographed in his Spider-Man costume, and at the garden, sloping steeply down towards the road, where his foster mother says the boy was playing at being a tiger. David seems to be limping slightly as he follows behind the others. They are filmed by the police force and the footage is released to the media. It plays out on newspaper websites. It's on Facebook and Twitter. People send me links to it in text messages. It is repeated on every channel that evening during the TV news.

In it, the detectives also visit what the film calls Location #2; a stretch of road where they go through another pantomime of unrolling an aerial photograph, laying it out on the bonnet of a pristine white four-by-four that just happens to be waiting for them, and standing round and pointing at something in the photo. In the background, street signs and a property name are clearly visible. It's a few hundred metres from the house where William was last seen.

This only provokes questions. Why are there two locations? What do the police know about that street? Rumours soon spread. I get more calls from journalists, trying to add the different things together. I watch the footage over and over, part of me thinking of the stick I would have got from inside the police if I had paraded myself like that for a B-grade piece of television, part of me thinking that there is something going on here, but I can't see the whole picture.

This is how you build pressure on a suspect, I think. It feels more like part of a considered plan to provoke a reaction than that wild, accusatory front-page story. My phone starts ringing again but I ignore it, thinking there isn't much I can say. The footage is obviously staged but I can only guess at the reason. Either the cops want to demonstrate how hard they are working or I'm right that this is something they are doing to gather evidence, by watching to see what their suspect does next. Either way, it's not going to help anybody if I start mouthing off.

But if this footage is being released now to gather evidence, it tells me the cops aren't confident in what they've got already. If so, then it was wrong to leak that story to the *Daily Telegraph* saying the police now have a suspect they believe is responsible for the death and disappearance of William.

Whoever is in the right or wrong here, I fear some badness has been done.

Yeah, I'm In

I still haven't found an answer to the question Kathy Nowland asked me when I visited to talk about her daughter, whose half-naked body was found lying in the dirt of Mount Druitt's Town Centre Reserve: who would do that to a person?

Since then, I've looked at all these killers: John Wayne Glover; the pack of hyenas that murdered Anita Cobby; Julian Knight; Ivan Milat; and Martin Bryant. Through the podcast, I've spoken to those who knew them, who spent time with them and who, as cops, pursued them. I've grown close to Bernie Matthews, who tried to bite out a man's throat. I've learned that evil people can seem ordinary; that they can be understood if not forgiven; that we all have violence in us; that those who do badness can also be victims; but that evil is also not inevitable; two people may share a past yet only one goes on to do badness; that evil is sometimes done because people see no reason not to; and that, whatever it is that causes evil, you can trace it back to childhood.

But I'm still looking for the answer. Who would do that to Kathy's daughter, Michelle Pogmore? Who would do that to William Tyrrell? I want there to be a simple explanation.

So I go looking for one.

* * *

'I'm OK. It's 10 am, I just got out of the jacuzzi.'

I don't know whether James Fallon is joking.

I'd asked him how he was going, as a way to start the conversation. He smiles at me. Like a crumpled teddy bear, he's big and round with a white beard and the dark outline of spectacles.

'All right. Here we go,' he continues, grinning. During our conversation, I notice how Jim swears happily, like a cop would. His eyes twinkle. I find I want to like him. You can imagine he is great fun at a family barbecue.

None of which helps explain whether this neuroscientist, a professor emeritus in anatomy and neurobiology at the University of California, Irvine, a former Fulbright scholar, would really have just gotten out of a jacuzzi at 10 am on a weekday morning. But Jim doesn't seem to feel the need to explain it. Instead, he waits for me to start talking.

'In essence, I'm looking at what constitutes evil,' I begin. I explain how I left the cops and have started looking at the badness people do to one another from a different perspective than I used to. How I've spoken to hardcore crooks, as well as hardcore cops, psychologists who've studied the mind of killers, and the families of homicide victims. That I've got a sense there is something about your DNA, or maybe your life experiences, particularly in childhood, that can help explain why some people do badness. But neither of those things seemed to fully make sense of it. And that I've started reading about the work Jim has done with brain scans.

'I suppose the first thing is, do you think there is something that is evil?' I ask Jim. 'Could you call me evil, for example? Can we talk about that?'

'Sure.' He is no longer smiling. 'I mean, you could start anywhere. You could start with Plato.' This is not what I was expecting. 'Or others, you know,' Jim continues. I guess the rows of heavy books lined up on the shelves behind him in his home office aren't there for decoration. He starts talking about the French humanists and I feel like a rabbit in the headlights, with a Mack truck rushing towards it. I say nothing. I cannot move. Now we're in the Enlightenment. I catch only parts of what he's saying: 'Philosophers who made the assumption that we are born *tabula rasa* – we're born clean slates and therefore any sort of sense of goodness, badness, morality, evil has to be taught to us.'

Later, going back over the conversation and reading up on what Jim is saying, I'll discover this idea is the opposite to Plato's. The ancient Greek philosopher argued that we all have some kind of in-built knowledge that we're born with, including of what is good. And, I guess, what is not good is evil. Other philosophers argue that we're born with no such knowledge – like clean slates – and learn about good and evil from our parents, or our friends, or church, or from the government.

Jim starts talking about baby rhesus monkeys. Different experiments have looked at whether those born in a laboratory have a natural fear of snakes or not. Some did and the idea is that, if those monkeys were afraid, they must have some in-born knowledge that snakes were scary, because they'd never met one before the experiment took place. If so, maybe a monkey could be born with something else, like an idea of good and evil.

The idea of scaring baby creatures with a snake seems pretty cruel, but I follow the argument. Jim seems to be siding with Plato and the terrified monkeys; that we are born knowing right and wrong.

'We seem to have a sense of it,' he says, 'and we seem to produce behaviours spontaneously that appear good or evil to others.' It gets complicated, because what is good or bad to one person might be different for another, but Jim says don't get hung up on those details. He reckons 95 per cent of what is considered badness is pretty much universal. No one is going to look at the murder of Michelle Pogmore, for example, and say it is a good thing. Or the Granny Killer's exploits.

So, Jim says, if evil exists and we can understand it, why do people do it? He thinks the cause is also something that you're born with – although, again, it's complicated.

As he talks, Jim starts pointing at different parts of his own head and naming the different areas of brain behind it – I catch the words 'amygdala', 'ventromedial prefrontal cortex' and 'anterior cingulate cortex' but after that, he's lost me.

The brain itself is physically different in different people, Jim says, tracing neural pathways around his skull with one finger. I notice another skull hanging on the door over Jim's shoulder. It's from a wildebeest, he tells me. Years ago, he was in Kenya, watching the animals' annual migration. Jim says he stood there as countless wildebeest struggled to cross the Mara River, then looked down and saw a head on the ground near him. A crocodile had taken the rest of the animal's body. Jim walked forward, keeping watch for crocs, picked up the head up and brought it home, where it hangs in his office.

Then I get what he is saying. Crocodiles are brutal, violent killers. But they're just doing what they are born to. Wildebeest were born to run rather than fight. Their brains are wired differently. Looking inside our skulls can help explain our behaviour, Jim says. Then he continues: it isn't just about the brain, it's also in your genes. And it's in how your genes interact with each other and how they are affected by the environment you live in.

I was happier with the baby rhesus monkeys, but Jim is moving faster now and so I try to keep up. Let's start with a brain that's hard-wired differently from others, he says. Imagine you have a brain that predisposes you to impulsiveness, maybe even to violence, and to not caring about other people – all the things you might expect from a classic psychopath, like the ones you see in movies. People like Tommy DeVito, the mobster played by Joe Pesci in *Goodfellas*. Manipulative, uncaring criminals who, like Tommy, can interrupt a game of cards he's playing to shoot a man in the foot for not getting him a drink, curse his victim for making such a big deal of the injury, then go back to playing cards, calmly saying to the dealer, 'Yeah, I'm in.'

People like this do exist. The character of Tommy DeVito was based on a real gangster, Thomas DeSimone, and that shooting at the card game really happened. So how do you explain them?

Jim points at his skull one last time, saying that's where psychopaths come from.

He knows this because he is a psychopath.

***

Jim's married, with three kids and several grandkids. He talks about them with real affection. He's done ground-breaking research into degenerative diseases like Parkinson's and Alzheimer's, which has helped to make the world a better place for other people. It's not what you'd expect from Tommy DeVito. Nor is the fact Jim was a happy baby and, he says, an attractive toddler – attractive enough, at least, for one grandfather to enter him in a national beauty contest.

Growing up, Jim says he was close both to his dad, who took him on fishing trips, and to his mum, who taught him to cook, sew and iron. The family were religious and, when Jim was 14, he was named Catholic Boy of the Year for the diocese of Albany, New York. He enjoyed school, had lots of friends, and had some wild times in his late teens and early 20s, just like I did. Later, he worked as a bartender, a schoolteacher and a carpenter – all jobs that brought him into friendly contact with people. None of this is what I'd expected a psychopath's biography to read like.

Jim had always been interested in the natural world; how animals and plants worked. Eventually, he became a scientist. He got into neurochemistry and neuroanatomy. His work involved looking at the human brain through different kinds of scans. One day, a university colleague called, saying he was consulting for some lawyers who were representing a killer who had murdered several people. The killer had been found guilty and the lawyers were hoping to find something that might convince the judge to show him mercy. Would Jim look at a scan of the killer's brain, to see if anything was wrong?

Sure, said Jim. He looked at the scan. It showed less activity than normal in the orbital cortex near the front of the brain and around the amygdala, two areas that help process emotion and inhibit behaviour. Jim says the two areas interact with each other to balance our more primitive, animal instincts, like the urge to fight, to flee, or to kill another animal for food, against our social instincts to maintain relationships with other people. I think about the crocodile and the wildebeest. Those animal urges are like our crocodile brain. Other parts of the brain control these instincts. When these areas of the brain are less active, Jim explained to his colleague, a person can become impulsive. They might do things that are destructive to others.

The lawyers took this to the judge, arguing that it was a matter of biology – their client couldn't control himself. The crocodile emerges. Word spread and Jim received more calls, asking him to analyse the brains of more than a dozen killers over the next decade. In 2005, another US psychiatrist asked if he would look at around 50 brain scans of different murderers, 'the baddest dudes you could imagine', Jim says, all psychopaths or impulsive killers. Could Jim find a pattern?

When he did he became transfixed.

At first, Jim found the same decreased activity in those areas he'd seen before, in the first scan. But Jim also saw another pattern repeated across the new scans; a darkness on the image, like a void, representing reduced activity in a thin strip running from the front of the brain to the back. This void ran through areas that helped connect different parts of the brain dealing with emotions and empathy – the ability to understand or feel another person's emotions. The scans seemed to suggest there was less activity in all these areas of the brain in psychopathic killers, while other killers — the impulsive crooks, who killed in a rush of emotion — showed less activity in some areas, but not all of them together.

These patterns of brain malfunction, Jim thought, could help explain why some people were psychopaths. He was no legal expert, but decided it was interesting enough for him to write up what he'd been doing, saying the results 'may offer a powerful new tool for understanding psychopathology and how it is viewed and adjudicated in the legal system'. His research threw up a host of questions; not just whether the worst killers are born or made, but whether it was fair to treat them like other people when they got to court. After all, they were only doing what their brains told them.

During October 2005, while Jim was finishing this paper, he was also working on his other studies, which involved looking at brain scans from people with Alzheimer's disease. Needing to see some healthy brains in order to compare them, Jim had his mother scanned, as well as his aunt, three brothers, his wife, himself and their three children. When he sat down to analyse his family's scans, one of them looked odd. It didn't fit. Like it was from the brain of a straight-up psycho.

Jim thought the scans had been mixed up. He figured that could happen. After all, the names of those people whose brains were pictured in each scan were kept hidden. So he asked a lab technician to check the name on this one.

It turned out there was no mix-up.

The brain scan was his own.

It's Like Rolling Dice, Right?

Jim Fallon laughed. He knew he couldn't be a psychopath. But then, he thought, he didn't really understand what one was. While he'd written about them in his research, he only had a general understanding, the same as you or I might; that psychopaths were violent, unstable crooks who didn't care about their actions.

Staring at the scan of his own brain, Jim could see it looked like those of the psychopathic killers he had studied – but he had never killed. He'd never even contemplated doing that kind of violence to another person. So he asked around among his university colleagues: what is a psychopath? But he couldn't get a decent answer.

Different people had different explanations. Some said they weren't even sure such a thing really existed. Just like 'evil' isn't in the psychiatry textbooks, Jim found that 'psychopathy' didn't appear in the book they called the bible of the American Psychiatric Association, the *Diagnostic and Statistical Manual of Mental Disorders* (although this has since changed).

Most of the experts he talked to traced the idea back to another US scientist, Hervey Cleckley. A professor of psychiatry and neurology, Hervey's 1941 book *The Mask of Sanity* describes 13 different patients out of hundreds he'd worked with who had strange, unexplained personalities and who probably, wrote Hervey, caused more unhappiness and confusion than any other.

To Hervey, they were baffling and fascinating people; difficult to interpret and almost impossible to deal with. While they appeared normal, they also showed no concern about other people's feelings. They were destructive of their own lives and others, but did not show remorse. Talking to his colleagues, Hervey found there was little agreement as to what was actually the matter with them. He argued that these psychopaths were unable to understand the common emotions and convictions shared by other people. They could mimic these but not feel them. Dealing with a psychopath, you were confronted with someone wearing a convincing mask of sanity but, beneath it, they had no concept of others' thoughts or feelings. Instead, there was a void – like that seen by Jim Fallon when he looked at those brain scans.

A generation later, during the 1970s, a Canadian criminal psychologist called Robert Hare built on Hervey's ideas to create what he called the Psychopathy Checklist. It consists of 20 separate qualities, such as lack of remorse or guilt, poor behavioural controls and impulsivity, each of which can be scored between 0 and 2. Score over 30 and you can be diagnosed a psychopath. Other measures, such as glibness or superficial charm and a grandiose sense of self-worth, closely reflect Hervey's idea of a mask of sanity – that a psychopath might be friendly, even charming, on the surface. Unlike Hervey, however, the checklist also draws a direct link between psychopathy and criminal behaviour by including qualities like juvenile delinquency and criminal versatility.

Today, the Psychopathy Checklist is used all over the world. What's often misunderstood, however, is that both Hervey Cleckley and Robert Hare said you didn't *need* to be a crook to be a psychopath. Instead, there is a whole other group of psychopathic people out there; those who share the same traits as some of our most terrifying killers but may not themselves be criminals. These people might seem cunning, driven, in control. They might have a lack of remorse, superficial charm or an inflated sense of their own importance. They might be business leaders, politicians, soldiers … or detectives. Some of them might not realise their own behaviours are psychopathic, Jim says. They may not want to accept it. What makes one psychopathic personality dangerous might make another successful.

Fundamentally, says Jim, in the brain of a psychopath, the relationship between our primitive, crocodile impulses and our more developed, social instincts is broken. As a result, the psychopath is less able to control those impulses and may not even realise that his actions are hurting others. 'That means the psychopath isn't really evil,' Jim says. 'They're predators. They're great white sharks.' If you lock up a psychopath over some crime, you can't just release them back into the kiddy pool, he continues. But, to his mind, the psychopath isn't evil because he is not choosing to hurt others. An evil person is someone who knows what they are doing is wrong but chooses to do it anyway – what Jim calls a sociopath.

* * *

It's Like Rolling Dice, Right?

When Jim told his wife about his brain scan, she told him, sure, you've got a lot of bad behaviours. And, as he happily admits, Jim sees the world differently from most. For a long time, he'd think nothing of skipping a relative's funeral, a friend's wedding or a work presentation to go to a party, to the racetrack or to a casino. He likes taking risks and will put others at risk to do so. Jim says he takes revenge when he feels cheated. His revenge is finely calculated, Jim says, and measured out exactly against the offence that provoked it. Say you're another academic who has offended him in some way. He might not steal your girlfriend, but he might make sure you don't get the research grant you're going for.

That didn't mean he was a psychopath.

Other people asked him what the scan meant but Jim didn't have all the answers. Two months later, he and his wife were hosting a family barbecue when his mum told Jim there was something he should look at. It was a book. She insisted that he read it. When Jim did, he found it was about one of his ancestors, Rebecca Cornell, who was murdered by her son Thomas in 1673. Another of Rebecca's descendants was also accused of murdering her father and stepmother, Jim discovered. Talking to his family, he learned there was a whole crop of murderers and suspected killers hanging along one branch of his family tree, as well as another branch of men who'd walked out on their wives and families, seemingly on impulse, either for other women or for reasons unknown.

Even among his own generation of brothers and cousins, several were decent boxers or got into street brawls, Jim says. It was as if they *liked* to fight. All this got him thinking. Maybe it wasn't just his brain structure that was different from that of other people, maybe his genes were violent as well. That was something he could study. As well as scanning his family's brains during his work on Alzheimer's, Jim's lab had also taken blood samples for genetic analysis. He decided to check them.

OK, Jim tells me, the link between our genes and our behaviour is complicated. Describing it simply, our genes influence how our body functions, which in turn affects our thinking, personality and behaviour. And everybody is different.

It's like being in a casino, Jim continues. You get half your genes from your mother and half from your father, just like how at the blackjack table you get dealt a hand of cards, or when you play craps, you are handed a pair of dice. Each basic human trait – like aggression – is affected by different genes, Jim says. These individual genes also have different variants, which are called alleles.

'It's like rolling dice, right?' Jim adds. 'If you've got a pair of dice, your chances of rolling either snake eyes or two sixes are pretty low.' Most likely you'll get something in the middle. It's the same way with the genetics of these traits. Most people are in the middle. They are normal. But some people are born with variants that make them likely to be less or more aggressive. 'That doesn't make them a psychopath or anything,' Jim continues, 'but they will really strongly have that trait, be it extroversion, aggression, empathy or openness.'

Jim gives me an example. Take the MAOA gene, which is widely known as the 'warrior gene'. It controls the body's production of the MAOA enzyme, which in turn helps regulate the supply of a chemical called serotonin. Serotonin is a neurotransmitter, meaning it helps transmit messages between nerve cells and, as such, it plays a role in different bodily functions including stabilising our mood and our feelings of well-being and happiness.

Variants of the MAOA gene between people can lead to differences in the supply of the enzyme. Scientists have linked the variants that produce low levels of the MAOA enzyme, or where the gene is not working, to aggression and violence.

So far, I'm following Jim's explanation, but like everything he tells me, it's more complicated than simply saying the warrior gene can turn you into a killer. For one thing, Jim says there isn't only one warrior gene. Other genes are also thought to be involved in aggressive and antisocial behaviour. Also, Jim says you need to look at how your genes interact with each other, and with other genetic material, meaning there are probably dozens – or more – of warrior genes inside us.

It took years to complete the genetic analysis of Jim's family, partly because the technology was constantly evolving. When it was done in 2009, he found that nearly all his family had the variant of the warrior gene linked to low levels of the MAOA enzyme. The analysis also showed that others in the family had around half or fewer of the other gene variants known to be linked to violence.

Jim had the full set though.

He grins, and at this point in the conversation, I am starting to wonder if he really is a killer and whether I've got myself into something more dangerous than I expected. Instead, Jim tells me this is where you need to look at environmental factors – particularly at early childhood.

As well as different variants between genes there are what Jim calls gene 'promoters', which help regulate their behaviour. He talks about the effects of stress and fear, which release different hormones into the blood system. These are like someone pressing down on the gas pedal of the gene itself, Jim says, holding up his hand in front of his face to mime a driver using the accelerator to rev an engine.

These effects are particularly strong in the first few years of childhood. At that point in life, the fear and stress caused by things like abuse, abandonment or witnessing violence is like putting a brick on the accelerator pedal. Over-revving can also cause lasting damage to the engine. If this kind of fear and stress happens a lot, particularly when a person is very young, it can have a permanent effect on them.

'Sorry, Jim,' I say, trying to keep up with what he's saying. 'You're saying in the early years of a child's life, their brain development itself is subject to the environment they're in?'

'Yeah.' And, in one way, this seems obvious. Yet it's also a revelation to get a glimpse of the science that explains it. 'But this is the proviso now,' continues Jim, 'that environment only matters if you have a certain collection of genes.'

'OK,' I say. So, as I understand it, you might be born with the genes of a potential killer, but whether they get turbo-charged or not depends on what happens during your life. And particularly your childhood.

＊＊＊

It feels like the pieces are falling into place now. One of those pieces is what Cesare Lombroso argued, way back in the nineteenth century, about how physical differences between people – including differences in their brains – can predispose some people to criminal behaviour. Jim is saying this is true and that also there is a genetic factor where some people are born with genes that can lead them into badness. The other piece of the puzzle is the one I've been trying to make sense of while looking at Julian Knight, Ivan Milat and Martin Bryant. Was there something about their life experiences that led them to do badness? My mistake had been thinking about these different pieces separately, in terms of whether it was nature or nurture that made people evil.

'So the nature/nurture argument, it's really asked incorrectly,' Jim says. 'It's not one or the other, instead, the different pieces fit together.' He starts telling me a story about how he once had a revelation while sitting in the jacuzzi and staring out the window at the garden, where his mother was pruning flowers.

For a moment, I'm distracted, thinking that Jim must have a home jacuzzi, which explains why he was in it on a weekday morning. He tells me how he was lying back in the bubbles and thinking over what he'd learned about himself: that he had the brain structure of a psychopath, with unusually low activity in those parts of the brain that deal with emotion, empathy and impulse; and that he had a genetic predisposition to violence. But he was not a killer. So what was he missing?

Looking out the window, Jim says, he saw his mum was sitting on a three-legged garden stool. He was missing the third leg, Jim realised – his childhood had been happy. He'd suffered no neglect or abuse. Growing up, Jim was part of a loving, supportive family. As an adult, he did not live in a violent community. Far from it, he was a university professor in sunny California. All that meant Jim hadn't endured the kinds of stress and fear that might have sent his genes revving out of control.

It's only when you put all these pieces together that you can make sense of the picture, I think. That, then, is the lesson. It's not nature or nurture on its own that makes someone do evil. It's both. At the same time.

I Regret It

This is a different kind of crowd from the ones I'm used to. Walking into the pub with Johnny Lewis, I've never seen so much gold chain in one place before now, all of it strung around the necks of the pack of solid-looking hard heads standing together at the bar.

There are a few faces I recognise. A couple of blokes from training, some ex-boxers and footy types. A few of them turn to look at me and nudge the man beside them, as if they're saying to each other, 'He's a cop'. The whisper seems to travel around the room and I start to feel I am not welcome. Then I see someone smiling at me. A tall man with greying hair whose eyes look like they've seen more than most people ever get to. *I recognise that face*, I think. *It's Graham Henry.* He raises a glass.

At first, we dance around each other, talking mostly about friends we have in common from growing up in the same part of Sydney. Around us, the others seem to have relaxed and are laughing, telling stories. A few come over, introduce themselves and ask if I will join them for a selfie. I'm having fun. At one point, Johnny comes up and says he has to go and train one of his fighters.

'Are you right, mate, if I leave you?' he asks me.

'I think I can hold my own here, Johnny,' I tell him. 'I'm fine. I'm not going to be attacked.'

Graham and I start telling war stories, him about his time as one of Sydney's criminal kingpins and me about my time in the Armed Hold-Up Squad, which was set up to bring men like Graham down. Both of us are cautious not to say too much and end up being disloyal to those we worked with. When I mention some of the cops I knew as a junior detective, Graham says he knew them. They were tough and honest, he says, at a time when there wasn't too much of that going round.

About another older cop, who always gave me a bad feeling, Graham says, 'He was fucking hopeless but he was staunch. He never gave us up.'

I realise that by staunch he means the guy was crooked and protected crooks. Graham laughs, saying how in his day it might cost $5000 to pay your way out of one criminal investigation, or $10,000 to buy yourself out of another. Graham was running Sydney's underworld at the time when Murray Farquhar was the State's chief magistrate. He went down for four years after perverting the course of justice. Two years later, in 1987, the State's former prisons minister, Rex Jackson, was jailed after taking bribes in return for ordering the release of prisoners. Graham mentions another cop I worked with, saying he was dirty. I find myself defending the system, saying that it's only ever been a small number of cops who were found to be corrupt.

'Yeah, it wasn't everyone,' he says, smiling. But it wasn't that small a number either. Which is how he ended up stabbing a police prosecutor on the street outside a pub like this one.

I Regret It

Graham says he first met Mal Spence in the company of another bent detective, Roger Rogerson, once a hero of the Armed Hold-Up Squad, who was later jailed for perverting the course of justice and jailed again, in 2016, for murder after a drug deal went sour. Like Roger, Mal was a bigmouth and a braggart, Graham says. Shortly before Christmas 1988, Mal had started mouthing off about how Graham had given him up to the cops' internal investigators for driving a stolen Mercedes.

That was the worst thing anyone could say about him, Graham tells me, because it was implying he'd broken the code: you don't dog. Graham got drunk, caught up with Mal outside the Lord Wolseley Hotel in Ultimo near Sydney's CBD, took him outside, then stabbed him in the stomach. With Mal collapsed and wounded on the footpath, Graham leaned over his bleeding body and drove his knife into the prosecutor's neck. Merry Christmas.

He went down for six years over that one, Graham tells me. 'I regret it.'

I lean in, thinking, *This is unexpected.*

'Using a knife cost me six years inside.' Graham smiles. 'I should have beat the shit out of him.' He would have got a shorter sentence.

I can't help laughing. It's unexpected, but I like him.

'What are you making of this?' Graham asks, looking around at the crowd that we're a part of.

I've been chasing half these people half my life, I joke.

Graham laughs.

That evening, I leave the pub at the point when I can't keep up with the drinking and walk home feeling peaceful. I think back, decades ago now, to when I'd just joined the cops and used to see Graham drinking in the pubs near where we grew up in North Epping. I didn't want a bar of him back then and would never have gotten into a conversation. That younger version of myself wouldn't believe we'd end up having beers together.

People change, I tell myself. *But I am still that same person.*

* * *

That feeling of peace lasts less than a week, until Monday, 15 November. The police announce a new, 'high intensity' search of the house where William Tyrrell disappeared.

It's been searched, I think. It was searched at the time he went missing. We conducted another long forensic search in 2018, before the inquest started. This time, the search is different. Bigger. There are TV cameras recording every moment as the cops go through the property again and pick at the bush with rakes and forks near the area they called Location #2 in the film footage released on the anniversary of William's disappearance.

Once again, the news is on every TV channel and repeated in the constant phone calls from people asking if I've seen it. Police dogs have been brought in, according to the TV reporters.

Cadaver dogs. Trained to smell out human remains. The police confirm it: 'It's highly likely that if we found something it would be a body,' says Detective Chief Superintendent Darren Bennett at a press conference surrounded by a forest of reporters. Darren's the boss of State Crime Command, sitting above the Homicide Squad, meaning the decision to reopen the search has been signed off at the highest levels of the police force. 'We are looking for the remains of William Tyrrell, no doubt about that,' he says.

The search is due to take three weeks, Darren continues. A huge effort. 'This activity is in response to evidence we have obtained in the course of the investigation. It's not speculative in any way.'

He's saying that they have a target. That they know what happened. He says the police will look above and below ground in three locations around the house where William was staying. That means they believe William was buried. It sounds, again, like they are trying to send a message. To put pressure on their suspect.

If so, the pressure is increased in the late afternoon, when the TV news reports the police are set to take out an Apprehended Violence Order against William's foster parents. Again, this has been leaked to the media. My phone rings all evening and on into the night. The questions friends and family are asking are different now. They want to know why didn't we look more closely at the foster parents. We did, I try to tell them. It's strange, people tell me. No one ever knew their names or saw them express any emotion. I try to explain that we weren't allowed to name them because they were foster parents, and the only interview they were allowed to give for years had them in silhouette, so you couldn't see their faces.

It seems to make no difference. After today, people seem to have made up their minds about the couple. If the police do have listening devices in place, I wonder if the cops monitoring those recordings are also thinking the same and how that might affect the way they interpret anything that is said. I barely sleep and, when I do manage to drift off, I wake up feeling sick, thinking, *Something isn't right here.*

I get up in the darkness and put on my shorts and T-shirt. I pack my gloves and handwraps. Try to eat but everything is tasteless. I walk outside, into the pre-dawn shadows, and the few people in the deserted streets all seem to have their backs turned to me.

Even the silence seems accusatory: you're wrong about the foster parents.

At Erskineville Oval, I bow my head to walk through the doorway towards where we meet for training. Inside, Johnny walks towards me out of the darkness.

'Don't worry, Gary,' he says, beckoning me forward. 'We've got your back now.'

Oh, It's the Foster Mother

I stand a little taller after the morning's training session. Wiping the sweat away with one forearm, I hear Adam Watt and Dave laughing. The rising sun chases shadows across the oval. Walking back, past shops selling the morning newspapers, the headlines are all about William Tyrrell. At home, the story still leads the news on the TV. The same images are repeated: uniformed cops sifting through dirt; digging in the garden directly underneath the balcony of the house where William went missing; in the forest stripping the ground bare of the young trees and undergrowth ahead of excavations due to begin that week

My phone pings, with one text message after another asking, 'Are you all right?'

That's strange, I think, replying, 'Yes. Why?'

A reply back: the commissioner of the New South Wales Police Force is on breakfast radio. I turn it on. He's criticising my investigation into William's disappearance. 'I think some time was wasted,' he says. 'The investigation was looking at some persons of interest who were clearly not.' The team of detectives who took over after I was gone 'inherited what was a bit of a mess'.

Although nobody names me, this feels personal. The commissioner knows I was the detective running the investigation then. The radio interviewer, Ben Fordham, also knows it. My phone starts ringing; another person out there listening to this and wanting my reaction. Everyone is being told I made a mess of the attempt to find a missing three-year-old. I wasted time.

I feel the same anger rising in me as when I walked out of court after being convicted. It's been almost three years since that day now. And I've kept quiet. I've made a point of not criticising the cops in public. When will this stop? I don't want it. Let me lead the life I'm making for myself outside the police force. Quit dragging me back in.

Later, I'll be told that none of the cops who is actually working on the case was expecting the commissioner to call me out so publicly. Just like they weren't expecting the newspaper story saying they had a new suspect. During the radio interview, when Ben asks him about that, the commissioner confirms they are now looking closely at one person.

He's confident the police working on the case now can solve it: 'I truly believe that.'

My editor at the *Sunday Telegraph* rings me, 'I've been told to call you for a welfare check.'

'I'm OK. These idiots aren't going to break me.'

'What the fuck is going on?' he asks.

I'm asking the same question. Neither of us has seen anything like this. A police commissioner criticising the running of an ongoing Homicide investigation. For one thing, he must know that, if they do arrest somebody, this is now the first thing a defence lawyer will reach for: 'But officer, your own police commissioner has described this investigation as a mess. So how can we trust you?'

For another, as commissioner, he was the boss. This case has been running the whole time he has been in that position. As investigation supervisor I wrote up monthly progress reports, setting out the work we'd done, our different suspects and our strategies. Each of these was passed up the chain and signed off by an assistant commissioner. At different times, I also handed up fortnightly briefing notes for a deputy commissioner, outlining our progress. There were countless written situation reports, operational orders and a comprehensive investigation plan, which I kept updated. There were at least three formal reviews, where I outlined what we were doing in person to a panel of senior police. The cops still have all of this paperwork. No one can say they didn't know what we were doing.

If this case was a mess, then it's also on him.

'Fuck him,' I tell my editor. He didn't need to do this. I've kept quiet. Before now, when people called, asking for my reaction, I've chosen not to speak out. I wouldn't be talking about William now if the commissioner hadn't just called me out in public. He wants to make me a target? Well, here I am.

***

The day doesn't stop coming. The news reports are now saying the police are looking at whether William died in an accident and his body was later moved and hidden. Reporters are reporting other reporters: 'Multiple media reports suggest police are now probing whether the three-year-old fatally fell from the balcony of his foster grandmother's home in Kendall.' There seems no doubt in the reporters' minds about who's right: 'Police close in on new person of interest'. Their language — closing in — suggests a hunt surrounding its quarry.

The theory William fell from the balcony is something we discounted. For it to be correct, all of this must have happened:

William was alive at 9.37 am, when he was photographed wearing his Spider-Man costume, playing on the front deck. Sometime after, he must have gone round to the back balcony, climbed up over the railing and fell from it.

His foster mother, or his foster grandmother, went looking for William. He was found, dead or badly injured. No one called an ambulance. Instead, either or both of the women decided to cover up what's happened.

If only one of the women is involved up to this point, the other was either deceived or agreed to keep the secret.

William's sister didn't see what's going on, or if she did, she must have been convinced to stay silent. She was five. Her account in every conversation and interview with police was consistent.

When William's foster father arrived back at the house, sometime around 10.30 am, he met his wife in the driveway. By then, the neighbours say she had already been outside, looking for William. She looked desperate, the neighbours will tell police, but she must have been pretending.

Her husband must also have been lied to. Or else told William was dead and convinced to join in with the conspiracy.

At 10.57 am William's foster mother called 000 and already had her cover-story ready. She told the operator William left the front deck, ran onto the lawn and went around the side of the house.

Nine minutes later the first police arrived. The foster mother told the cops that William was playing at being a tiger. 'We heard him roaring round the garden.'

That afternoon, William's foster grandmother told police the same thing. William was 'pretending to be a tiger. He was running around roaring.' This story has remained consistent.

From the time the first cop got there, the family were with people constantly, including police, well-meaning friends and neighbours, but also staff from the Department of Family and Community Services, who oversaw William's foster placement. These people are trained to watch the parents in cases of missing children, looking for anything suspicious. William's foster mother, and maybe her husband also, must have managed to deceive them.

That morning, or in the days that followed, while hundreds of cops and SES volunteers, and mums and dads, and teenage boys on trail bikes and girls on horseback from the local pony club, and TV crews from what will feel like every station in the country searched through their home, the street and the surrounding bush for any trace of William, somebody must have hidden William's body.

One of the things that was raised with me in 2016, when we decided to re-interview the foster parents, was that his foster mother did drive down the road from the house that morning for a few hundred metres, then got out and ran around, apparently looking for the three-year-old.

Maybe she used the car to move his body, I was told.

Maybe. But what would you do if your child went missing? You'd run around looking for him outside, like she did. Then you'd get in the car, drive it a little way and get out to keep looking.

The best I could say at the time about this whole idea is that it wasn't likely. With nothing to suggest that is what happened, we decided to look elsewhere.

* * *

I start getting messages from cops, in South Australia, Victoria and Queensland. They're watching what's going on. Some reckon it's a disgrace for a commissioner to be criticising his own police force. Others say the commissioner knows exactly what he's doing.

Think back over the press coverage, they tell me: the *Sky News* documentary in July, where David Laidlaw said he knows what happened to William; the *Daily Telegraph* story in September saying police had zeroed in on a new suspect; the new searches in November; the Apprehended Violence Order the police have applied for against the foster parents; the commissioner going on the radio this morning. The whole thing might be orchestrated. What if, these cops argue, William's foster parents have been under surveillance this whole time, with listening devices and telephone intercepts ready to capture anything they might let slip in conversation. Today, the commissioner might be trying to drive a divide between you and the foster parents. He knows they trust you. They wrote to him asking that you be allowed to attend the inquest with them.

Oh, It's the Foster Mother

So making them believe I messed the case up would leave them feeling isolated. Some people suggest it's the kind of strategy I might use. As a detective, if I was going to use listening devices, I'd want to have a plan in place to get the most from them, often by provoking a reaction. The commissioner's doing a Gary, one cop tells me. Building pressure.

That's not right. I've worked many more homicides than he has and have been accused of playing hardball when working those cases, but I understand actions have consequences and there is no way I would have done this to a person. With a strategy like that, if you get it wrong, you destroy lives. One thing the commissioner will achieve by going on the radio, though, is to help justify the cops' failure if the police never manage to find William. Now everybody can look at it and say, 'It's Gary's fault. He messed it up.'

I get a call from another colleague at the *Sunday Telegraph*, who says there's going to be a non-publication order on the upcoming court hearing to decide on the Apprehended Violence Order. It means the media cannot reveal the identity of anyone involved, including the person the order is supposed to be protecting. Nor can we report the evidence, or any information about the evidence, including what the police are alleging has happened or what the couple say by way of explanation.

The order will stay in place until the court case is decided and any appeal has worked its way through the system, or until the findings of the inquest into William's disappearance are delivered, whichever is the latter. That could take years. In the meantime, for people reading about it in the paper, there will be the news that the police are seeking an AVO, then silence. In that silence, people will whisper rumours.

**

A reporter has tracked down one of William's biological grandmothers, asking for her opinion. She's glad about what the detectives are doing, saying her eyes have been on the suspect from the beginning. One of the detectives has just rung her, she says, telling her they are digging up the garden bed beneath the balcony and that William was probably going to be found there.

I doubt that's true but it all gets reported. Inside my apartment, I'm still sitting in the same, sweat-stained shorts and T-shirt I trained in that morning. On TV, at the search site, I can see the wind blowing through the stand of trees around the house where William went missing. A cadaver dog is sent running over the garden, including the bed beneath the balcony. The TV reports that the police will wait until nightfall to test for blood by spraying special chemicals that glow blue on contact. I watch uniformed cops searching the rainwater tank. *We already searched it.*

Some journalists are passing round copies of the foster father's witness statement, given to police a few days after William went missing. There's nothing in it I haven't seen but the fact these confidential documents seem to be floating around adds to the feeling that this is becoming a shitstorm.

Another journalist calls me, asking, 'What do you think?'

'What the fuck do you mean, what do I think?' I'm tired.

'Well, I don't believe it is the mother. But there's the AVO. And they've clearly got evidence.'

Oh, It's the Foster Mother

'On what are you basing that idea?'

'Well, she drove down the street.' It's the same theory we looked at years ago now, that William's foster mother got into her own mother's grey Mazda, which was parked outside the house, and drove down the road between the tall, dark gum trees, stopping near the local riding school, where she got out. How has this got picked up and thrown about again today?

The journalist says she knows what's in the police's application for the Apprehended Violence Order. If that is true, I'd love to know who leaked it.

'I've got it on good authority there's a typed-up murder warrant ready for [the foster mother's] arrest,' she tells me.

'I thought you were smarter,' I say. 'We don't use warrants to arrest someone for murder. So you don't type up a murder warrant. I don't know where you're getting your information.'

She is silent.

We end the conversation.

***

I'm powerless, reduced to reading the constantly updating news stories in the empty lounge room of my apartment. A headline reads, 'A suspect in the disappearance of William Tyrrell has had a child removed from her custody.' My heart sinks.

Again, the paper doesn't name the suspect, or the child that has been taken from her, but you don't have to look far to work out their identities. The same paper says the suspect is one of those against whom the police want to get the Apprehended Violence Order. Another paper reads 'Police seek AVO against Tyrrell's foster parents.'

I close my eyes, running my hand over my bowed head. It's the child I feel sorry for. Where is that child now? In the care of the State Government. Or in another foster home. Alone. I have a sick feeling in my throat, thinking about what that child is going through. The court order means nobody can name them. They can't speak out. Already in their short life they have seen William go missing. Now they have been taken away.

Is that child reading the same headlines I am? If they have a phone, or a computer, or can see a television, they could barely miss it. The AVO. Cadaver dogs. The water tanks. The balcony.

Looking up, I see the sky is growing darker outside. Right now, half of Sydney, if not half of the country, must be watching the evening news and saying, 'Oh, it's the foster mother. They've got an AVO against her.'

The newspapers are now saying the police will go to court and allege something happened to the child this month. That the child had been bruised. Only the application has not been heard in court yet, meaning these details should never have been made public. *If this is a deliberate strategy, I would never have gone this far.* But it feels like everybody is against me on this one.

Another newspaper story reads: 'The chief suspect in the disappearance of William Tyrrell has had a child removed from her custody.' That's a low blow, calling someone the chief suspect. It's only because the newspaper can't name the person that they have the courage to say that. Were they to name them without being certain of their guilt and they would have a case to answer for defamation. Call them only 'the chief suspect' and, it seems, you can get away with almost anything.

Late that night, I'm still sitting alone and unwashed in my apartment, a silent witness to the constantly repeating news on television. The State Police Minister, David Elliott, has waded in, responding to questions about the claim that we wasted time chasing the wrong people. He says there will be an internal review of the investigation. 'It's the least that we can offer the family and it's the least we can offer the community,' he tells the pack of reporters.

Bring it on. Take this to a review. But let's do this in public. Allow people to see what has really been done here.

You Know that Now

Believe the newspapers this morning, Wednesday, 17 November, and you'd think this will be over by the week's end. One paper says detectives, 'believe they are close to cracking the country's most baffling missing child case'. In another, police have 'precise new information' which led them to search a five-metre square of bush near the home where William Tyrrell went missing. A third reports that the Australian Federal Police are now involved in the investigation. They've brought in ground-penetrating radar, 'that can show inconsistencies in the soil at the tract of bushland'. The cops even allow themselves to be photographed inside the garage of the house where William went missing, scanning the concrete slab that has been laid there, searching for his body.

Photos have also been released to the media of a grey car being winched up onto the back of a tow truck, ready to be taken for forensic examination. It's the Mazda that William's foster mother drove down the road on the morning he went missing. No one seems to mention how that car was taken for forensic testing days after William disappeared, and nothing was found. Instead, the reports describe the foster mother as the 'lone person of interest in his disappearance'.

No one is questioning this story. Instead, the reporters are knocking on the door of her home in Sydney's upper north shore. When no one answers they start knocking on the neighbours' doors. One neighbour tells them she didn't know the couple were the same people now being pursued by the police force. 'I didn't realise that they lived so close to us.'

Well, you know that now, I think. *And you know what people are saying they did to William.*

* * *

The police raise the stakes higher. William's foster parents are being charged with the common assault of a child. Again, a court order prevents the details from being reported, as well as the child's identity. But we've all seen the stories. Parents who do terrible things to children. There are more whispered rumours; maybe this was like those cases.

The newspapers track down William's biological mother and run her quotes under a headline that reduces the complicated family situation – a young child taken from one set of parents and placed with another for his own good – to something misleading by calling the biological mother William's 'mum' while his foster parents are now only his 'carers'. The woman is photographed standing on her front step with a beer in one hand. She says William's biological father has just got out of prison.

At the search site, outside the house in Kendall, TV reporters scramble to get on air as a group of cops digging in the bushland cluster round a patch of soil. A detective I recognise as the officer-in-charge of the investigation strides into frame, carrying what looks like a folded Spider-Man costume.

You don't have to let the cameras record this. You can put up screens. You can keep the press back.

On TV, one reporter calls it a heart-stopping moment. The police have found some threads of red material. Could they be part of William's Spider-Man suit, which he was wearing when he vanished? 'Officers believe this is his graveyard.'

I find all of this offensive: the choice of words, likely to upset anyone who cared about William; the way a tragedy is presented as drama; the dumb parroting of any leak or information handed out by the police; piling on a woman you cannot name but are happy to say is a suspect; even going door to door, making sure her neighbours know who you are talking about.

I think back to what Jim Fallon told me, that people can do badness because they don't realise the harm they are doing others. On TV, the scraps of red material are bagged and taken for forensic testing. It is on every channel.

We used to find that kind of stuff all the time when doing searches. Every time you dug near where people have been living, you'd find cloth scraps, discarded clothes and other rubbish. You'd check it but it rarely meant much.

Days later, after the tests come back, the reporters say they've been briefed by the police that the red threads don't mean anything at all.

* * *

In the evening, I put on jeans and a T-shirt and head to the Sydney Super Dome to watch the boxing. I hope to lose myself in it. For the past year now, boxing has been a way to do that. To stop thinking, if only for that hour every morning when we're training at the oval.

Tonight, two super welterweights are fighting: Tim Tszyu and Takeshi Inoue. I'm here for Tim. He is defending his titles and unbeaten record. Johnny Lewis will also be there, somewhere in the crowd of thousands, watching. He once trained Tim's old man, Kostya, to a world title. Graham Henry sends me a text message, asking, 'Are you going to the fight? We'll try and catch up there.'

Tim's good, stalking around the ring before going about his business. In the first round he lands a right that knocks his opponent back and follows with a left hook to the body. He keeps on at him, delivering more trauma. The crowd roar. By the eighth round, people are on their feet and cheering when Tim delivers an uppercut that snaps Takeshi's head back. He takes the fight by a unanimous decision.

After, the reporters say Tim devastated his opponent. They call it a brutal contest. People walk out like it was some kind of celebration. When I catch up with Johnny, he says it wasn't bad. But he has seen better.

With the fight running late, I get three hours' sleep then wake in the small hours of 18 November to make sure I am ready. I've agreed to do an interview, on the same breakfast radio program the police commissioner used to pick a fight with me over the investigation into William's disappearance. This is me standing up to say, 'Enough'. Both for myself and for

William's foster mother, because what others are saying about her now is shameful.

*　*　*

I respect the police, I say, knowing there will be many in the force listening. I know there are some good cops on the strike force. But we've investigated every theory, including whether William was run over in the driveway, whether he tripped and hit his head on a rock or toppled off the balcony. I explain how the foster parents were cleared once, then I cleared them again when I took over the investigation, then we went at them a third time when I ambushed them at Parramatta for another round of questioning. That time, I say, we also had a covert operation running.

'You had a listening device in their car?' the host, Ben Fordham, asks me.

I have a split-second to answer. 'Yes.'

As I walk out of the radio station building, I get papped by a camera crew that's waiting there to film me. The story becomes how I went on breakfast radio and talked about a listening device. They say I revealed a covert police operation. That it's confidential information.

It's not. That information came out in court when the police put me on trial. It's like no one heard what I was saying. One news report says the cops have put me back under investigation. I wonder which cop leaked that to the reporter and whether there will be an investigation into the leak itself.

*　*　*

At the same time, more journalists are waiting outside the home of William's foster parents, although they must know the couple will say nothing. They photograph them going in and out. They write how the foster mother is wearing slippers and that she goes back into the house to change them. One newspaper will later run photos with their faces pixelated under the headline, 'Inside the privileged life of William's foster mother', calling her a 'wealthy professional worth several million', who lives in 'an exclusive suburb'. Beneath the article online, a reader will leave a comment: 'Is that why their identity has been protected for so long – because they're rich?' The question goes unanswered.

Another newspaper claims to take its readers 'inside the police thinking on the case'. It says detectives became suspicious when they looked at that last photograph of William, wearing his Spider-Man costume on the front deck of the house where he went missing.

The paper says that this is 'crucial evidence'. William is barefoot in the photo. It says this contradicts the evidence from his foster mother that he was wearing shoes at the time that he went missing.

That isn't crucial evidence. We looked at that in 2016, more than five years ago. William could put his shoes on. There is nearly an hour and a half between the time that photograph was taken and the 000 call reporting him as missing.

If that is the police's thinking, then they don't have anything new; they've just gone back and looked again at the evidence we gathered then and have raked up some old suspicions.

Over the coming days, the media continue to wait outside the home of William's foster parents. They quote experts speculating on what state his remains will be in. How were they wrapped? Are they in a sealed container or in plastic? Had his body decomposed before it was buried?

The police drain a creek and find a piece of blue material. Three large gazebos are set up in the forest outside Kendall and beneath them, the cops rake the dirt dug up during the excavation, shovel the dirt and sieve the dirt. The next day they repeat this.

The same line is repeated, that the cops have 'new information'. What this is, is not made public. The search continues: clearing the bush; piling dead branches high; finding other scraps of cloth, a green hessian bag and a replica pistol. The police collect an unknown number of things like this, which the media describe as evidence. This evidence is sent for forensic testing. In time, the police dig up around 15 tonnes of earth before a thunderstorm arrives, lashing the site like God's wrath and flattening the gazebos.

Sodden cops and TV reporters shelter together beneath the gum trees. Elsewhere William's foster parents choose not to appear in court for the first hearing on the assault charge. Outside the court, news crews park their satellite trucks on the footpath while, inside it, reporters cram together on the benches. Court orders restrict their reporting to little other than a comment from the magistrate that 'the allegations are not the most serious that the courts see, by any stretch'. Despite this, there seems to be no chance of the case being resolved any time soon.

The search outside the house in Kendall is also likely to stretch on for months, according to a police spokesman, far longer than the three weeks they originally expected. It will go on partly because the storm has made it harder and partly because the police say they're confident that they will find fresh evidence.

It will go on, according to the police commissioner, 'until investigators believe the job is done'.

It will go on because they have 'new information'.

I Went Straight to Parramatta

I keep my promise to Bernie Matthews. Before he died, Bernie asked me to contact a woman called Wilma Robb and when I call, it feels like she has been waiting for me to do so.

'It's so good to speak to you,' says Wilma, in a gentle voice that makes me want to trust her. In person, she has pale eyes, a wide smile and a sweet, open manner.

'Bernie told me a lot about you,' I say. He told me Wilma was put in a children's home at five years old and ended up at the Parramatta Training School for Girls in western Sydney and then later at the Institution for Girls in Hay, deep in the Riverina in southwest New South Wales. Both girls' homes were set up to house children found by the State Government to be neglected, uncontrollable or who had been convicted of a crime. At the time, the law said a 'neglected' child was anyone who was either so poor they had no obvious means of support; was being ill-treated; had parents who were not looking after them; did not attend school regularly; had fallen in with a bad crowd; or was in some other way exposed to 'moral danger'.

I Went Straight to Parramatta

The girls were raped and beaten, Bernie had told me. At least 11 of the staff were alleged to be abusers, including five of the superintendents who ran the Parramatta girls' home.

Is this why he wanted me to contact Wilma? Neither of us mention it at first.

'Bernie told me a lot about you as well,' says Wilma.

She's been going through some of his things and collecting old photos of him. For a while, we talk about how much we miss him. She reminds me how Bernie's laughter used to come from deep inside him, bubbling up from way down in the bottom of his belly.

I think how Bernie was in too much of a hurry before he died to do anything without good reason. I think about Adam Watt asking, why was I chosen? It reminds me of another conversation I had with a sifu, or master, I met while training in martial arts. We all have a purpose, he told me. For some of us, it is very hard to find that purpose.

Talking to Wilma, I'm amazed at how easily the conversation moves forward, as if Bernie has prepared the way. Wilma is 73 and tells me about growing up in Griffith, something over an hour's drive east from Hay. When she was five, her mum went into hospital with cancer. The hospital, in Sydney, was a full day's journey from Griffith and her dad worked away a lot, so Wilma was put into a children's home.

She remembers looking out through wire mesh on the balcony at the road in front of the home, where cars used to pull up and drop other kids off. Wilma sat there, waiting for her mum and dad to come back and get her, she says, but they didn't. Decades later, Wilma went back and visited the children's home but couldn't find the balcony. She asked someone who'd worked there about it.

There was never a balcony, Wilma, they told her.

Wilma said she remembered looking out from it at the road outside.

'Most likely you were in a cot.'

'But I was five years old.' Too old to be shut up in a cot, thought Wilma. Too old to be left there, staring out the window.

'Yes, but it was easier for us to control you that way.'

Looking at old photos from the children's home, Wilma saw the cots had wire mesh across them. They were like little prisons.

***

Too many times, since I've left the police force, have I heard stories like this. Of crooked cops, prison officers who beat the inmates, or children's homes where the staff abused them. I've stopped thinking that the world is simple, like I used to in the police force, and that it can be divided into evil on the one side and us, on the side of the angels, standing up against the darkness.

Evil is far closer to home for all of us, I've realised. After a year, when her mum came back from hospital, Wilma's parents did return to collect their daughter. Only, her mum still wasn't well, she says. Her dad was angry and violent. Growing older, she got sick of listening to them argue, so she used to take off.

There was a policeman, Wilma tells me. A detective. I'll bring her home, he used to say to Wilma's father. Sometimes,

I Went Straight to Parramatta

when she was walking to or from school, the detective would pull up beside her and tell her, come on, Wilma, jump in the car. Then he'd take her to the police station or out into the bush or anywhere and Wilma wouldn't tell anyone what he did to her.

Because she ran away from home, Wilma was put into foster homes and later sent to another institution, the Thornleigh Training School for Girls in Sydney. She calls it Ormond House.

That name is familiar. I remember visiting the place when I was a young policeman, looking for kids who were in trouble. Wilma remembers the high wire fences. She was 12 or maybe 13 then. Still a child, but old enough to get together with three other girls and manage to break out.

They ended up sleeping in a phone box, she says. Grabbing bottles of milk and loaves of bread from shopfronts to try and keep from going hungry. As a runaway, Wilma had nowhere to go, nor any way of contacting her family. So when a woman riding a motorbike asked if Wilma wanted to go with her, she said yes, jumped on and the woman gunned the engine.

'We went out and she turned off onto a dirt track and it went down to a creek and there was a heap of bikies there,' says Wilma. I sit in horror, listening to what they did to her. After, the woman took Wilma back, the cops picked her up the next day, or maybe the one after. Not because she was a victim but because she'd run away from Thornleigh.

'When the police picked you up, did you tell them what had happened to you?' I ask.

'No. No. No,' she repeats softly.

'Did anyone ask you what had happened?'

'No, nothing,' she says.

What happened next? I ask her.

'I went straight to Parramatta.'

***

Wilma says this isn't just her story; it's also about the other girls. There are estimates that over 30,000 of them went through the Parramatta girls' home during its century of operation, before it was closed in the 1970s. No one knows how many of them were abused because there are no records. A few have spoken out, like Wilma.

I ask if she will come on the podcast so more people can hear what she has to say about it.

She is uncertain for a moment, then agrees.

***

I start with a warning to the listeners: 'I think one of the most important roles of society is to protect our children. Sadly that didn't happen for our guest, she was let down by the very people who should have been protecting her. When you hear Wilma's story it might make you cry,' I continue, 'but you may also be inspired by the woman who is telling it.'

Wilma smiles a little and says she is nervous.

I like that honesty about her. It's painful for her to talk about this, but she will, because she worries what happened to her in the past might still be happening today.

Do you think it happens because people don't realise what goes on behind closed doors, I ask her, or because people blindly trust society to look after our children?

I Went Straight to Parramatta

'I think, unless you have experienced it, you don't understand it.'

I ask her to describe what happened when she got to Parramatta.

***

Wilma copped it.

'I was acting out a bit, you know? Like, I was naughty. We were all naughty, but it was fun naughty, you know? It was girl naughty. We were kids.' Because she was acting out, she got given Largactil, an antipsychotic drug, to control her behaviour. It made her drowsy. 'Gives you the shuffles if you take it long enough.' Zombie-like, she calls it.

Wilma used to spit the medicine out, but she got caught doing it and sent to the superintendent. She waited on the step outside his door until he came out. He whacked her around a bit, she says, before telling her to go down to the shower block and scrub the floors. While she was down there, he came down with his deputy carrying a bottle of Largactil.

'They handed it to me and said, "Take this",' says Wilma. She put it in her mouth and spat it back. One of the men grabbed hold of her and pulled her arms up behind her back; the other took her hair and bashed her head into one of the sinks.

Wilma had some teeth knocked out. 'I couldn't see out of my eyes. I couldn't move my head, I was hurting so bad. There was blood everywhere,' she says. The men kicked over the bucket of water she'd been using to scrub the floors and told her, 'Now clean up your mess.'

Still bleeding, Wilma was then thrown in isolation. For three weeks she was shut inside a mouldering wooden cell, allowed out only to shower in a little yard where she was forced to strip naked and stand under a stream of cold water while the grown staff stood there, watching.

Other girls were raped by the staff inside those isolation cells.

Some of the girls fell pregnant. The staff called them nobodies, or sluts and liars. They would demand to see a girl's soiled sanitary pads before providing them a new one. Some of the girls started sticking pins into their bodies. The pins were to show they were tough, or to get back some control over themselves, or to offset the pain they were suffering.

No one ever asked Wilma why she ran away from Thornleigh or what happened to her after. She kept silent about the rapes she suffered at the hands of the detective and the bikies because nobody would listen. Because she couldn't trust them, Wilma continued to rebel against authority, earning more beatings and time in isolation. One of the staff would grab her by the ears and lift her off the ground. Another big, hawk-like man who ruled the roost, would punch her with a closed fist. At 15, she required a set of false teeth.

By rebelling, Wilma earned a reputation as a troublemaker. As a result, she was sent to Hay, a former colonial jail in regional New South Wales, set up as a maximum-security facility to house the most difficult and rebellious girls from Parramatta.

I think how similar this sounds to Bernie's stories about his time in the prison system.

When Wilma arrived, handcuffed and doped-up with Largactil on the train from Sydney, they sat her down in a big old chair, with two men standing either side. 'They held my hands down on the arm rest and a female, the matron, cut my hair.' Wilma watched her hair dropping onto her knees as the two men told her what the rules were.

The girls would march, not walk. When told to do something, they would come to attention. They would sleep in cells. No eye contact. No talking. It was called the silent system.

'I looked up at them and they said, "Eyes down. Welcome to Hay. We are either going to make or break you."'

Wilma managed to defy them.

She tells me about being locked in an isolation cell, sitting on the bare floor with her back against the cold, stone wall. I may as well do something, she decided, so she plucked her leg hairs one by one with her fingers. The institution didn't allow the girls to shave their legs, she explains. There is a lightness in her voice as she describes her way of fighting back against the system.

When Wilma got out of isolation, one of the staff noticed her bare legs. Wilma was told to stand at attention.

'And I knew straight away,' she says. 'I knew I was going back.' She marched herself back to the isolation cell door, took off her shoes, her bra and belt, the way the girls were told to, so you couldn't hang yourself while in solitary confinement. Then Wilma stood there waiting to be locked up. She did another 24 hours that time, she says. Watching her smile as she tells me the story, I think that it was worth it.

That's the difference between her and Bernie, I think. Bernie attacked the prison guards. Her rebellion wasn't violent.

Wilma is living proof that a childhood full of badness doesn't mean that child is always going to grow up and do bad to others. Both she and Bernie were violently abused in the care of the State Government, but only he responded by trying to bite a prison guard's throat out. What is it that made their responses so unlike each other? Well, for one thing, Wilma is a woman.

Men make up the vast majority of violent criminals. Scientists have measured differences between girls' and boys' use of physical aggression from as young as 17 months old, while a global study by the United Nations in 2013 found 95 per cent of all perpetrators of homicide around the world are male. It's in our genes. Men are violent. If brain scans and the genetic analysis of killers are now being used in court — which they are — then maybe we have to accept this evidence, too. Thinking about this reminds me of the US forensic psychiatrist, Dr Dorothy Otnow Lewis, who once sat in a nursery watching a toddler upset his basin of bubbles in an act of violent desperation. She suggested 'being male' could be used as a defence in court. I think she was joking.

Joking aside, even if Wilma didn't grow up to become violent, her time in the girls' homes has still left its mark on her and others. After leaving the institution in Hay, she attempted suicide by taking an overdose of medication. Even today, she tells me, every so often, she thinks about ending it all. She won't do it, she says, because she is too close now to her children and grandchildren. Their lives have also been harder due to the damage done to Wilma in the girls' homes, she says. They grew up with a mother who felt shame and guilt about what happened to her. Who could not sleep with the door or windows closed because she felt claustrophobic.

'I don't know how many times my daughter used to ask me, "Why can't you be like a normal mother?"' Wilma tells me. 'And I told her, "Because I'm not a normal mother."'

In that way, the violence done to her in the children's homes did get passed on.

It Sort of Comes Up as Strength

Both girls' homes, at Hay and Parramatta, were closed in 1974 after people started to speak out in public about the abuse. But no one went to prison for it. Decades later, in 2014, a national royal commission found evidence that several staff, including female officers, must have known what was happening to the girls at the time. None of them tried to stop it. After being released from Hay, Wilma Robb told her mum what had happened to her, who said to leave it alone for fear of being punished. So, like many others, Wilma kept silent.

It wasn't until she was in her 50s that Wilma found her voice. In 2004, she made a submission detailing her brutal treatment to a senate inquiry looking at the experiences of children in institutional care. That inquiry found she was only one of many who had been silenced. The *Forgotten Australians* report said more than half a million Australians had been put in orphanages, children's homes, training schools or foster care over the past century and 'their stories outlined a litany of emotional, physical and sexual abuse, and often criminal physical and sexual assault'.

It Sort of Comes Up as Strength

Today, Wilma wants her abusers brought to justice. But it hasn't happened.

She went to the police in 2006, reporting the beating she suffered in the shower block at Parramatta, where the home's superintendent Percy Mayhew and his deputy Gordon Gilford knocked her teeth out. The cops said they would look into what happened, but, finally, told Wilma they would not be prosecuting the men because so many years had passed and the men were either dying or had Alzheimer's.

In 2014, the royal commission named 11 different alleged abusers who had worked at Parramatta and Hay, most of whom had not been previously investigated by the authorities. A few had resigned or been quietly dismissed after inquiries into their conduct. The commission's report lists half a dozen instances where other staff were believed to have been aware a girl was being abused, 'but nobody supported her, nobody said anything and nobody did anything'.

* * *

I feel numb. 'Sometimes you've got to stand up to things, and the people who were there and knew this was happening and didn't stand up to it, well they are complicit in it,' I say.

Wilma doesn't reply. She doesn't need to.

This is why Bernie Matthews wanted me to meet her. He wanted me to help give her a voice. As we come to the end of our conversation, Wilma thanks me for the chance to speak on the podcast.

'I need to be thanking you,' I tell her. Listening to what she's been through has taught me something. It's not something

I expected to face up to when I started looking at evil a couple of years ago now, but it has forced me to ask, of all those people who mistreated Wilma, who is worse? The detective who raped her, the bikies, or the abusers in the girls' homes?

At least the bikies admit they are outlaws. What can you say about those others, who knew evil was being done to girls like Wilma but said nothing and did not act to stop it? The lesson is an old one; sometimes doing nothing is the same as doing evil.

Looking back, I can see other examples, right back to the death of Michelle Pogmore, the first act of badness I looked at after my own conviction. There was the cop who sat there playing cards on his computer during the first, frantic days of the investigation. And the silence from the media, who barely reported the 13-year-old's death. Or the way her mother, Kathy Nowland, had to keep calling me up, asking what was happening with the case, because no one else in the police had told her.

No one was speaking up for Kathy or for Wilma.

Maybe this is why I was chosen. I wouldn't be here talking to Wilma today if I hadn't gone through what I have since becoming a criminal. Without being forced out of the police, I wouldn't have this podcast. I wouldn't have a new career as a newspaper journalist. I wouldn't have met Bernie.

Today, Wilma has her family. She's been on the steering committee of the Alliance for Forgotten Australians, campaigning for recognition of the damage done to those people like her, who were put in children's homes, institutions or other out-of-home care. In November 2009, Wilma was sitting in the second row from the front of the audience when then Prime Minister, Kevin Rudd, formally apologised for their treatment, saying sorry for the physical suffering, emotional starvation and tragedy of their lost childhoods.

The apology was lip work, Wilma tells me. It did not go far enough, so she stood up in the Great Hall at Parliament House in Canberra and held up a linen napkin, on which she had written 'What about children's prisons?' Because she wanted the prime minister to admit that's what those institutions were.

Today, that napkin is held by the National Museum of Australia. It has become part of the way the country understands its history.

'I can't think of a better way to show you haven't been broken,' I say to Wilma. 'You're still here, you are thinking about all the people who shared that same experience and you are speaking on behalf of them. Did you get kicked out?'

'No. I thought I would but I didn't.'

'I don't know how you've managed it,' I tell her. I still don't fully understand how she has taken all the anger and the pain of her experiences, and turned them into something positive.

'It's still all there,' says Wilma. A psychiatrist once told her that she had no anger in her. 'I thought, well, I feel it, but it sort of comes up as strength.'

Maybe she is using her anger as a weapon, I suggest. 'Making sure the story's been told and people don't forget about it and people don't let it happen again.'

'Yes.' She smiles again and her pale eyes look straight at me.

You Look Ready

Johnny Lewis has us doing seven-punch combinations: left jab, right cross, left hook, right rip, right rip, left hook, right cross. He's paired me with Adam Watt for the whole session so far this morning and now he's standing right beside us, getting in Adam's ear and saying, 'Let your left hook go, Adam. You're holding back on it.'

Adam lets it fly.

Even with Johnny's warning, I barely see the punch coming. I take it on the glove, thinking Adam is on another level.

'That's it, Gary,' Johnny growls. Adam and I keep trading punches, glove to glove. I'm making strange noises with the effort, sweating so hard in the cold, early morning that steam is rising from my shoulders. I'm determined not to give up before Johnny says this is over. The only consolation is that everyone on either side is also hurting. *I'm part of something here*, I think. *Something I didn't have before starting to train with Johnny.* We stand together, legs shaking with the effort, our breathing coming hoarse and heavy. No one quits.

Afterwards, we lean forward, hands on knees, almost broken. Almost.

'I've signed you up for a six-rounder, Gary,' Johnny jokes. A six-round boxing match. 'You look ready. You up for six rounds?'

I laugh.

Spirit Of

Ken Marslew tells the story like it doesn't hurt him. He was in bed he says, in the dark hours of the morning when two young cops came knocking on the front door.

'Are you Ken Marslew?' they asked him.

'Yes.'

'Do you have a son called Michael?'

'Yes.' The panic rising.

'He's been shot.'

'How is he? Where is he?' Ken was desperate.

'Can we come in?'

Ken let them in. They said he might want to sit down.

***

We're sitting at a picnic table near the water's edge in Gosford, on the Central Coast of New South Wales, where a flock of boats is gathered around the sailing club. Ken looks out at one that's running up its white sail, ready to leave the shore behind it, and tells me how he used to sail himself but gave it up, then started heading out to sea again after Michael was murdered.

Spirit Of

It was salt-water therapy, he says. His boat was called *Spirit Of*. It could have been the spirit of Michael, he says. It was the spirit of whatever you needed in that moment. Turning back to shore, the weathered lines around Ken's eyes grow deeper. He says what drives him now is trying to prevent others from getting hurt like he was.

Michael was 18 and working at a Pizza Hut in Jannali, southern Sydney, when there was an armed robbery. He was shot at close range in the back of the head with a 12-gauge shotgun. This was in 1994, Ken tells me. Back then, he was still looking to the future. He and Michael had had plans together; Ken had just put down the deposit for a franchise business selling ribs and pizza. Michael was going to come and work part-time to help pay his way through uni.

When the police came to his door and told him his son was dead, Ken says he didn't know whether to believe it. It was like he was dreaming. Leaving the house, he went to tell Michael's older brother, a born-again Christian who suggested they find a church, so the two of them went round looking for one that was open. They finished up at the police station, for Ken to give a statement. He was still in a daze, babbling on to the detectives. Then Ken found out he was a suspect.

In any murder investigation, the victim's family are among the first people the police look at. Often, they are right to do so. But Ken came to accept that only later. Instead, in that moment, 'It fired me up like you wouldn't believe,' he says. That helped, because his brain fog lifted. But all that he could feel was anger.

* * *

'I hated the world,' Ken says. 'I hated everybody in it.' He hated himself. He was either in a rage or in tears. 'I started to live my life that way and I blew away my marriage. Friends of many years couldn't get near me.' What made it harder was his hatred had no focus. After ruling Ken out as a suspect, it took four months for the police to catch the first of Michael's killers.

Ken learned there'd been a gang involved in robbing the Pizza Hut. The police caught two more of them soon after, then the fourth a few weeks later. 'That's when the hate and anger really flared up because I had a target,' Ken says. 'You would know that, as a dad, if anybody touches your kids, you want to kill them.'

'Yes,' I tell him. If anyone hurt my children, I would be an animal.

Time passed. The four accused men kept changing their stories. The fact there were several different suspects also meant there would be three separate trials, stretching out over two years, and the long, disjointed court process was confusing. During the early, procedural, court hearings, while the lawyers argued over administration and admissibility, Michael's family found they didn't understand what was going on, or even some of the words the barristers were using. The first time Ken walked into court, he believed in the justice system, but soon found he was questioning that faith. This felt like an offender-friendly process, he says. The suspects all had lawyers. The family had no one.

One magistrate even told Ken that it was now a matter for the prosecution and defence to deal with. It had nothing to do with what he, the victim's father, wanted.

I remember lawyers saying much the same when I was a detective. 'What you've got to understand, Gary, is that this is an adversarial system,' they told me. And I understood that; we dealt with some great prosecutors and there were some defence lawyers who you might not like but who you respected. But there were also lawyers who seemed to treat people as pawns in a game no one else knew the rules to, with themselves as grandmasters. When I tried to argue that a victim's family were getting hurt as the legal process dragged out by another month, or six months, when we all knew who the killer was, they told me, 'It's not about right or wrong, Gary. It's not about the truth, it's about what we can prove.'

I felt like telling them to fuck off, because what's the point of a court if it's not there to protect the good and punish evil? In the trials of Michael's killers, Ken says, he listened to the mothers of his son's killers give evidence, saying what great kids they were, but Ken was not allowed to say that Michael was a good kid; that he'd just finished his first year at uni and was studying to become a primary school teacher; that Michael had been pretty smart; that he had a beaut group of friends; he loved his parents; and that he and his son used to spend a lot of time together. Ken's experience of the court system, he says, was that the suspects all got defended, while 'you go to court as a victim and you get victimised and re-victimised.'

His eyes narrow so the life-lines cut further into the skin around them. Ken says he wanted to tell the judge, 'My son is dead, there are a lot of people who loved him.' His plans for the ribs and pizza franchise crumbled. For months, Ken says, he was unemployed and unemployable. 'Anger got me out of bed in the morning, anger drove me all day and I didn't sleep a lot those days either let me tell you. I just lived on anger.'

During one of the trials, Ken physically attacked a suspect. The accused man was sitting in the dock, he says, 'and I sat there and boiled and boiled and boiled and had to do something'.

He thinks it was a sheriff's officer who grabbed him. They took him out of the courtroom and Ken punched the wall outside it. He shrugs, flexing his fingers. 'My knuckles are still damaged from doing that. Turns out sandstone walls aren't really forgiving.' And so, outside the court, he started to speak out, saying he wanted the death penalty brought back for Michael's killers.

***

Working with the parents of other homicide victims Ken began campaigning against a State MP who'd attempted to bring back the old system of 'dock statements' – which allowed an accused crook to give an unsworn statement during their trial. It was another way of giving offenders the right to speak out, Ken thought, while the victim's family could say nothing. The campaign got them noticed. At the 1999 election, a new Labor state government came to power, promising to do more on law and order, and Ken was given a place on the Attorney-General's Victim's Advisory Board and on the Premier's Council on Crime Prevention. As he started to find his own way through the maze of the justice system, Ken formed a support group called Enough is Enough, to help other victims' families, like his, but who were just starting out.

People would call him at all times of night, he tells me, explaining that when you've lost someone the demons always come for you at night. When people were left alone with their thoughts and had no one else to talk to, they would call Ken. 'Foolishly, I would answer,' he said.

I think of my own sleepless nights spent speaking to the families of different murder victims. Sometimes they wanted to understand what would happen next in the court process. Sometimes they just wanted to speak to someone.

'I felt like I could do something for them,' Ken says. 'At that stage it was a case of the blind leading the blind.' The support group grew, with Ken funding it at first using his superannuation savings. He started to give talks, urging people to report street crime and domestic assault. He started working with young people on conflict resolution. The group produced an anti-violence video for schools.

All of it was fuelled by anger, Ken says. 'It was almost like I split into two. There was the grieving dad, who wanted revenge, and then the crusader, trying to find a way to end violence.'

* * *

After the four men were found guilty of Michael's killing, but before they were sentenced, Ken asked the prosecutor if he could give the judge a written statement, describing how his son's death had hurt him, damaged his marriage and caused great stress to his family. He was told the judge would not accept it.

Later, Ken met with judges, arguing that homicide victims' families should be given the right to make a public statement about their loved ones. The judges were reluctant. They said it was not relevant to the task of assessing the seriousness of a killing. 'Nobody wanted to change the bloody legislation,' Ken says. So he stormed into parliament and demanded the politicians do something. 'I did a lot of storming about in those days.' It worked.

The law was changed, giving families the right to submit a written statement to the judge in homicide trials. It became known as the Michael Marslew Amendment. To Ken, it was a win. He had beaten the system. But, inside himself, he still felt divided.

He kept busy, lobbying politicians, sitting on umpteen dozen government committees, making submissions on different bits of legislation and to the State Sentencing Council. Ken thought the people he met there would be consumed by their desire to deal with violent crime, like he was, but what he found made him angry. 'You sit in amazement as to where some of these people are in their head,' Ken says. 'They're not people who talk to victims, they don't talk to offenders, they don't talk to coppers.'

I tell him about my own frustrations in the police force. How those people who decided which cases got priority, or which would be abandoned, rarely met the victims' families. How I used to get angry with my bosses, slamming doors or shouting to try and get more resources or time on an investigation. That I'm still working out how best to use my anger at leaving the police force. Sometimes I think I have moved on from it, I tell Ken. And sometimes I want to storm into police headquarters and lay them all out.

'I'll come with you,' he says, laughing, then adds, while looking straight at me, 'So you're divided, also.' Anger can only take you so far, Ken says. For him, everything changed in 1999, when a police sergeant asked if he would be prepared to sit down, face to face, with Michael's killers.

Whose Values Are Working?

The meeting took place in Long Bay prison, inside a conference room with blinds drawn over the windows. Michael Marslew's parents sat on chairs that had been laid out in a wide circle, along with several prison officers, a member of the Salvation Army and the police sergeant who had arranged this meeting, Terry O'Connell.

It wasn't the first time Terry had done something like this. A country cop, from Wagga Wagga in southern New South Wales, he'd started holding what he called restorative conferences after being assaulted by a 14-year-old he was trying to arrest over a fight. Rather than charge the kid, Terry invited him and his mother to a meeting in the police station. It turned out the teenager's father had been killed 14 months earlier and the kid had been lashing out ever since as he struggled to deal with his own trauma.

It got Terry wondering if punishment was the best thing for him, and whether the whole criminal justice system had got it wrong by focusing on the what of crime – that this murder happened – and how to punish the offender, and not enough on the why, and what could be done to stop it.

Ken wasn't thinking about the why as he sat inside the meeting room in Long Bay prison, he tells me. A life for a life, he figured, even after all the campaigning he had done about reducing violence. When Terry offered him a chance to meet the men who'd killed his son, Ken had said yes, but really he was thinking, *You'll need to bring a bag with you.* Because one of the people in that room wasn't going to walk out alive after the meeting.

Only two of the four who'd been jailed over Michael's killing had the balls to show up, Ken says. They walked into the room wearing their green prison uniforms. Neither was the man who'd physically pulled the trigger, though the courts had found them all to be jointly responsible for what had happened.

Ken didn't launch himself at them, not this time. He said his piece. Told them what they had done to his family and listened to their apologies. One of the two, Karl Kramer, looked Ken in the eyes as they spoke. Karl had helped plan the armed robbery but hadn't gone into the Pizza Hut himself. Instead, he was the cockatoo, staying outside in the car park on the lookout.

Karl seemed genuine, Ken thought. Afterwards, he asked to meet Karl again in private. During that meeting, Karl talked about his own son. Ken asked him, 'How would you feel if it was your son who'd been murdered?' Both of the men were crying.

Over the next few years, they met again and spoke on the phone. Karl asked if Ken could send him some self-help books. When Karl said he didn't have the cash to make phone calls in prison, Ken sent him a little money. He got insulted when people tried to suggest that he was trying to be Karl's father. They weren't that close. And he wasn't going to forgive him.

'I still haven't,' Ken says. 'Only Michael could do that. What I did was let go of the hate.' He realised that it was hurting him more than anybody. Moving on meant letting that poison drain out. 'And that, to me, is a completely different thing than forgiveness.'

In 2009, Karl was released from Goulburn prison and Ken was there to meet him. The two had talked about what Karl could do now. Ken knew that there were programs out there where local cops or social workers met with young offenders, trying to steer them away from a life of violence, but too often the kids came back saying that the adults didn't know their backgrounds or couldn't understand the world that they'd grown up in.

They were missing something Karl could offer. As a convicted offender, he could sit down with those kids and show them where he had taken a wrong turning, to keep them on the right path. I think back to what Bernie Matthews told me on his deathbed: 'What are you going to change? Where it begins,' – catching those people who might go on to commit badness. Ken could see that being useful. To Ken, Karl was a tool he could use to continue the work he was doing on reducing violence.

For it to be successful, Karl needed to have accommodation and employment, so he could show people that he had rebuilt his own life after doing wrong. Ken helped with that, offering him a job with Enough is Enough.

'Are you ready for a new world?' Ken asked as Karl walked through the gates at Goulburn.

'Yeah, very much.'

The two of them walked away together across the cold, grey car park.

* * *

On 6 December 2021, three weeks into the search of bushland near where William Tyrrell went missing, the TV cameras show uniformed cops digging through a creek bed, uncovering another faded scrap of fabric. The TV reporters gather round, pecking at this latest piece of information: could it be part of the Spider-Man suit that William was wearing? No one seems to believe it. A bone fragment is recovered later, not the first that's been found in the forest, the reporters tell us, and sent off for testing to confirm if it's human or animal. Watching, I notice the detective leading the investigation, David Laidlaw, standing at the edge of the search site. He looks tired.

The police force seems to have thrown everything it has into this effort. They've had divers going through the dams, brought in a mechanical digger to strip the ground of topsoil and consulted with experts to help guide the search, including a forensic archaeologist and a hydrologist who once helped the Queensland Police Service recover the body of another missing child, Daniel Morcombe. Fewer senior cops seem to be doing interviews these days, though, leaving the newspapers to recycle quotes from last month. In this way, the boss of State Crime Command, Detective Chief Superintendent Darren Bennett, is quoted again as saying the search is 'not speculative', is being done 'in response to evidence we have obtained' and 'we're very happy with the items we've found'.

* * *

Whose Values Are Working?

I can't help thinking that the cops just came too late for William Tyrrell. It was only minutes between his foster mother making the 000 call, saying the three-year-old was missing, and the first police officer arriving at the house in Kendall, but it was still too late when they got there.

Whatever evil had been done to William took place before that 000 call. That's the problem with all the police work I did, I realise. We only ever got the call-out after the badness had happened. Every case I ever worked in Homicide we arrived too late for.

'It took me years to come to this realisation,' Ken tells me. What we should be talking about is how to stop people from becoming victims in the first place. Ken says that I have got a role to play in this work; talk to people about crime, he tells me, but do it in the way you understand it now, from both sides. Talk about where badness comes from. If that means giving a voice to criminals, then do it, he continues. How else are we going to understand them? Talk about it with compassion. Talk about redemption. Being a cop means people are going to listen. Because the way we've been dealing with crooks up till now doesn't seem to have stopped crime.

When the invitation arrives, with the gold crown on top and beneath it, in black letters that Her Excellency, the Honourable Margaret Beazley, Governor of New South Wales, requests the pleasure of my company, I guess Ken had something to do with this. It's to an evening reception of something called the Justice Reform Initiative on 10 December. I look at it, feeling stunned for a moment. Ken can't know how much this means to me. Every time I sit down for a drink with a former copper these days, I hear the same story; about how those in charge of the police force are bagging me out, saying I was a dangerous loose cannon and the place is better off without me. I thought all the judges and lawyers felt the same. I don't want to be part of the problem. In my heart, I'm still a cop. I still want to fight crime. That's why I get so angry when I see police work that isn't working. This invitation feels like a chance to rejoin those on the right side of the criminal justice system. Looking at it, I realise that's something I didn't know that I was seeking.

I can still stuff this up, though. I'm nervous getting dressed in shirt and tie and walking up to Government House. I'm familiar with the setup — close-cropped lawns and sandstone walls, the flock of suits and dresses gathered beneath a giant Moreton Bay fig tree — but that's not from coming here as a guest. Years before, in the cops, I worked on close personal protection for dignitaries, meaning I was one of the people I see now standing in the background wearing dark suits and sunglasses among the evening shadows. I feel out of place walking up the driveway and my doubts return as I get closer.

It is a crowd of heavyweights. I count two former federal Cabinet ministers, two former State attorneys general, a Director of Public Prosecutions, a prisons inspector, four judges and the former leader of the State Liberal Party, as well as the vice-president of the National Party of Australia. *These people are those at the very top of the system*, I think. *And they're saying it isn't working? If these people believe the justice system needs reforming, why are we still sending accused crooks into the courts and prisons daily?*

Ken waves me over. I make small talk and mostly listen. The conversation is about how prison fails Indigenous people, who make up about three per cent of the country's population but closer to a third of its prison population. People say the system's also failing young people because most of those in the juvenile justice system have previously suffered neglect, abuse or been taken from their families. It's failing those with mental illness, who make up more than half the adults in prison. It's failing victims, because half the people imprisoned today will be back in custody within two years of being released, having committed another crime, with another victim. And the system is failing taxpayers, who are spending around $110,000 per prisoner every year for a system that is failing.

I'd never really thought this in the cops; that the justice system doesn't stop people committing badness.

'It's like any corporate approach to a problem,' Ken says, as the evening shadows lengthen. 'Your problem is you want to stop people from becoming victims. What's the source of that problem? It's the offenders.' Particularly, he says, he's thinking about those crooks who get out of prison and offend again. That's a cycle, he says. So how do you stop it?

It was a woman from the Salvation Army who first suggested Ken go into prisons. She saw what he was doing with his charity, Enough is Enough, and told him he was doing God's work. That pissed Ken off because he was still dirty with God for letting his son be murdered. He still hated anyone wearing a green prison uniform.

Then Ken stopped and thought, *Maybe she's right.* Maybe the prisoners would listen to him because of what he'd been through. So he started working with Corrective Services, visiting different prisons. He wanted to prevent the crooks from committing further crimes when they got out and the way he thought to do this was by getting them to accept responsibility for what they'd done that put them in there. The way Ken saw it, the four men who shot Michael never had to do that. They'd been allowed to stand up in court and tell everyone they weren't guilty. It was only after, when he sat down at that private meeting with Karl Kramer that he'd seen the guy come close to accepting what he'd done to Michael's family. And he reckoned Karl was better for it.

So Ken went into prisons and he told the crooks, 'Don't make out that you never hurt someone.' When one armed robber tried to argue that his gun wasn't even loaded, Ken got in his face, saying, 'How would you fucking feel if I put a gun to your head that you didn't know was loaded or not? What would you do?' Before these conversations, Ken would say to the guards, 'I don't want anybody in there with me. I don't want a psychologist in there. I don't want a guard. I just want to talk face to face with these people.'

That takes balls, I think to myself. Those prisoners were dangerous, almost by definition. But Ken didn't want anything to interfere with his message. Sometimes one of the crooks would storm out. He got threatened. On one occasion, a couple of prisoners started shaping up, ready to assault him.

'How did that escalate?' I ask him.

'I probably told the bloke he was a fucking idiot,' replies Ken. 'You try telling them that they're responsible for being in prison. Victim blaming is a huge thing: 'Oh, I wouldn't have done this if they hadn't have done that', you know. But to me, the key to reform is in accepting responsibility. Once you can own what you've done, you can then start fixing it.'

The blokes backed down after some other prisoners in the room came to Ken's rescue.

Today, after spending 25 years visiting different prisons, Ken reckons about five per cent of the offenders inside them are pure evil, and nothing anybody says will change them, 35 per cent are career crooks, and 60 per cent are stupid bastards who thought they could get away with something and didn't.

He concentrates on the 60 per cent; those who've committed a stupid act of badness. If he can stop them from reoffending when they get out, that means fewer victims.

It's not forgiveness, Ken says, but it does mean welcoming these people back into society. They need to find somewhere to live. They need to work. It means politicians spending money. Without those things, these former prisoners are going to be desperate – and likely to commit more crimes, if only to get some spending money.

Other people have different opinions, Ken says. One time, he was giving a talk in Long Bay prison, in Sydney's eastern suburbs, when a bloke at the back of the room called out, 'You're a fucking coward.'

Ken was lost for words at first. Looking over, he saw a balding head he recognised as Arthur 'Neddy' Smith, the gangster who used to run drugs, protection rackets and armed robberies with Graham Henry before going down for two murders.

'Where's that coming from?' Ken asked him.

'You should have killed those bastards when you had the chance,' said Arthur. He meant Ken should have murdered Michael's killers, not sat down with them.

That's the code among the underworld, Ken thought. If someone does badness to you, you do badness to them in return. But if violence breeds violence, all you're left with is another grieving family.

'Look at it this way,' he told Arthur. 'I'm going to leave here in about an hour and I'm going to get into a car in the parking lot that my company pays for, and I'm going to drive it home to a loving wife who's going to make me a dinner that I really like, and you are still going to be in here. So whose values are working?'

Arthur didn't answer and he left before the session ended. But the next time Ken was in Long Bay, Arthur walked up to him in the prison yard and nodded. They shook hands.

* * *

Leaving Government House, the bright lights of the city buildings are pushing back the late evening darkness. I walk along the harbour, heading for the train station. A mass of people are spilling around outside the ticket gates, looking like office workers who've stumbled out of Christmas parties and have not yet decided whether or not to kick on.

'Jubes! Jubes!' a voice yells out.

I look around and see a grinning face I recognise. He's from the cops, someone who works closely with the police commissioner. He's also drunk and eating ice cream.

'How are you, mate?' He shakes my hand. A blob drops from his cone onto his shirt, unnoticed.

'How the fuck do you think I am after what your mate said on the radio about me?' I stare at him for a moment. Saying the investigation that I led into William's disappearance was a mess. Saying that time was wasted. 'What the fuck?'

He looks surprised.

'Oh, mate,' he says. Another drip of ice cream trails over his fingers as he thinks what to say next. 'Mate, he had to go out and defend the strike force because people were saying the investigation was stuffed up when you were taken off it.'

That's it? That's the reason the commissioner hung me out and took a shot at me in public? It's a lame explanation. I don't know if I believe it or if Mr Soft Serve here is just saying something he thinks will defuse me.

I let it go. He approached me out of friendship and it's nearly Christmas. Also, he's dead-drunk and I am sober.

He asks where I've been this evening.

Government House, I tell him. Lots of politicians, legal people, people from the prison system. All talking about the justice system. No one was there from the police, though. He looks at me. I hope that finds its way back to the senior cops he works with. We say our goodbyes. He takes another lick of ice cream. We walk away in opposite directions.

On the train home, I think it's not so bad being out of the police force. Maybe I can do more good outside it.

Risk of Harm

The police publish a press release, shortly before the end of the working day on Tuesday, 14 December. It runs to seven paragraphs: the search for William Tyrrell is coming to a close.

There are no leaks to the press this time. No front-page stories. Just a brief statement, saying, 'forensic examinations of seized items and a significant quantity of soil remain ongoing'. When those examinations are done, the police will send their findings to the coroner, whose inquest into William's disappearance has been running off-and-on for two years and nine months now, without any date confirmed for its conclusion.

'The NSW Police Force remains committed to finding William Tyrrell,' says the statement. I'm out with some other journos from the *Sunday Telegraph* when I read the email on my phone and pass it round. It's pathetic, I tell them. The cops stood up and made a song and dance of it when they launched this. Senior cops gave interviews on television. They were quoted saying, 'It's highly likely that if we found something it would be a body.' But nobody is fronting up for the cameras this time. Instead they drop a media release to say, it's over.

'Where's the commissioner?' I ask the other journalists. He was out there, in front of all the media when the search started. Where's the head of State Crime Command, who was giving interviews the day news broke that the cops were going to get an Apprehended Violence Order against William's foster parents? Where's the boss of the strike force, who was being photographed at the search site when the parents were charged with assaulting a child?

The journalists say nothing. Later, watching the evening news, I wait for someone else to ask those questions. No one does. Instead, the reporters talk about how the cops have left a metal rake embedded in the ground at the search site, on which people have written, 'We will never give up', 'We will not stop till we find you', and 'May you rest William'.

The TV journos carry on like it is something beautiful. To me, it's a symbol of what the cops have really been doing; raking through the dirt. By the week's end, all that's left of the search is the scars it made in the ground around Kendall, deep enough for a man to stand up in, and a few strips of blue and white police tape flapping in the forest. On Friday, 17 December, William's foster parents are back before a court in Sydney to face the charges they assaulted a child.

Again, details of the case cannot be published. The magistrate says this is necessary for the couple's protection: 'There is a very real risk of harm,' she says. 'All persons charged must be presumed innocent.' She criticises the 'relentless media attention' on William's disappearance, saying the State's local courts, including hers, hear up to a hundred assault cases every day but none get the full-press attention from every major newspaper, radio and TV station this one has attracted.

There is a risk the parents' assault charge will also somehow be connected to what happened to William 'based on innuendo and misinformation', the magistrate continues. She says one recent headline seemed to make the 'hopefully unintended' suggestion that the foster parents are suspicious because 'as child abusers they probably did it'.

The damage is already done, I think. Online, among the headlines that come up on a Google search for news on today's hearing, are two saying William's foster parents pleaded guilty to the assault. But they didn't. The couple pleaded not guilty. I am embarrassed for my new profession.

***

This is shameful. There is a child out there, somewhere, who has been taken away from William's foster parents. We cannot name that child, nor say anything that might identify them. With Christmas coming, the child cannot contact the couple. The child cannot speak to old friends of the family. The child cannot receive presents.

Instead, the child is in State care. Who knows what that child is thinking? Their doubts. Their fears. Their sense of isolation. What they are reading in the news or being told by others. I think of what I've learned about the long-term impact on a child who feels they've been abandoned. Of what James Fallon said about how stress works on a young brain, like putting a brick down on the accelerator, sending the machine revving out of control until it causes damage.

That damage can last a lifetime.

This is what's at stake now. I know I'm on my own here, saying there are questions we need to be asking about this police investigation, but this is why I ask them. Because we are no longer only talking about the likely death of William, but about the life of this other child.

* * *

I've spent the past two years studying badness. Working on the podcast, I've spent dozens of hours sitting down with cops and crooks, including those who have killed and those who have investigated killings – enough, all told, to fill almost four entire days of back-to-back recordings. Enough to saturate in evil, and I'm still getting started. Today, the podcast has hundreds of thousands of listeners. Our total downloads are measured in the millions. Which means there is a whole world out there made up of people fascinated by the subject of evil.

Well, if you are looking for an example, I have found it. In the disappearance of William Tyrrell, only one of two outcomes is possible: either the cops are right and their suspect has done something to William, or they're wrong. If they are right, then she has committed an evil act. If they are wrong, then all of this – the leak to the *Daily Telegraph* saying police believe the suspect is responsible for William's death and disappearance; the leak of details about the Apprehended Violence Orders; allowing TV cameras to film a cadaver dog running over the flowerbed beneath the balcony; taking a second child away from the family; the unquestioning repeating of all these things by the newspapers and on television; the reporters gathered outside the foster parents' home and knocking on their neighbours' doors, making sure they all knew who was under suspicion; the fact that, still, no court date has been set to hear the truth or otherwise of the assault charges; that no date has been set to restart the inquest into William's disappearance – all of this, instead, is the real badness.

Over the coming months, William's foster parents will plead not guilty to the assault charges. Both will be charged again, with giving false or misleading information to the New South Wales Crime Commission during secret hearings that were not and cannot be reported. An unnamed police officer will tell one newspaper 'we can prove' William's foster father made a false statement to the commission, a line that will be picked up and repeated in other papers. None of these papers will say what that false statement was, what the proof is, nor will they admit they would never have the courage to say this – that, in effect, an alleged criminal is guilty before a trial has been held to decide that – if it weren't for the fact they are not naming William's foster father. Both foster parents will say they are not guilty of these charges. Both will also be charged for a third time, with stalking and intimidating a child. Again, they will fight the charges. Everyone will seem to be pursuing them. The newspapers will continue to pick over small details of the couple's life – including when they hold a sale of children's bikes, car seats, prams, furniture and a 'WATER TANK' in thick, accusing capitals. The newspapers keep running the same few allegations from their criminal charges, over and over and over.

Eventually, a trial date will be set for the assault charges, in January 2023. That is more than a year off. Until then,

William's foster parents will stand accused in the eyes of their friends and neighbours. The same justice system in which half of all prisoners are released only to end up back inside within two years also leaves those who should be presumed innocent waiting over 12 months to face justice.

For now, over the Christmas holidays, William Tyrrell barely gets a mention in the papers. On Wednesday, 5 January 2022, it is reported that detectives are conducting a fresh round of interviews. The next day one newspaper reports a bone fragment is still being examined by the State Forensic and Analytical Science Service.

Nothing will be said about what those tests find, if anything. Instead, there is only silence.

Piss and Wind

Karl Kramer, who killed Michael Marslew, lasted around four weeks outside prison before being charged with breaching an Apprehended Violence Order. Michael's father, Ken, stood by him. The case was dropped.

Six months later, Karl was charged over a home invasion. Again, the case collapsed, but he was back in court in 2014 and, this time, went down for reckless wounding and causing grievous bodily harm.

Today Ken says Karl is full of piss and wind. He never earned his redemption. Not everybody will.

Some don't deserve it. Not the animals that murdered Anita Cobby. Not Julian Knight, who never seemed to accept responsibility for his own actions. Not Ivan Milat, who died in prison. Not Martin Bryant who, when questioned by detectives, didn't seem to understand the enormity of what he had committed.

But there are other people.

* * *

I get accused of doing more badness. The white goods repairman who we arrested while I was leading the investigation into

William Tyrrell's disappearance decides to sue and the case is heard in the New South Wales Supreme Court. After his arrest, the repairman was charged over unrelated child sex allegations, which were ultimately dismissed, and he's now claiming we brought the case to punish him, hoping to crack him open, revealing what we believed he was hiding about William.

Unfortunately, the fact we were going to arrest him at home was leaked to the media by someone above me in the police, meaning the TV cameras were waiting when we arrived there. The arrest and his first appearance in court were on the evening news and the next morning's front pages. That made it worse for him, but it was not my doing. I was furious about it.

In court, his lawyers play anonymous phone messages left on his answering machine after his arrest. They call him a 'weak paedophile dog', a 'maggot dog' and a 'paedophile cunt'.

'Where's William, you dirty fucking paedophile,' one of the callers asks him. Another: 'Hey, mate, you better return little fucking Will because we all know you fucking got him.'

So, yes, I know he suffered. And, yes, I did go hard at him after he was arrested. I saw an opportunity to ask him about William. There were questions I needed to have answered: he'd been due to visit the house where William went missing; William's foster mother called him on that morning to talk about the broken washing machine; when I took over the investigation, no one had confirmed whether he had an alibi. I would not have been doing my job – which was to find a missing three-year-old – if I did not ask him about those things.

And I knew it would be unpleasant for him. In court, he describes being assaulted by a prison guard while waiting for his trial. Later, after his release on bail, he says a woman came up to him in public, saying she didn't want him to be there around children.

He claims I told him, 'Mr Nice Washing Machine Man, I'm going to ruin you'.

I don't remember saying that, I tell the court, when my turn comes to give evidence.

I did not threaten the white goods repairman. I admit he did look shocked during our conversation, but he did not ask to end it. Again, I stress, we did not charge him with child abuse to further our investigation into William's disappearance. We did it because there were allegations of child abuse against him. Once he'd been charged and interviewed about those, only then did I ask him about William.

I don't consider what I did to him, or to Paul, the witness whose conversations I recorded, to be badness. In those recordings you can hear me questioning Paul about his actions around the time when William went missing. I'm aggressive. I push him hard, wanting to get answers. Listening back, I found myself thinking, *Who is this bastard beating up on an old man?* I don't want to see myself in that person. But that's my job. I'm not a saint. I have done things in the police that other people might not. They needed to be done and I believed it was right to do them. A three-year-old boy was missing. I have answered for it in court.

Circle Up

The bell sounds the beginning of the session.

'Partner up!' Shane Phillips calls, and the dozens of people who just a moment ago were milling around this strip of bitumen in a park near Redfern, central Sydney, suddenly have a purpose. It's hot, a summer morning in January 2022, and I'm thinking, *This is going to be hard work* as I walk into the crowd, looking for a partner. One girl who looks like she's in her mid-teens raises her hands. We start to warm up, my boxing gloves tapping her pads like raindrops on a window. The sound spreads out, repeated through the crowd, with Shane raising his voice above it to call out combinations: 'Left, left, right, hook.'

The noise of glove on pads increases like heavy rain. I can feel a prickling sweat. The girl gives me a smile of encouragement and I start to land my punches harder. She smiles again. That's good. It feels good to be so quickly accepted.

After a three-minute round the bell rings and we change partners, just like the drills I've been working with Johnny Lewis. Speaking to Shane before the session started, he told me there are some hard heads here: addicts who've cleaned up their acts; some people serving time in prison, who've been brought here on day release. For some of them, this is a kind of redemption. I pair up with an older bloke, who stays silent, throwing heavy punches, sweat running down the dark skin of his forehead.

The bell sounds. Shane calls out another combination. It's just after 7 am and the sun is throwing early-morning light between the tower blocks.

* * *

'I guess I got in trouble as a young bloke,' Shane told me before I got here. 'I made all the mistakes. I saw the violence, the drugs. I saw the death and destruction.' His mother's family got taken away, Shane said, meaning they were members of the Stolen Generations, where people of Aboriginal descent were taken from their families and placed in State care by the white authorities. 'That trauma was passed down.' So was the anger and resentment.

'We all thought authority was bad for us,' Shane continued. Growing up in Redfern, he'd watch the police drive past without talking to anyone who lived there, unless they had come to arrest them. 'We were the same, looking at them. I thought, it's us against the world, we mean nothing to anyone. It was consuming me. It was festering.'

Growing older, Shane saw the same bad blood running through the generation coming after him, who were then still children. They were taking drugs and drinking, getting caught up in petty crime and violence. And every drunken bashing or bruising domestic violence meant someone getting hurt.

Circle Up

On the bitumen, the rounds continue. This time when the bell sounds, another of the older men calls out an unforgiving combination: jabs, straights, hooks and uppercuts. Looking around, I start to see that the crowd here isn't just a rough-and-tumble crew from Redfern. There are trained heavyweights and kickboxers, some are lawyers, even the Governor-General of Australia, David Hurley, a decorated former soldier, has come down here to train in the mornings.

This morning, nobody is shirking. Everyone is breathing heavily. The sound of glove on pad increases to a thunder. I don't know if I can get through this.

Finally, the bell sounds a last time. Shane calls out: 'OK, circle up! Let's go!'

The crowd breaks apart and re-forms in a circle, standing silent. A young lad, his T-shirt soaked with sweat and sticking to his body, steps into it.

'The hard work we do here replicates the discipline and the routine that we carry through the days, the weeks, the months and the years. If this is the hardest thing you do today, well, you're going to have a good day,' he says. I get goosebumps. Everyone applauds.

A teenage girl repeats the pledge in the Eora language, spoken by Indigenous people throughout what is modern-day Sydney. One of the old blokes talks about respect and people listen. Shane stands there, his own clothes wet with effort. He looks at me and says, 'All right, we've got Gary here. This is his first morning. Gary, could you come into the circle and tell us your impression of what you've seen here.'

I walk forward. My words stumble. First, I thank them. I'm honoured that they let me join them. I was not expecting it to be so tough this morning, I say. I was not expecting it to be so powerful.

'What I am seeing here is pride. Pride and respect. It's just coming out in bucketloads.' I see people who've done crimes and want to find a way back. I see people who are prepared to let them. I see people who want to be stronger versions of who they are. I see a whole community, standing in this circle together. It's humbling, I tell them.

Shane says they call this program Clean Slate Without Prejudice.

I'm Telling You

It took a cop to start the conversation. A new Detective Superintendent, Luke Freudenstein, took charge of the Redfern Local Area Command in 2008, a year when there were robberies happening almost daily. Every evening, the main street looked like something from a sci-fi movie; the sun went down and so did the metal shutters on the shopfronts.

Luke started turning up at meetings of the Babana Aboriginal Men's Group of local leaders. He said there were 15 names that kept appearing on the night-time crime reports, all teenagers and young men, all seen there or thereabouts when some badness happened.

'I can arrest my way out of this, or we can do something together,' Luke said to the men's group.

Shane Phillips, who was at the meeting, says they palmed him off. They didn't need a copper to tell them they had a problem. Shane had seen before how this would play out, he says. Those 15 names were going to the Big House or they were going to the graveyard.

But Luke came back. Shane learned he used to be a boxer and had a couple of exhibition fights during his 20s. Shane's old man was a former middleweight champion. The two of them got talking. Shane says the men's group looked at the names on Luke's list. They knew the boys. They knew their families. Together they chose the 10 most influential, knowing the other kids would follow.

Maybe they could do something, Shane says. Talking to Luke, they settled on some boxing.

That first early-winter morning, the men went round to the 10 boys' houses, knocked on their doors and dragged them out of bed. It was still freezing cold and raining outside but they had gathered together, ready to start, when they saw a cop walking down the road towards them.

'I hate him,' one of the boys said.

'We're going to go in,' Shane told him.

Inside, the two sides looked at one another. The tension was freaky at the beginning, Shane says. Then they started training; working those exhausting combinations. Every time a round ended, they swapped partners.

'Do you know what's crazy?' Shane asks. 'We get in there, we do this training, we were all fucked at the end of it and afterwards, it was like we saw each other for the first time.'

Ever since, the training has continued.

***

What Luke and Shane set up here is simple: Monday, Wednesday and Friday, you get up early to train. You follow the drills. When you are told to run, or jump, you do it. Afterwards, you feel good. You feel like you've achieved something.

You start to crave that feeling. Good habits are addictive.

Three nights a week you're more likely to head to bed than out onto the streets, because you're going to be training at six the next morning.

Both sides got shit from their own communities at first, Shane says. The blackfellas were getting called dogs and informers for talking to the police, and the police were getting called worse by the few out-and-out racists in the force. But that just helped unite them when they met for training. The two sides started saying hello to one another in the streets.

Luke got some of the young blokes to go into the police station once a fortnight, to tell their stories. At first, the feeling inside the room was so thick that you could cut it, Shane says. 'They came in and one or two would present their case and say, "Listen, this is what I am doing, I have been arrested by you and you and you but I'm trying to change my life, I've got a routine, I've been training."'

It was quiet when the boys finished, Shane says. Then one of the cops spoke up, saying, 'Let me know if you need anything.'

Outside, the young blokes started to hear people saying good things about them. Meeting them so often in the mornings also meant that Shane and the older men could talk to the younger blokes. They talked about community and culture. About some things that didn't get discussed much, like domestic violence. Some of the older men had grown up in violent families. Who better to talk to the young blokes and tell them it wasn't right than men who had lived it also?

A year later, not one of the boys on Luke's list had committed an offence.

'It was freaky, man. I'm telling you, we still pinch ourselves now that we were part of it. That we really got to see it in our own lives,' Shane says. In the first five years after Clean Slate Without Prejudice was set up in 2009, robberies in Redfern fell 73 per cent. Assaults on police were down 57 per cent. Break-and-enters almost halved.

Since then, the program has expanded. They talked to the Redfern Chamber of Commerce about removing those metal shutters from the high street. Mentors were employed to work with kids who'd been referred by school, social services or the police, in return for them signing a contract saying they would turn up at training. The mentors would also drive around in the mornings, making sure they did so. After training, the kids would sit down at tables laid out with Tupperware containers full of cereal, so they wouldn't start the day hungry. They had lessons with their Elders, learning their traditional language. Then their mentors drove them to school.

Luke approached Corrective Services NSW, asking if they'd let some prisoners take part in the training. His argument was simple; no one would get any time off their sentence and it wouldn't cost a lot of money – just enough for some shorts, T-shirts and runners. It would mean Luke getting up even earlier on those three mornings each week to be at Long Bay prison in time to escort the prisoners to Redfern, but that would give him and some of the mentors time to talk to the crooks during the journey. At training, the prisoners would have a chance to talk to people, to apologise for what they'd done and to start rebuilding. They'd help serve the kids breakfast. They'd also get a chance to do some employment training.

If any of that could help stop these prisoners committing more crimes after they got released, then surely it was worth trying, Luke argued. The prison governor agreed. That show of trust meant something to those who were involved, Shane tells me. His own brother was among the first prisoners allowed out to take part in those early training sessions.

Not every day is a success, he says. Nor is boxing the answer to all of Redfern's problems. But something was happening. The cops were better able to do their jobs because they knew the people who they were policing. The community was helping make sure those people who were out there, already carrying out little acts of badness, were brought back into line before they went on to commit greater evils.

'It was unheard of, some of us were going out on the beers with a couple of cops,' Shane says. A few of the cops got involved with the local Aboriginal footy team, the Redfern All Blacks. 'Luke just became part of the community. You know, we would go to a game at Redfern Oval and there were police holding the bump pads, warming people up. And it was crazy.'

Listening to him describe what they built here, I feel fired up. Partly, I think, that's the good chemicals that get released into your body when you get up to train in the morning. And partly it's just being in the room with Shane. *I thought I was a crime fighter*, I find myself thinking. *How many other people are there, out there, doing just as much as Shane is? You never hear about them. But this bloke is having an impact I could only dream of as a detective.*

* * *

But, it isn't easy. Luke Freudenstein retired in 2018, after 37 years in the police force. A year later, under a restructure led by the police commissioner, the Redfern Local Area Command was merged with its neighbour and moved into a new, bigger police station.

'What's the relationship with the cops now?' I ask Shane.

'It's starting to creep back to the way it was because it's become a super-station,' he says. 'We've lost the personal contact. It's grown big and some of the new police don't have the same relationship.

'So it's back to the old days of driving past and looking at each other without talking.' The lesson is you have to sweat to earn redemption. And it won't last if you stop sweating.

Are You Confessing?

Leaving the cops isn't simple. The police commissioner announces his retirement, saying he will stand down after a single term in office, with his successor replacing him at the end of January 2022. After that date, when strangers ask him what he does, or who he is, I don't know how long it will take for him to find an answer, but it's taken me a long time. I am only starting to feel comfortable about it, I'm no longer just that ex-cop. I have built a new life and am a better person, I think, for becoming a criminal.

On 20 January, the papers say my old boss at the Homicide Squad, and the man who made the decision to charge me with criminal offences over recording those conversations with a witness, has resigned from the police force. Later, I learn the truth is he got told his contract had been terminated during a phone call with the incoming commissioner. When the current police commissioner announced he was leaving, my old boss from Homicide had been expected to get the top job. It didn't happen. After spending decades working his way up the ranks of the police force, his career was ended with that phone call. He was on holidays at the time.

That's how the cops deal with their own, I think to myself. An email has gone round the force this morning saying he served his last day yesterday. I'd like to say I wish him well but cannot bring myself to do it.

***

Graham Henry sends me a message saying he and I should do a TV crime show together. He says we'd kill the opposition.

It's a measure of how much he thinks I've changed since leaving the cops that he even suggests this.

It's a measure of how much I've changed that I say I'll think about it. In the end, I decide against it, though I do ask Graham if he will do an interview for the podcast.

***

The new Commissioner of the New South Wales Police Force is formally appointed on 1 February. The State Premier, Dominic Perrottet, says she has the integrity and honesty to lead the force into the future. On 15 February, one of the Sydney newspapers reports the previous commissioner is a frontrunner to join the board of Racing NSW after hanging up his uniform. Racing NSW regulates the State's thoroughbred racing industry, a business worth millions or maybe billions, depending on how you slice it. His name is expected to be presented to the State Cabinet for approval, the paper says.

The next day, 16 February, I meet Graham in a pub in Rozelle, in inner-city Sydney. He asks me if I want a beer. While he's at the bar, I get talking to one of his mates, who I later learn has done time for accessory to murder. He only helped dispose of the body after, Graham will tell me. He was staunch. He didn't give his mates up.

Graham returns with the beers and a few others drift over to join our conversation. One of them keeps scowling. He raises a finger.

'You don't know how lucky you are for us to let you into the circle,' he says, pointing at me. He means you're lucky because you were a cop and once a cop, always a cop and we fucking hate cops.

I understand, I tell him. This is unusual for both of us. But I am not a cop any longer. I'm here because I'm going to do an interview with Graham. I want to get to know him better. This is what I do now.

We leave the pub and Graham takes me on a tour of Sydney, showing me where he hid while planning to kill Arthur 'Neddy' Smith after they fell out. He shows me the laneway outside the Lord Wolseley Hotel where he stabbed Mal Spence, the police prosecutor. We go back to the first pub and he asks me if I want another beer. Inside, the same crew from earlier are still drinking. Graham and I take our drinks and sit together, apart from the others.

During the podcast, I don't intend to sit in judgment on him in the interview, I tell him, and I don't want him to judge me either. The whole point of this, I tell him, is to help people understand crime. Why do people like him do badness? If we can understand that, then maybe we can stop it happening again.

That means I'm going to have to ask about some of the badness he's committed. And, particularly, I am going to ask about some of the people who made attempts on Graham's life and were later found dead or who went missing.

'That's their bad luck,' he says.

'Are you confessing to anything?'

'No, I don't confess.' Graham says he doesn't know what happened to those people and he has never been charged over any killing. He says he's going straight and the only people he hurt when he was a gangster were also in the same game he was – except for those he beat up after arguments in pubs, and they were asking for it.

He talks about badness like it is a transaction: one story starts with a drunken businessman inside a restaurant in Double Bay who walked over and took a prawn cutlet off Graham's plate. Graham shrugs, telling me he stabbed him straight through the hand.

I say that he hurt a lot of people.

'It's not something I'm proud of,' he says.

I wait.

'I shouldn't have done it.'

He doesn't say that he is sorry.

But at least he is honest.

* * *

The next day, 17 February, the ABC publishes an investigation about the former police commissioner, alleging he did not declare his ownership of shares in racehorses while he was in uniform, even though the cops' own code of conduct said he had to. Other shareowners in the same horses allegedly included people working in the liquor, gaming and security industries, according to the reporting. One had been investigated by police over an alleged fraud but never charged.

The former commissioner is quoted, saying he 'legally and ethically complied with all government policies over my 34 years of loyal service'. The report causes a commotion. That evening the state's Racing Minister, Kevin Anderson, announces the former commissioner will not be given a board role with Racing NSW. The next day, 18 February, the cops confirm there is an internal investigation into the horse racing interests of other, serving, police commanders. It is being conducted by the force's Professional Standards Command, the same people who investigated me over the recorded conversations with a witness.

A month passes. Then, on 15 March, the State's Law Enforcement Conduct Commission reports on its own inquiry into the allegations. It has found no substance in any of the claims made against the former commissioner. Instead, it says, there is a history of anonymous complaints being made against him, dating back to 2016, all of which had been considered or investigated by different authorities at the time and no misconduct found. This inquiry clears the former police commissioner. Instead, it blames 'disaffected officers who have mounted a campaign to harm [his] reputation ... someone is prepared to throw whatever mud they can, in the hope something sticks'.

If that's the culture of the place, I think, *then I really am better far from it.* Today, on a Thursday afternoon, Graham and I take our seats opposite each other in an old warehouse in Erskineville, near the oval where I train with Johnny Lewis, which has been converted into a recording studio. The two of us are confident in each other's company now that we've spent some time together. Graham's smiling. There's still a menace to him, though. A hardness. I can sense it in his eyes when I look closely.

There was a time when I'd have loved to arrest him. Or when, just like with Bernie Matthews, if Graham and I had met in the street, either one of us might have come up shooting. Back then I thought he was a monster, but now I see the person in him. He is like me in some ways: loyal, honest to the code he lives by, a product of the place and time that he grew up in. That place and time was similar for both of us, North Epping in the 1960s separated by a few hundred metres and a few years. Graham became a kingpin. I became a detective. All I want now is for him to explain how he got there. How he wound up committing badness.

'Are we ready to go?' I ask the sound engineer sitting on the other side of the glass window. He gives me a thumbs up. The tape is rolling. This is like those recorded interviews I used to do when I was a detective. For a moment, I think back over what I've learned since leaving the police force: Dennis O'Toole told me about the Granny Killer and how evil people can seem ordinary; Sarah Yule, who studied under one of the pioneers from the FBI's Behavioral Science Unit, taught me those who do evil can be understood, if not forgiven; Ian Kennedy showed me that we all have violence in us but he was able to control it during the pursuit of Anita Cobby's killers; Bernie Matthews told me about his childhood friend called Wobbles, who was both a criminal and a victim; Tim

Watson-Munro spent months talking to the Hoddle Street killer, Julian Knight, inside prison and showed me his evil was not inevitable; John Killick shared a prison yard with the serial killer Ivan Milat and taught me that different people might have the same life stories but not all of them go on to do evil; Bob Gibbs worked the crime scene at Port Arthur and saw the devastation caused by Martin Bryant. From that, I learned evil can be done not because someone wants to, but because they see no reason not to. Talking to Bernie again showed me that the causes of our badness reach back into childhood. The neuroscientist, Jim Fallon, sat in his jacuzzi and realised that it's not nature or nurture that makes people do evil, it is both at the same time. Wilma Robb helped me see that sometimes doing nothing is the same as doing evil – yet she has managed to live a life of purpose despite the badness done to her. Most recently, Shane Phillips showed me that redemption is possible, but that you have to sweat for it.

I haven't finished learning. I'm sure Graham has more that he can teach me.

For a moment, I wonder if my old colleagues in the police would judge me if they knew I was sitting down with this old gangster.

I don't care. They have already judged me.

Graham and I start to talk.

Postscript

I have spent most of my adult life as a police officer fighting evil in the best way I knew how. If someone committed a crime under my watch, I did everything in my power to catch them. I was ruthless in the way I went after criminals and make no apologies for doing so. I like to think I made a difference.

Since leaving the police I've been forced to look at the world differently. It's taken me down a path of self-discovery, towards the realisation that a badge and gun are not the only weapons to fight crime. In fact, I've learned there are a lot of people out there fighting just as hard as I was, if not harder, but doing so with different weapons. Often, they don't get the recognition given to law enforcement officers and sometimes they are dismissed for not being tough enough on crime. Make no mistake, they have a strength of character and commitment to the cause equal to any of the most dedicated police officers I've had the honour to work with.

This book is dedicated to William Tyrrell. The fact I could not provide answers for William's family is one of my great regrets. Like everyone, I want answers about what happened to him but in recent years I have been astounded at the amount of misinformation and leaks from the police that have been reported without question. Dramatic statements have been made by those in power, and life-changing insinuations have been allowed to stand in public, without anyone taking responsibility for the effects these have on people. Different potential suspects have been hung out in public and discarded without explanation. And the public are still expected to keep trusting those in power.

It is time those in power are held accountable for their actions and for the mistakes that have been made during the investigation into William's disappearance. I would like to see a public inquiry into what has happened, with the power to compel evidence and require witnesses to appear before it. I would welcome the opportunity to be questioned on oath about my handling of the investigation. I would hope such an inquiry could take place before any more lives are ruined. Sadly, I doubt those with the authority to make this happen will have the courage to do so.

At the time of writing, the inquest into William's disappearance has been running for over three years with no date set for its completion. The legal action described in this book as having been launched by the white goods repairman against the New South Wales Police Force has not yet resulted in a judgment. The criminal charges against William Tyrrell's foster parents have not yet been tested in court, though some details were made public during a brief hearing in June 2022. The court heard William's foster mother is alleged to have kicked a child once in the thigh, to have hit the same child with a wooden spoon and to have said that if the child were to defecate on the floor, then she would rub the child's face in it. William's foster father is alleged to have physically restrained the child to make her sit down.

In court, the police alleged these actions were part of a 'pattern of ongoing violence'. A psychologist's report, which was tendered in evidence, said the foster parents had been attempting to intervene in the child's 'problematic behaviour'. The magistrate said the child had been 'acting up' and 'misbehaving', noting that parts of the police case were 'not particularly strong'. William's foster mother had also been dealing with severe, accumulated stresses at the time.

For myself, I am enjoying my life outside of the police and am challenging myself in ways I never thought I would before this. I have no idea what the future holds but, for the first time in a few years, I am looking forward to it.

Acknowledgments

*B**adness* has only been possible because people read a previous book I wrote with Dan Box, called *I Catch Killers*, and told me they liked it. When Dan and I talked about writing another, at first I was not convinced I had enough to say. That changed after I met a man called Ken Marslew, who appears in this book and whose 18-year-old son Michael was murdered during an armed robbery. Since then, Ken has dedicated his life to trying to reduce crime.

Whether I like it or not, Ken told me that my past experience in the police and current work in the media mean I have a platform to change the way people look at crime and, by doing so, change the way we deal with it. Ken's pretty persuasive. He virtually challenged me to do something with this opportunity. That got me to thinking about what I've learned since leaving the police. I realised there was something I wanted to say, as a result of my exposure to so many people who've been caught up in the world of badness.

Acknowledgments

Many of these people have contributed to this book by helping me understand what evil is and how to prevent it, or how to fight it when necessary. People such as retired police officers Dennis O'Toole, Ian Kennedy and Bob Gibbs, who spent their careers facing up to evil and did so with courage, dedication and compassion. Or those like Sarah Yule, Tim Watson-Munro and James Fallon, who have looked deep inside the criminal mind so we can understand it better. Few others would dare to see what they do.

Other people, like John Killick and Graham Henry, are included in this book not because of their criminal activities but because they had the strength of character to sit down to talk with an ex-cop. I think we all came away a little bit wiser. My close friend, the late Bernie Matthews, taught me everybody has a story that somebody can learn from. He also showed me that it's never too late to turn your life around. All three of these ex-crooks have sought redemption in their own way. I respect that and have enjoyed getting to know them.

I wouldn't write a book about badness without mentioning the victims of crime who suffer because of the actions of others. People like Kathy Nowland, whose beautiful daughter Michelle was brutally murdered. Or William Tyrrell's families, who still have no answers. I cannot comprehend your suffering, though I know it is something you will always live with. Another person who had a huge impact on me was Wilma Robb, a beautiful lady who has made the best of life despite being brutalised by a system that was meant to protect her.

It has also been humbling to meet those who do not wear a uniform but fight crime with as much passion as anyone in the

Homicide Squad. People like Shane Phillips and Ken Marslew, who are included in this book.

Thank you all. This is your story as much as it is mine.

Countless others have helped me understand the issues surrounding good, evil and what is right and wrong with our system of justice. Among them, I particularly want to mention Simon Fenech of Fruit2Work, Russell Manser who runs The Voice of a Survivor, Jeffrey Morgan from The Lifestyle Program, Mindy Sotiri from the Justice Reform Initiative, Bernie Shakeshaft, the founder of BackTrack, Peter Rolfe of Support After Murder, and Alyson Colquitt who has worked with the Women's Justice Network. They are people I've had the honour of meeting since I left the police force, and most likely I never would have met had I not left in the way I did. All of them are taking a stand against the badness in the world around them. Thank you for opening my eyes to what can be done.

I also want to thank the team at HarperCollins for once again trusting me enough to write a book, particularly Helen Littleton and Barbara McClenahan.

To Dan Box, we have now been working together for a number of years and we still have not had a fight. That's almost a record for me. Your professionalism and integrity shine through in your work. I wouldn't do this project with anyone else.

In part, this book documents my experience of working on the I Catch Killers podcast over the past few years. I want to thank all of the different guests who've trusted me to tell their stories. Thanks also to those who have worked with me

Acknowledgments

on it, and particularly to Claire Harvey for having faith in the project from the beginning, when it really mattered. And huge thanks to the people who have listened to the series and made it a success. There are some great episodes coming up.

Outside the book itself, there are other people I want to thank, for helping me navigate myself through this strange world I now inhabit.

Nick Fordham and his team at The Fordham Company have provided me with sage advice since leaving the police and it's been much appreciated.

To Johnny Lewis and his 'Erko' boxing crew, thank you for accepting me into your group. It's great being in an environment where you are judged solely on the effort that you put in. You guys came into my life at the right time and have given me the strength to fight the fight when needed.

Finally, I had no idea how dramatically my life would change over the past few years, or how much that would change me. While I'm happy with where I am now, there were some obvious low points and there is no way I would have gotten through them without the support of my family and friends. It might only be a small group but I know you have my back and you have given me the confidence to pursue a career away from policing. I love you all.

PODCAST

TRUE CRIME AUSTRALIA

I CATCH KILLERS

WITH GARY JUBELIN

After 34 years in the police and 25 years working homicides, Detective Chief Inspector (retd) Gary Jubelin is tracking down the detectives who inspire him – and the odd hardcore criminal – to extract their tricks of the trade in his podcast series.

Over beers, they reveal the untold true stories of Australia's most terrifying murders – and the cases that still haunt them.

Equal parts hilarious and horrifying, this is 'shop talk' like you've never heard before.

Listen to I Catch Killers with Gary Jubelin at icatchkillers.com.au or on your podcast app of choice.

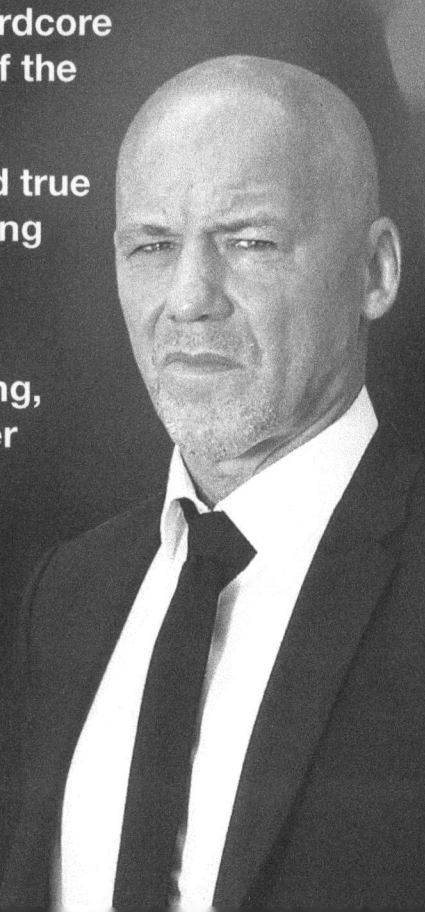